ANTIQUE TOY TRAINS

ANTIQUE TOY TRAINS

The Hobby of Collecting Old Toy Trains

Howard Godel

First Edition

© 1976 by Howard Godel

Copyright © under the Universal Copyright and Berne Conventions

Library of Congress Catalog Card Number: 76-10932

ISBN 0-682-48600-0

Printed in the United States of America by
Exposition Press, Inc., 900 South Oyster Bay Road, Hicksville, N.Y. 11801

I dedicate this book to Robert Lesser, who gave me the final push that got me started, and to the many collectors I have come to know, who have made the hobby of collecting old toy trains a thoroughly fascinating and enjoyable experience.

CONTENTS

ACKNOWLEDGMENTS

I wish to make it clear that many friends, fellow collectors, and acquaintances have directly and indirectly contributed to what you are to read here. I am forever indebted to the many evenings of countless bull sessions devoted to train talk, where most of the learning in the hobby takes place. My sincere and deepest apologies to anyone whom I may have failed to mention.

I especially wish to thank: Ed and Sheila Minkoff, John Henderson, Joel Cane, Ed and Pat Prendeville, Peter Tilp, John Marron, Roger Arcara, Dr. Gerald (Doc Robbie) Robinson, Phil Rosen, Joe Ranker, Elliot Smith, George Tebolt, John Daniel, Ward Kimball, Tom Sefton, Herb Morley, Ted Sommer, Tom Sage, Alan Stewart, Steve Papa, LaRue Shempp, Don Fernandez, Bob Lesser, George Henglein, Bob Hauser, Bob Willey, Ernie Davis, Ralph Scull, Ed Kraemer, George Martin, Glen Stinson, Lou Hertz, and Alex Acevedo.

Of course special thanks go out to my parents, immediate family, and relatives, who all helped and encouraged me throughout this very trying period.

INTRODUCTION

Hardly a child exists today who cannot recall with fond memories the many mornings of Christmas Days gone by. One of those very wonderful days in our lives brought us a toy train and, whether it was big or small, windup or electric, we loved it. It's no wonder, then, that people in all walks of life have an appreciation for electric trains of all sorts, and it's no surprise that these old trains would someday be collected by many people for many reasons. Some collect trains in order to run them, some collect them for the many memories that they provide and some, like myself, are fascinated by learning about the trains and the many models made of them, both old and new, and big and small.

The hobby of toy train collecting is less than forty years old. In any hobby so young there is much to learn and many facts and finds yet to be uncovered. For me, that is why collecting trains is so very interesting. I feel like a pioneer in the days of the Gold Rush when I acquire a rare and desirable new train for my collection. I feel like an explorer when I discover new facts about variations that certain models came in or when I see for the first time a rare train of which only a few are known. I enjoy collecting trains because it's so new and there are still so many discoveries yet to be made.

Why call the book *Antique Toy Trains* when most of the trains discussed in the book are far newer than the one hundred years necessary to label an item a true antique? Simply because no matter how collectors think in regard to the correct usage of the word *antique*, it is still a word that new collectors, dealers, and especially members of the public will continually use when referring to any collectible that is no longer made. It has long been considered acceptable to refer to very old autos as "antique cars," even though none are older than the required one hundred years and in fact most are actually no older than fifty. Technically, then, the word *antique* may be incorrect when used to describe trains made after the turn of the century, but when used in the context of old toy trains it is readily acceptable, for the word *antique* is immediately identified with any collectible deemed worthy of a serious following.

My objective in writing this book is not to put together a numbers list of every known variation or mention everything ever made, but rather to give a generalized overview of the hobby today. I tried to make the book of interest to total beginners and yet also to cover some of the rarer and most unusual items made. It is a tough compromise to try to write a generalized book on the hobby and every step of the way have to decide how deep I should go, what to include, what to omit, minor facts and variations, all the while hoping not to offend those collectors who thirst for greater detail and those who wish to be told of the obvious and the common. By its very nature a book of this sort, a generalized book that deals with practically every important subject in the hobby, can never be totally complete. The very idea of having a complete collection in any one field is a fantasy, for the fact is that new discoveries are still being made every day.

In my own collecting pursuits I have met train collectors from all over the country and I have found them to be as fine a group of individuals as you will ever meet in any hobby. Truly there is no typical train collector, for the hobby has attracted people from every race, ethnic group, age, and occupation. In a large and growing hobby as diverse as train collecting is today, it can naturally be expected that specialties and interests will vary, sometimes greatly, in each individual's goal as a collector. It is my sincere hope that I have mentioned the subject of your interest, for I realized early on that, to attempt to define and detail every facet of the hobby, I would need to write a series of volumes almost equal in size and scope to a regular encyclopedia.

Because there is so much to know in this hobby about variations, numbers, prototypes, and oddball and display pieces, any work of this kind that encompasses so many different manufacturers and such a large span of time will naturally have omissions. I have tried to verify all facts and data from many different sources, but naturally there will be mistakes. I will be happy to receive corrections and responses from those who care to write. For the many facts and information that are new to you, there are too many friends and collectors to thank. Please try to forgive me if your name is not mentioned. Writing this book and photographing the trains have been quite an experience for me. I hope everyone can learn from this book as I did while writing it.

Happy Collecting!
HOWARD J. GODEL

ANTIQUE TOY TRAINS

1

HISTORY OF TOY TRAIN MANUFACTURERS

One could easily fill an entire book with information on the many different companies that made toy trains. There are many too numerous to mention. Most people have at least heard of such makes as Lionel, American Flyer, Ives, and Marklin. Besides these more famous companies there was Dorfan, Carlisle and Finch, Howard, Knapp, Voltamp, Boucher, Beggs, Weeden, Carette, Hornby, Bing, Karl Bub, Issamayer, Hafner, Electoy, Marx, and others. Only a handful of these companies survive today, for few were fortunate enough to withstand the onslaught of time and the tremendous competitiveness that exists within the toy field. I could not possibly attempt to mention every manufacturer of toy trains that ever existed; there were far too many. What I will try to do is mention something about the history of some of the more well-known companies, and with due respect I must apologize for the lack of information and unanswered questions that you may have on the lesser-known early tinplate manufacturers.

Toy trains as a field of collecting can be said to include the early cast iron, tin, and wooden pulltoys of the later half of the nineteenth century, not to mention the early alcohol burners and similar types that were made. It is beyond the scope and depth of this book to mention too much in the area of pulltoys, so I will try to restrict myself to electric models. Most train collectors are interested mainly in "electric trains" and are almost totally unconcerned with early pulltoy or clockwork models. This is of course contrary to popular opinion, which would have you believe that the older something is the more desirable and valuable it naturally has to be. Because these very early models of trains are not as widely collected as are the later period mass production electric trains, I will not try to detail their history.

Early Manufacturers

The first electric trains were probably made by Carette. In 1893 Georges Carette and Co. of Nuremberg, Germany, advertised that they were manufacturing electric streetcars, but I am not sure if they were actually in production at that early date. Who was the first American company to manufacture electric trains? The Carlisle and Finch Company of Cincinnati, Ohio, an electric novelty company, made a four-wheel brass streetcar in 1896. The track used was three-rail strip track having wooden ties, and the company reputedly ran off 500 cars. They received more orders than they could handle for an item that at that time seemed to most people like some sort of scientific invention. On the next run they changed to two-rail track and they eventually expanded their line to include two styles of trolleys, a steam-type freight set, and a mining locomotive with little ore cars. Although Carlisle and Finch made the first electric trains in America, others have, in ignorance, at times tried to credit Lionel and Ives with this feat, but that is untrue. Carlisle and Finch stopped making electric trains in 1916, which probably accounts for their relative obscurity among most collectors today.

Another of the early pioneer manufacturers was the Knapp Electric & Novelty Company, which started making electric trains about 1905 and discontinued their train line in 1913. Knapp was located in New York City and made its success based on a game they sold called the Electric Questioner. In later years Knapp's founder confided that the reason he dropped the train line was that he thought it was a "passing fad." In 1938 Knapp made a line of HO gauge trains that didn't sell well and were therefore discontinued.

There was also the Howard Miniature Electric

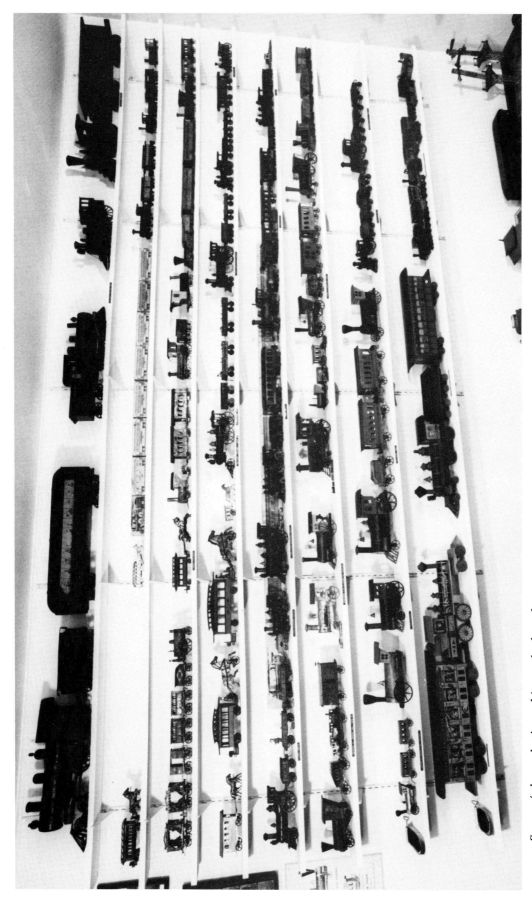

Some of the early tin and iron, clockwork and pulltoy models from the Ward Kimball collection. The two large sets pictured at left on the bottom shelf are wooden pulltoys with colorful paper label sides.

*A Carette No. 1 gauge alcohol burner and cars
from about 1905. This engine is particularly interesting
because it has an Americanized cowcatcher
as it was especially made for the American market.
Early sets such as this one in good condition
are becoming increasingly hard to find.*

Lamp Co., also of New York City. Howard made trains from about 1905 to 1910, yet not only were they the first company with an illuminated headlight but in the short period of time in which they made trains they produced four different electric trolley cars and four different locomotives. They also made a variety of passenger and freight cars to go with these engines. The locomotives all had brass drive wheels, unlike most other makes, which usually used cast iron drivers. The sets came with dry cells, and rheostats to control the speed were unavailable.

Voltamp Electric Mfg. Co. made large impressive trains, starting production about 1903 and lasting until 1922, when their train line was sold to Boucher, Inc., of New York. Voltamp used two-rail, two-inch gauge track, which was commonly used in the early years of electric trains. This type of track was also used by Carlisle and Finch, Knapp, and Howard. Two-inch track, sometimes called No. 2 gauge, is not to be confused with Standard gauge, which is 2⅛ inches between the rails.

Electoy trains were manufactured by the J. K. Osborn Mfg. Co. in Harrison, New Jersey. Electoy trains were made to run on No. 1 gauge, which is 1¾ inches between the rails. Ives, Bing, and Marklin had been using No. 1 gauge for clockwork trains for years. Electoy trains started production in 1911 but lasted only until 1913, which would account for their scarcity today.

Among the most well known of the foreign train manufacturers is Marklin. One of the earliest German manufacturers, it is Marklin that is credited with producing the first sectional tinplate track. They accomplished this feat in 1891 and at that time it caused quite a sensation. Bing and Carette were also large German toy manufacturers. In the years prior to World War I they dominated the American market

with cheap windup or clockwork sets, many of which sold for one dollar or less. These sets were made of stamped tin and were decorated with lithography. The engines and cars were often modeled after European trains. This would account for the odd-looking appearance as compared with American-made windups.

American-produced trains were better made, and the various American manufacturers would urge the public to buy American-made toys. In 1916 some of the major American toy concerns got together to form an American toy industry association. A. C. Gilbert (of Erector Set fame) was elected president, and Harry Ives (of Ives Toys) was elected the first vice-president.

I would not have you go on believing that Marklin and Bing produced only inexpensive trains of inferior quality, for that simply is not true. Although for the most part their trains for export were inexpensive clockwork sets, these companies were producing some of the finest No. 1 and No. 2 gauge sets ever made. I hasten to admit that I could devote an entire book to Marklin if I were to attempt to mention everything of note they ever made, but I will mention two sets in particular. They made a No. 1 gauge live-steam model of the Stephenson Rocket and a set of No. 1 gauge circus cars, which consisted of wagons that were fitted into flatcars.

Another foreign train manufacturer of note was W. J. Bassett-Lowke & Co. a British concern. Bassett-Lowke, established in the late 1890s, produced many

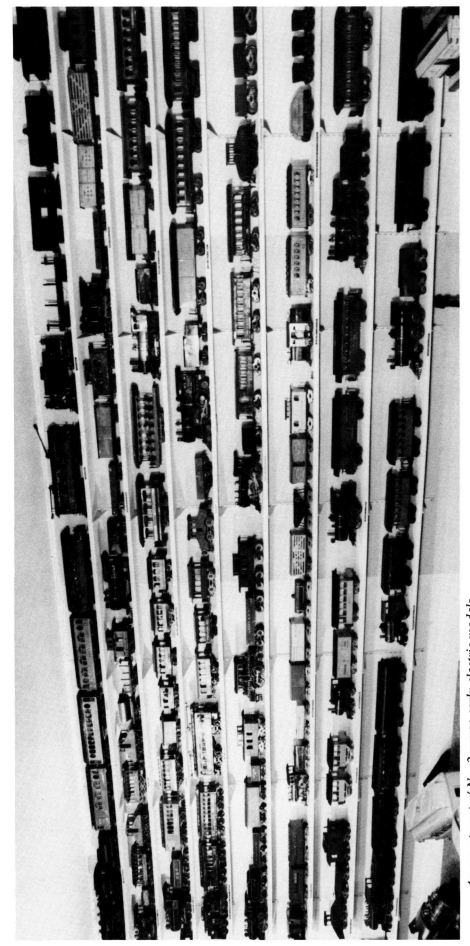

An assortment of No. 2 gauge early electric models from the Ward Kimball collection. Some of the models shown are made by Knapp, Howard, and Garlick and are virtually impossible to find today in any condition.

*Examples of two Marklin electric trolleys
complete with their seated figures.
These two trolleys, in excellent condition,
attest to Marklin's superior craftsmanship
and fine attention to detail.*

Some of the Buddy "L" toys and trains pictured underneath the layout of Tom Sefton. These large models from the Buddy "L" Outdoor Railroad of the late 1920s were never made as electric trains. These "indestructible" trains were made for a child to sit on and push or perhaps pull, whatever the case might be.

20

live-steam models of varying sizes; some were large enough to ride on and were actually made for that purpose. Basset-Lowke had a reputation for quality, and some members of the British Royal family owned their trains. Anyone who has ever handled or seen their trains knows what a finely made "toy" is like. Bassett-Lowke made trains in many different gauges, and the founder of the company is credited with first conceiving the idea of HO gauge. The idea for a gauge the size of HO started out as half O. The O gauge was seen to be too large for many households, and so HO was born. Little did the hobbyists of those early days realize that HO was soon to become the most popular gauge of all!

Dorfan

Joseph Kraus & Co. of Nuremberg, Germany was founded in 1910. They exported trains under the name Fandor. Fandor limited their line to O gauge models, and many of their freight cars are mistaken by collectors to be Bing, which also manufactured an extensive assortment of lithographed freight cars with different heralds. From the name Fandor comes the name Dorfan, and the connection is simple. The founders of the Dorfan Company, Milton and Julius Forchheimer, were cousins to Mr. Kraus of the Fandor line. The Forchheimer brothers both had a similar dream: to create a line of tinplate trains of unequaled quality and technical construction. Dorfan began production about 1924. Sad to say, it made trains only until about 1934.

Dorfan trains were pioneers in their field and are well known among collectors for their unusual design die-cast locomotives, typified by the No. 51 "Loco-Builder" engine. Dorfan contracted out much of what was needed to produce their engines, for their ideas and designs were ahead of their day. Many added refinements went into the construction of their trains, including heavier gauge steel and supporting braces for cars, ball bearing wheels, high gear ratios, and their famous die-cast construction using a metal called "Dorfan Alloy" employing zinc and copper. Their heavy die-cast engines were among the best pulling ever produced. Dorfan made up some figure-eight loops for store displays that had a 25% grade, which their engines pulling cars were able to handle. Dorfan was also the only American manufacturer to use colorful lithography on their Standard gauge freight cars, which had highly detailed die-cast trucks.

The Dorfan Company was located in Newark, New Jersey, and was proudest of their take-apart engines, which could be easily disassembled without soldering or a screw driver. It is ironic that the die-cast engines that made Dorfan famous were to spell its doom, for in later years it was found that the castings were sensitive to weather and, over a period of time, perhaps years, many of these castings were to warp and crack. Many collectors are fearful of Dorfan for this reason, but I believe nonetheless that if you see a Dorfan engine today that has survived intact for thirty- or forty-odd years and you do not subject it to extremes of temperature, it will undoubtedly survive for many years to come. Another odd Dorfan characteristic is that many of their deluxe passenger cars, both in O and in Standard gauge, had metal figures simulating people in the windows.

American Flyer

One of the biggest and most famous names in electric trains is American Flyer. Edmunds-Metzel, originally a Chicago hardware company, decided in 1907 to produce a line of clockwork trains using the name "American Flyer." W. F. Hafner had persuaded them to give it a try, under his direction of course. This venture proved so successful that the name of the company was changed to the American Flyer Mfg. Co. Mr. Hafner was a Chicago manufacturer of toy windup automobiles. In 1914 he went on to form his own Hafner Mfg. Co. Hafner produced a line of O gauge clockwork trains and never made any electric trains. American Flyer made O gauge clockwork trains and did not start producing electric models until 1918. The Flyer clockwork trains were inexpensive and mass-produced. Their sales department stated that in 1918 Flyer had made over 2,000,000 sets!

American Flyer started manufacturing Standard gauge trains in 1925, at which time Ives and Lionel had control of most of the market. It was quite a late date for Flyer to come out with the larger 2⅛-inch Standard trains, which they dubbed "wide gauge." The Flyer Standard gauge line was well made and their passenger sets had lithographed car sides, which were distinctively different from the Lionel and Ives Standard of that period. It seems that since many of the more inexpensive clockwork trains were fully lithographed it would be too "cheap" for Ives or Lionel to allow any of their larger deluxe passenger sets to be anything other than sprayed or baked enamel. It is a shame that they felt this way, for lithography was not only less expensive as a manufacturing process but the lithographed trains tended to resist scratches when in the hands of children and would not chip, as painted trains tended to do at times. The Flyer "wide gauge" line developed quickly and soon included a large assortment of quality freight cars using a distinctive style of truck. The trucks had a rivet in the center to equalize them; they are usually referred to as flexible-type trucks by collectors. They were similar to early

*Pictured above is an American Flyer windup set
with its original box. The original price
for the set was only one dollar
and seventy-five cents!*

Lionel trucks, which were riveted in a similar manner. Flyer went on to produce some of the most beautiful passenger trains ever made, topped off by the magnificent "President's Special" and chrome-plated "Mayflower" train sets. Sadly enough, the increasingly popular O gauge forced the discontinuation of American Flyer Standard gauge trains after 1936.

In 1938 the A. C. Gilbert Co. of New Haven, Connecticut, took over, and from that point on all the trains were made in the New Haven factory. Both O gauge and HO were made, until 1946, when Flyer started their new two-rail S gauge. Halfway between O and HO gauges in size, their S gauge trains were a good attempt at scale tinplate. The Flyer S trains of this period were less expensive and not. as well made as the Lionel O gauge trains being made at that time. American Flyer ceased production in 1965 after slumping sales and the then-current fad for slot cars and road race sets had taken their toll.

Ives

Another Connecticut firm that is perhaps more famous to toy collectors than just to train collectors is

Ives. The Ives Co. started in Plymouth in 1868 and by 1870 had moved to Bridgeport, a city now well known to collectors as the "home of Ives trains." They started making toys with the intention of producing good quality merchandise and they quickly rose to become America's greatest toymaker. The first Ives trains were painted tin trackless pulltoys with iron wheels. Most of these trains were clockwork-propelled, as were all of the first track trains made by Ives. The Ives factory had a disastrous fire in 1900, when the entire building burned to the ground. This was not enough to stop a prosperous and growing company, though. Ives went about immediately and had a new and larger factory built on Holland Avenue in Bridgeport; the building still stands.

In 1901 Ives was producing the first clockwork track trains in the United States using O gauge track. (O gauge is 1¼ inches between the rails.) Ives was receiving fierce competition from a number of German train manufacturers who were making trains on tracks (somewhat of a novelty for windup trains in 1901), and Ives decided to outdo their competitors. The Ives models followed American-design locomotives and were more attractive than foreign-made trains. Soon many of the foreign manufacturers were closely copying Ives, which may account for close similarities found between these early clockwork trains. Ives went on to produce No. 1 gauge trains in 1904, and finally in 1910 they came out with the first O gauge electric trains in this country. In 1912 they issued No. 1 gauge electrics and continued until 1920. In 1921 they produced the then-popular 2⅛-inch Standard gauge trains.

Harry Ives, who had taken over the business from his father, Edward, was determined to continue the tradition of excellent service and quality-made trains that his father had established over many years. The Ives company was a family-run business, even though they employed many people and were nationally famous. In this day and age of large and indifferent corporate monsters, it is hard if not almost impossible to imagine a company run the way Ives was. Harry Ives insisted upon catalogs being included in every train set, no matter how small; he never allowed even his least expensive sets to be cheapened in quality in any way; factory repairs were almost always done free, and rather than repaint the scratched locomotives they often replaced the engine with an entirely new one off the assembly line. Harry Ives would not allow their line of toy clockwork boats to be discontinued even though he was aware that the company was losing money on them! Policies such as these finally caught up with the great Ives Co., and they declared bankruptcy in 1928.

Perhaps it is too sad to think that such a tradition in toymaking could go under, but it did. Ives still produced trains in 1928, 1929, and 1930, but they used car bodies of different manufacturers (Lionel and American Flyer) in many of their sets. These trains, produced in those three years, have come to be known as "transition period Ives." Ives transition sets are generally scarce and are highly sought-after collector's items, as are most Ives trains for that matter. Lionel quickly acquired Ives and produced Ives trains in 1931 and 1932 at the Lionel factory in Irvington, New Jersey, but in 1933 they discontinued the Ives line and announced that they had absorbed Ives. Lionel then auctioned off the remains of the Ives factory, and the Ives dies were sold for scrap. Lionel had finally gotten rid of their chief competitor; the Ives tradition had completely ended.

Lionel

To the majority of train collectors today the name Lionel represents the biggest and most successful name in electric trains, and Lionel is by far the most popular and widely collected of any make. Its history dates to 1900, when a young man (only twenty years old) named Joshua Lionel Cowen established the Lionel Manufacturing Company at 24 Murray Street in New York City. Cowen was an inventor and his success had started at an early age, for he was only eighteen when the Navy Department gave him a contract to produce fuses for 24,000 mines. He had just invented a highly reliable fuse that was being

used by photographers to ignite the magnesium powder for their cameras. When the contract was completed he developed a device that consisted of a slender battery in a tube with a light bulb on one end. He thought this would be useful to illuminate the flowers in a flowerpot, and he sold one of his first models to a man named Conrad Hubert, who immediately went on the road to try and sell this new invention. It probably didn't do too well, and Cowen sold the invention to Hubert. Hubert then went on to develop it into what is today known as the Eveready flashlight.

Cowen's next invention proved to be more fruitful. He developed a small electric motor (tiny by 1900 standards), and decided to use it in an electric train. Using his own large 2⅞-inch gauge track with wooden ties, he produced a large wooden gondola car in 1901, his first year of production. From a two-man operation his company grew quickly, and he had his first catalog out in 1903. He numbered his line in a series with the No. 100 (the model of the B.&O. tunnel locomotive) first, continuing through to the number 800. I mention the numbers chiefly because some might imagine the No. 1 trolley (or Nos. 2 and 3 for that matter) to be the first Lionel trains made, but they are not. They are among the first Standard gauge models made. It was in 1906 that 2⅞ gauge was dropped and Standard gauge train production begun. Since at that time a few American train manufacturers were using 2-inch (No. 2 gauge) track it is safe to assume that the 2⅛-inch (Standard gauge) track was probably a mistake. Also up until 1913 Lionel catalogs still mistakenly stated that the "gauge of track is 2 inches."

Lionel introduced O gauge electric trains in 1915. It is interesting to note that there were no clockwork models made in the entire Lionel line until the mid-thirties, yet, without the high-volume sales usually generated from inexpensive windup sets, Lionel was employing 700 people by the year 1917! Many years later, in the dark Depression year of 1934, Lionel came out with their first windup handcars. These Disney character cars (Mickey and Minnie, Donald Duck and Pluto, and so on) at one dollar apiece generated such tremendous sales that they are credited with saving the Lionel Corporation from bankruptcy.

Due to the tough years of the Depression, Lionel found itself faced with a continually growing debt and was forced to go into receivership in May, 1934. In August, Lionel went to Walt Disney to contract to produce the famous Mickey Mouse Handcars. These windup toys were produced for the Christmas trade, but they soon developed into year-round sellers. A number of different models were made, all of which

SUB-ASSEMBLY work was clumsy in the early days and there was virtually none of the automatic equipment now in use. Thus manufacturing costs were high, there were fewer sales and, consequently, fewer jobs for Lionel folks.

TODAY'S PAINT ROOM employs both spray and dip processes. Work is streamlined and easy, and modern ventilating system carries off all paint fumes for the protection of employee's health. Mass production methods prevail throughout department.

OLD-TIME PRESSES, while a vast improvement over the days when all work was performed by hand tools, lacked the speed and precision of present-day methods. But Lionel was a growing concern and constantly in search of better production methods.

MODERN DIAL PRESS is one of the many pieces of equipment used to reduce unnecessary handling of parts and promote efficiency. Streamlining of assembly operations boosted production. This in turn cuts manufacturing costs and increases earnings for employees.

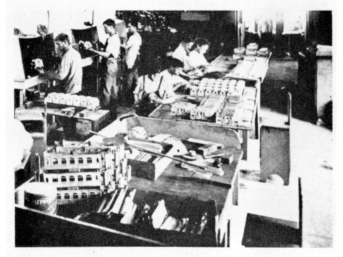

PAINTING has always been an important factor in providing eye-appeal as well as protection against corrosion. Paint Room of the 20's lacked efficient equipment of today and work was slow and tedious, as can be seen in photo above.

ROWS OF FAST, efficient junior presses help perform multitude of small assembly operations and are a big factor in cutting production costs. Modern safety equipment provides complete protection for operators while at work.

An assortment of factory photos from the Lionel Corporation magazine,
All Aboard at Lionel, *issued to Lionel employees. These pictures*
from the Golden Anniversary Issue of 1950 give you a glimpse into the past
of the once vast Lionel production.

sold in terrific volume. By February of 1935 Lionel was discharged from receivership and had paid creditors close to $300,000; it came away with assets of $1,900,000. The tremendous success of the Lionel handcars had literally saved the Lionel Corporation from bankruptcy.

The late 1920s and early 1930s were the main years for the production of what is now called "Classic period" Standard gauge. There is of course no accounting for individual tastes, but most collectors believe the Lionel Standard gauge passenger sets, such as the famous State set, Blue Comet set, and Stephen Girard sets, to be among the most beautiful trains ever made. In the latter part of the 1930s Lionel made some of its most beautiful O gauge trains, among them the scale Hudsons, semiscale 0-6-0 switchers, and scale freight cars that were doubtless the finest scale tinplate production models ever made.

During World War II Lionel ceased train production entirely and helped greatly in manufacturing items for the national defense. Lionel perfected an oil-filled compass that was declared the best in the world by many experts. Lionel also made azimuth circles,

peloruses, binnacles, fuse-setters, and other devices for the Navy, which caused the firm to receive the Maritime "M" Production Award—one of the proudest moments in Lionel history.

After the war Lionel resumed the line, the major change being the all-new knuckle coupler, which instantly created a division between prewar and postwar trains. Most collectors today collect postwar O gauge trains, and today the main emphasis of the hobby is not on the older trains, as one would assume, but on the collecting of diesels, passenger cars, and operating accessories, many made as late as the 1960s. Lionel discontinued Standard gauge trains in 1939, but you can bet their popularity lingers on.

After World War II, when full production of toy trains was under way, Lionel had more than 2,000 employees. By 1950, when Lionel was celebrating their golden anniversary, they were very similar to any major corporation, from their pension and profit-sharing plan right on up to their board of directors. They introduced Magne-Traction that year. This magnetized the steel driving wheels of the engine to improve traction and prevent derailment. There was

The doom of the Lionel Corporation was apparent, as the cover of this 1963 accessory catalog shows. Lionel motor racing was an attempt to regain the market lost to electric racing cars, which were a popular fad of the 1960s.

5-DAY AUCTION

Monday, Tuesday, Wednesday, Thursday, Friday

AUGUST 7th, 8th, 9th, 10th & 11th

Starting at 10:00 A.M. Each Day

CONSISTING OF

MACHINERY & EQUIPMENT

USED TO MANUFACTURE THE PRODUCTS OF

THE LIONEL TOY CORPORATION

Hillside, New Jersey

In late 1966, the Board of Directors of the company decided to close the Company's plant at Hillside, New Jersey, to discontinue the manufacturing of certain of its product lines and to transfer certain other product lines to other of its facilities. Plans have been made to dispose of the land, buildings, machinery and equipment of the Hillside facility.

TERMS OF SALE

Everything will be sold to the highest bidders for cash in accordance with the auctioneer's customary "Terms of Sale", copies of which will be posted on the premises, subject to applicable federal, state and local taxes, if any.

A deposit of 25%, by cash or certified check, will be required on all purchases with balance to be paid before purchase is removed from the premises.

ONLY CASH, CERTIFIED OR CASHIER'S CHECKS, MADE PAYABLE TO SAMUEL L. WINTERNITZ & CO., WILL BE ACCEPTED. FIRM OR PERSONAL CHECKS WILL BE ACCEPTED ONLY IF ACCOMPANIED BY BANK LETTER OF CREDIT.

Although obtained from sources deemed reliable, the auctioneer makes no warranty or guarantee, expressed or implied, as to the accuracy of the information herein contained. It is for this reason that buyers should avail themselves of the opportunity to make inspection prior to the sale.

One of the 20th Century's Largest Auction Sales!

PARTIAL LISTINGS ONLY: Due to the Great Quantities of Equipment and the vast ... be covered it was impossible to have the

As sales slumped Lionel was forced to close their Hillside plant in 1966. The auctioneer's folder boasted that it was to be "One of the 20th Century's largest auction sales!"

also a postwar version of the famous Hudson locomotive numbered 773. The 1950s were definite boom years for Lionel, with their name a household word and a Christmas tradition.

Alas, all good things must come to an end, and so arrived the decade of the 1960s, which brought about changes in quality so severe that they hastened the fall of the Lionel Corporation as we knew it. The famed lawyer Roy Cohn, nephew of Joshua Lionel Cowan, headed a syndicate that took over complete control of the company. It was during Roy Cohn's administration that plastic truck cars were first made, and, while company assets were being sold, stock prices remained high until the company was sold to another group. By that time stocks had nosedived and the company put together one final dying effort when they ran off many former O gauge locomotives in 1965 in an attempt to regain their market. They failed.

The Lionel Corporation still lives on by manufacturing items other than toy trains. In 1970 the General Mills subsidiary Model Products Corporation leased the Lionel name and manufacturing rights. MPC started to produce a new line of O gauge trains. In February, 1975, the remaining dies of the old Lionel Corporation were shipped to Mount Clemens, Michigan, and the Lionel Irvington, New Jersey factory will never again produce the old trains as we knew them.

Louis Marx

Last but not least, we must pay tribute to a company that not only thrived during the Depression but went on to survive and outlast the tinplate giants. The unfaltering Louis Marx & Co. provided an inex-

This photograph, taken inside the Lionel plant at Irvington, New Jersey, before they closed for good in February, 1975, shows the Lionel parts inventory that was kept up for so many years.
(Photo by Peter Tilp)

The outside of the Lionel factory building in Irvington just before its close. Model Products Corporation of Mt. Clemens, Michigan, which currently leases the Lionel name, had decided to shut the facility and consolidate their operations in Michigan. At the time of the closing Lionel had only the bottom half of their once huge factory building. (Photo by Peter Tilp)

A small and inexpensive Joy Line passenger set with its set box, part of the continuing giant, Louis Marx & Company.

pensive train to millions of people who might otherwise have had none. The Joy Line toy trains date from the early 1920s, when they were producing a cheap line of clockwork and electric trains. Louis Marx was a toy salesman who originally contracted to have toys made from the Girard Model Works of Girard, Pennsylvania, the makers of Joy Line Trains.

By 1932 Marx had obtained control of the Girard Model Works, and the famous Marx symbol was being used. Marx trains were mostly small lithographed types, but the variations of lettering and colors are astounding. Two of the most famous Marx prewar models (all in O gauge) are the M-10,000 articulated and the many versions of the Marx Commodore Vanderbilt. Interestingly, Marx actually made one Standard gauge train, a model without a motor that had flanged wheels and was designed as a pull-toy! Louis Marx & Co. survives today alive and well

because they served a need that was great at a price that was right.

I know the need is great for a definitive history of the major tinplate manufacturers that will include all the details and tell about the hows and whys of production. My only attempt here is to present a brief history and summary of a handful of the more well-known companies. Perhaps justice will never be done and many companies may never see the full story in print. The only thing I can say is that by collecting the trains we may learn a little of the history from the trains themselves, every time we repair them, every time we run them, and certainly every time we stop and admire them.

2

THE BEGINNINGS
OF THE HOBBY

The hobby of train collecting as we know it is a lot older than most present-day collectors would imagine. While it is for obvious reasons impossible to pinpoint an exact date at which it all began, we can at least document the first creditable efforts at an exchange of information. The first article written from a train collector's point of view was in the *Model Railroader* in 1935. Soon afterward, articles appeared in other publications, but the one magazine that did the most for the hobby was *Model Craftsman,* now known to many collectors as *Railroad Model Craftsman.* Their first article appeared in August, 1937, and many articles of interest to tinplate collectors appeared for many years thereafter. One of the earliest of the first known collectors was the late Lee P. Ridgman, who devoted a column to old train models in his tinplate magazine, *Model Railroaders' Digest.* But the man who is usually associated with the beginning of the hobby is a pioneer collector named Louis H. Hertz.

Lou Hertz

Over a period of years Lou Hertz wrote many magazine articles solely on old toy trains and the tinplate-collecting community he knew so well. His most important achievements are the detailed research he conducted on the history of the various tinplate manufacturers. He is probably best known for his books on train collecting, namely, *Riding the Tinplate Rails, Messrs. Ives of Bridgeport,* and *Collecting Model Trains.* While these books are without a doubt the best ever written on the subject of collecting old trains, many have been out of print for years and have become collectors' items in their own right, bringing fifty dollars or more when they can be found. This of course has created a situation in which, if a copy were to be found in a public library, it could be

highly profitable for a collector to borrow the copy and then declare it "lost," because the library would more than likely be unaware of the book's collector value. While this is a practice I do not encourage, I will say that I have seen many an ex-library copy in the hands of a collector! This only goes to show the demand that exists for information within the hobby, and it is the need for more informative books of this kind that led me to tackle such a project. Naturally, as I am a relatively "new" collector this book could not have been completed without a little help from my friends and assistance from the many older and more knowledgeable collectors I have come to know.

More mention should be made of Lou Hertz, who devoted many years of his life to researching the history behind tinplate trains. He is regarded among many train collectors as the "Father of Our Hobby," a title he definitely deserves. It must be stated that there were and still are many enthusiasts who can date their collecting efforts from as far back as the early or mid-1930s, but rather than try to mention all of the older collectors I know and by omission end up offending certain people, I will refrain from listing them here.

Most of the older collectors who began collecting in the 1930s and 1940s have extremely large train collections by today's standards, or any other standards for that matter. To the novice collector such a collection may seem to have great merit for its size alone. This may be true, but if you were to ask most older collectors about the rarity of a certain model or what variations a certain engine can be found in, you would be very surprised. You would quickly find out that their detailed knowledge on most train subjects is vast and perhaps greater and more creditable than merely a large accumulation of trains alone would be. Simply to collect trains and run them may have been the initial goal of most collectors, but it quickly de-

An early Lionel No. 2 trolley car of 1906-1907.
Even in the beginning days of the hobby,
in the 1930s and 40s, many items
were still hard to find.

velops into the desire to learn more about these models
that fascinate us to no end.

In the early days of the hobby, collectors were surprised and excited to find someone else who appreciated the older tinplate trains. Many of the early
associations started out with a letter written in re-
sponse to an ad in a magazine. Since there were
fewer collectors, many of the letters were from all
over the country, and many of the early hobbyists
saw the need for a collectors club or an organization
of national size. There were many independent clubs
of all kinds and their interests mainly centered on
running the trains rather than on simply exchanging
information. The train-collecting community was small,
but it was about to grow at a very rapid pace.

The Train Collectors Association (TCA)

Bill Krames and Ed Alexander invited collectors
to a meeting at Alexander's Train Museum in Yardley,
Pennsylvania. The meeting was held in 1954. After
a second meeting and a gathering of collectors on
the West Coast, a national organization was formed—
the Train Collectors Association. Burton Logan was
elected the first president, Evan Middleton vice-president and Lou Redman secretary-treasurer and editor
of the quarterly magazine. The organization, known to
most collectors today by its initials, TCA, is the largest

organization of its kind devoted to the hobby of train
collecting.

Other organizations had been tried but they never
got off the ground. Lou Hertz proposed the National
Tinplate Model Railroad Association as early as June,
1937. Burton Logan and Lou Hertz together tried to
form the National Tinplate Historical Society in
September, 1944. It was not until 1954 that the beginnings of an organization came about. By 1957 the
TCA had been incorporated and was beginning to
develop growing pains.

The purposes of the TCA are to further the hobby
of collecting tinplate trains by publishing a periodical,
issuing other information for collectors, establishing
standards on descriptions and valuations, and having
meetings to provide for the exchange of trains and
information and to promote fellowship among collectors.

While there are some active collectors who have
never joined TCA and some who never will, I, as a
current member, can testify to the fact that the TCA
has done an outstanding job in promoting an interest
in the hobby and has a very fine and professionally

The Train Collectors Quarterly
SUMMER 1975
VOL. 21, NO. 3

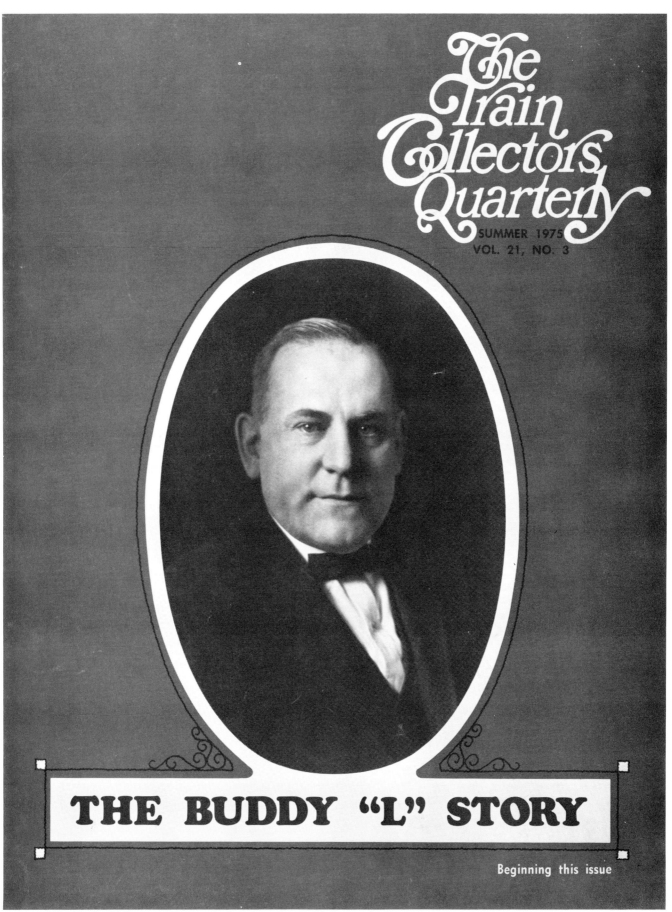

THE BUDDY "L" STORY

Beginning this issue

The Train Collectors Quarterly *is a popular and informative magazine issued by the Train Collector's Association.*

JULY, 1974

VOL. 9, NO. 7

The T.T.O.S. Bulletin, *issued monthly, is the magazine of the Toy Train Operating Society.*

34

produced quarterly magazine that is worth the price of membership alone. It must also be noted here that the TCA provides all its services with the help of a number of volunteer members, too many to mention. Without men to act as officers, head committees, edit the magazine, write articles, serve as directors, run the business office, and organize train meets there would be no organization.

The TCA has a strict set of bylaws to be followed by all its members. To prevent unsavory characters from joining the organization you have to be signed in by two current members on your application. Once you have been signed in you become a probationary member for three months and if your membership is not contested you finally become a member. The TCA has its own collection insurance plan for its members. Another very important item is the national directory, which lists all the members and their addresses or phone numbers, so that a collector can visit another member when out of town. It is the sincere hope of the TCA to establish a permanent museum and head-quarters for the use of the membership. The Train Collectors Association was and still is the single greatest motivating force behind the train-collecting community today.

Other Clubs

Another old collecting club, which was basically a local affair, was the Standard Gauge Association. Their first meeting was held on December 8, 1957, and although the group was made up of many train collectors the initial idea behind the club was to organize an operating society to run trains. Even though it was called the Standard Gauge Association, it did include O gauge and was not exclusive to Lionel, Ives, or any other particular make. The late George Brink was elected president, and Lou Hertz was elected vice-president. Because I was not actively collecting trains at that time I never got a chance to join. I have been told the group lasted only about two years, which is a shame. To its credit, the SGA published a very fine journal; about seven issues were printed. I have been told that copies of the last journal still lie in the hands of Lou Hertz, never having been mailed.

Another club that grew from a small operating and collecting group to a national association is the Toy Train Operating Society. This group originated out of Pasadena, California, unlike most other clubs, which are invariably headquartered in the East. In 1966 a group of five collectors got together and formed the TTOS to pursue their hobby of collecting and operating trains. The original five were Bill Harris as president, John Bentley as vice-president, Leroy Lowden

as secretary, Ed Warner in charge of publicity, and Betty Warner as director. The TTOS was incorporated in 1968 and grew rapidly to become an organization of national size. There are no requirements or prerequisites to joining TTOS, other than the fact that you must operate or at least collect toy trains. While this group is still smaller than the previously mentioned TCA, it is rapidly catching up and already has more than 2,000 members. It also publishes a monthly magazine, as compared to the TCA quarterly.

Both organizations have a number of divisions in all parts of the country. The various divisions host a national convention; the TCA convention is held at the end of June and the TTOS convention during the first week in August. Both groups contract to have convention cars made up for sale to members only at the convention. These so-called "convention cars" are especially made up by Lionel and are therefore always limited-production items. As with many other scarce trains, the prices of the early convention cars have become exorbitant.

There are other clubs and organizations devoted to the hobby of model railroading, namely, the National Model Railroad Association. The NMRA is a fine organization but is basically devoted to the building and operating of HO trains and equipment. Within the train-collecting community there are very few who will number HO trains among their interests. This is not because they consider HO scale inferior but rather because of the recent vintage of most HO equipment and its size, which is appreciably smaller than O gauge and tiny by comparison with Standard trains. The only other group devoted to collecting trains that I know of is the Lionel Collectors Club of America. The LCC of A originally headquartered in Pittsburgh, Pennsylvania, is a small and growing organization somewhat similar to the TTOS.

To sum up, it is important to remember that toy trains were sold in all parts of this country and all over the world. There were and still are train collectors everywhere, as is evidenced by memberships in the TCA from a number of foreign countries. The hobby has grown and will continue to grow, and we can assume that many of today's youngsters will grow up to discover the magic and beauty that characterize old toy trains.

When did the hobby start? Who can say? Perhaps it goes back a lot farther than we will admit, perhaps to the days when men sat down in the 1840s and tried to model the first real railroad engines that were just beginning to take over the minds and hearts of a growing country, a country in which they would play a vital role in building America to what it is today. And what is America today? A fine place in which one can live free and collect trains—what else?

3

HOW TO COLLECT
OLD TOY TRAINS

As ridiculous as the title of this chapter may seem, you may be surprised to learn that there are no books available that can tell you "how" to collect trains. Unlike the situation with coins and stamps or antique cars, there are no guides available on just how to collect. Some will immediately answer that they don't need someone to tell them how to collect trains; after all, it is obvious that you just go out and buy up whatever trains you like and throw them on some shelves and, presto, an instant collection! There is of course more to it than that. There are fundamental principles of collecting that have developed over the ages, as people have been collecting furniture, clocks, paintings, vases, sculpture, and other forms of classic art for many years. To understand train collecting it is necessary that we put it into its proper perspective and try to see just what we are collecting.

Toy trains, those models that are most popularly collected, are manufactured products. They are mass-produced for a large market in tremendous quantities. This quickly differentiates them from paintings and sculpture, of which there is usually only one original. When comparing toy trains we must therefore keep in- mind that they are manufactured and compare them with other related collector fields, such as coins and stamps, antique cars, and antique guns. Most trains were made as toys, and we must bear this in mind, for their play value and durability are some of their virtues, as well as their more obvious features, such as eye-appealing paint colors, glistening brass and nickel fittings, and the piping and detailwork that went into the design of almost every engine.

When a manufacturer designed a train, he first had to consider it as a working toy and then try to make it as realistic as possible, keeping in mind all the while that it could not be too expensive or it would not sell. It is the failure of a manufacturer to produce an exact-scale replica and yet still come up with a realistic and beautiful model that would last in the hands of a child as a well-made toy—it is this failure that we collect. Perhaps I have chosen the wrong word; maybe the word *compromise* would be better. Most toy trains are a compromise between scale realism and a durable and practical toy and, where details and size were cut down, you had a child's imagination believing he had an engine "just like the real ones."

When a designer sits down to model a train, he puts a certain amount of time and energy into seeing that it will be both beautiful and practical to make. He designs the train with its esthetic appeal in mind, just as an artist designs his sculpture. When the train designer uses different paint colors he weighs their appeal, just like a painter about to start a painting. In the end he has designed an object that is definitely appealing and beautiful. He has created art. Who is to say that collecting trains is unlike collecting art, for surely art, like beauty, is in the eye of the beholder. All one needs to do is to stop and consider that all the inanimate objects that surround us, such as cars, houses, tools, furniture, and clothing, were especially designed by man. Since many men devoted great time and energy to creating these objects, it is no surprise that they were designed with beauty in mind, as are practically all inanimate man-made objects.

Before I get carried away and start having this chapter sound like a philosophy thesis, I would just like to say that trains are collectible for their beauty alone. They may have many other features, such as the joy of running them, building large and elaborate layouts for them, or collecting them as a field of toy collecting, but they do not have to run. Most collectors will tell you how they someday aspire to construct a large train layout, but very few ever do. Most collectors do not care whether or not their trains run at all. This is not because they don't appreciate or

Glass-enclosed bookcases are a handy way to store and protect your trains.

enjoy operating trains but rather because the time involved in just acquiring and learning about the trains is tremendous. Many collectors feel, although I do not agree, that their trains are too valuable to be run, for they might damage the trains and thereby lessen their value. I disagree, because, if the trains are handled with care and run on properly laid track, they will operate well, provided of course that the wheels and axles of the train are in good condition. I can readily understand that, when a train is in superior condition, in order to keep it "mint" the owner does not want it handled; still few collectors run their trains.

Whether or not to run trains is a familiar argument in the hobby, with no definite solutions. Certainly toy trains were "made to run" but I personally have found that collecting them alone has given me great pleasure and then there is the age-old excuse "I haven't got the room." This is often a legitimate excuse, for, to compare trains to stamps, a hobby in which a large collection can be housed in one or two books, I have seen many a collection of trains that took up not one but a few rooms. This is fine if one has a large basement, attic, den, or even better a large mansion with rooms to spare. An understanding wife wouldn't hurt either, the poor thing!

Displaying Trains

Many collectors do not have the facilities to display their collections properly, creating another dilemma for those collectors fortunate enough to have large collections. Where does one put the trains? When the trains are properly displayed, you will usually find them where they belong, that is, on a train layout, but since most collectors don't run their trains they prefer to have them on shelves. Book cases and china closets with large glass fronts are old favorites. Also store display cases make fine use of space, and many collectors will also build or have built for them custom display cases to fit their particular needs and be tailored for the particular gauge of trains they collect.

Most collections, though, are usually housed on open shelving. This creates a problem that all collectors are familiar with—dust. While dust usually does not damage the finish of the trains (some people have gone so far as to say that they thought dust protected the finish), it is certainly unsightly. That is the chief reason for wanting to house a train collection behind glass, but I can think of two other reasons. One is moisture, which can produce rust and cause paint to flake. Another reason would be itchy hands, the hands of individuals, both infant and adult, who love to grab and touch everything they see. I wish

I could say that most collectors do a good job of displaying their trains, but most do not. This brings us to another problem.

Storage

Many collectors keep their collections packed away in boxes. Although most will say that this is just a temporary situation until they find room to display the trains, there are those who never intend to display their collection. To these collectors the idea of "collecting" has become the primary thing, rather than experiencing the full-time appreciation of the hobby, which can come only from a collection that one can see. Because it is not at all uncommon to find most collectors having at least part of their collection boxed away, we can readily understand the demand that exists for trains in their "original boxes." When a train is found in its original box it usually tends to be in fine condition, since it's safe to assume that any original owner who managed to save the boxes must have taken good care of his trains or else used them very little. Also, the original boxes are not only often attractive in their own right but are an integral part of the train though to a collector more than to a runner (one who runs trains). Thus there is a higher demand for trains in original boxes, also sets in their set boxes, outside of the fact that these trains are usually in superior condition. In terms of storing trains, nothing beats being able to pack them back in their boxes. For many reasons, therefore, original boxes have begun to take on a value of their own and continue to enhance the value of the trains with which they are sold.

When storing trains it is always good to remember that your two worst enemies are moisture (humidity) and extremes of temperature such as are most often found in unheated attics and garages. If you avoid these obviously adverse conditions, then chances are you'll have no problems with keeping your trains in their present condition.

Cleaning

One other important thing to mention is that when cleaning your trains try to use a cleaner that will not work so well as to remove paint, as some cleaners do. Even with a mild cleaner you may leave some residue after cleaning your trains, which may eventually get between the paint and the metal, causing the paint to flake. That is why it is important to remove all cleaning agents completely if you ever have to use them.

While on the subject of cleaning your trains I hesitate to recommend anything in particular, for I

Open steel shelving can also solve the never-ending problem of storing and displaying your trains.

What are closets for? Why to hold trains, of course, as shown in this photo of the author's closet. Original boxes sure come in handy, as you can see.

tend to go along with the line of thinking that has developed in coin collecting. If you clean a coin you will invariably lessen its value, because it is rightly assumed that any old coin would look unnatural if it were worn with age and at the same time appeared clean and bright. Numismatists (coin collectors) go back to the days before our hobby began, and theirs is a popular hobby. Indeed, if you try to count the coin dealers in any major city, they will far outnumber the train shops; so perhaps we can learn something from a hobby with so wide a following. My reasoning simply is that an old train should have an amount of dirt and smudges corresponding to the amount of scratches it has. If the item is in excellent condition with few or minor scratches, then I say go right ahead and clean it. Only remember to clean all trains with care, because all trains, from plastic-bodied diesels to Standard gauge engines, can be damaged if not cleaned properly. Two problems you might encounter are that paint can be worn down if the original paint isn't a thick coat and that some colors have a tendency to run when cleaned, causing some streaks to show up.

There is one product that not only cleans but works to protect the finish of trains as well. The item I have in mind is a wax cleaner, of which there are many types and kinds. I have personally tried lemon wax, commonly used for dusting furniture around the house. I have never known of any of this type of spray can lemon wax to cause harm to trains, or anything else for that matter, if it is applied properly and gently.

Specializing

To get back to the problem of space, I must mention something I have seen many collectors do to try and cope with a lack of room and also a constant lack of money. The answer is to specialize. Try to narrow your interest, possibly to one manufacturer, such as Lionel or American Flyer, or to collect one period, such as prewar or postwar trains. Within time periods you can also narrow your field into one particular gauge, such as collecting only Standard gauge Lionel made from 1926 to 1939 or postwar O gauge Lionel only. Many collectors specialize in a series or rare type of trains. Examples would be Lionel trolley cars, Ives transition sets, Lionel 6464 boxcars, or Lionel Standard gauge steam engines as types of trains in a series. A specialist has advantages over an "everything collector," since the specialist is usually more knowledgeable within his field and he knows what to look for. If he comes across a rare item outside his field of interest, he can use it to trade for items he needs. Great satisfaction can be derived from specializing, because a "complete" collection can be had if the field one chooses isn't too rare to start with.

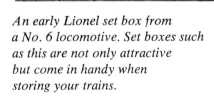

*An early Lionel set box from
a No. 6 locomotive. Set boxes such
as this are not only attractive
but come in handy when
storing your trains.*

*This scarce Dorfan set box pictures
the famous Milwaukee Road
Olympian on its cover.*

I will have to admit that I am myself an "everything" collector. I like all types of trains and could never have the self-control necessary to limit my collecting desires. Many collectors feel the same way, for I have seen very few "specialists" in the true sense of the word.

Buying Trains

Once you have an idea of what you want to collect you'll probably find yourself bitten by the "bug." As in any other collecting hobby, once you get started you feel like an addict needing a constant fix, the only problem being that you could go broke trying to finance your new habit. Soon you'll be trying to figure out ways to get trains from their original owners. While coins and stamps are fairly established hobbies, toy trains are not and you'll find that on occasions you can make a "good deal." Collectors of trains must frequently resort to buying trains from the public, and it can be fabulous and fantastic or discouraging and depressing, depending upon your luck. While there's no accounting for an individual's luck, there certainly comes a time when buying trains right can depend on your skill.

Today we are in an era of a new consciousness about the supposed great value of "antiques." Because of the tremendous number of antique shops selling everything from rare Oriental art, fine old clocks, and mass-produced items such as Depression glass to literally all kinds of basement junk, people, the public that is, have come to believe that everything is an antique or a collector's item and is naturally valuable. Because train collectors run ads in almost every paper in America wanting to buy old toy trains, people have naturally become suspicious. They assume that trains must be worth a lot of money. This is perhaps one of the most disheartening things a collector can hear, for it spells the end to all the great deals you hoped to make.

Years ago people were glad to get rid of their trains and they might have remarked, "Boy you're sure doing me a favor hauling off this junk." Although things weren't always that easy even then, most train sets were purchased for twenty-five dollars or less. Today most people won't bother with you unless you're going to offer them a hundred dollars to start with. You have to hope that they have a train that is worth some money, because most members of the public wouldn't know the difference between a Scout set (Lionel's economy model) or a State set (Lionel's most deluxe Standard gauge set). The trick is to get the people to give you an idea of what they want for their trains. This of course is more easily said than done. Usually most people want you to give them a free appraisal of what their trains are worth, and they sometimes fail to mention that they spoke to two other fellows before you or that they are planning to visit a hobby shop the next day. There are people out there who are kind and decent and willing to sell you their trains at a very reasonable price, but these people are few and far between.

In order to receive phone calls about trains you must start out in a number of different ways. Collectors run ads in local papers, put up signs in supermarkets or where they work, put up signs on their cars, canvass local antique shops and thrift stores, and generally harass their friends and relatives for their old trains. All these methods can work or fail, depending upon the time and energy you put into seeing them through. You can try different hobby shops and check papers that sell used merchandise, but sooner or later you'll end up having to buy from fellow train collectors. Train collectors buy, sell, and trade at train meets held in all parts of the country. These train meets are usually similar to most flea markets, except that they are always held indoors and are usually exclusively devoted to toy trains. There are two types of meets: those that are open to the public and those that are closed, so that you must belong to the club or organization that sponsors the meet. If you are at all serious about collecting trains, you should attend these meets, because you will not only be exposed to all kinds of trains and prices, but will end up meeting fellow collectors from your area.

While you will probably end up paying the full price for many items, you must also realize that many collectors have not gotten their trains for nothing, as many sometimes assume. Also any advanced collector will tell you that some trains are rare and you're lucky just being able to find one for sale. That is one of the major differences between our hobby and coin and stamp collecting. Many times you must come up with an equally rare item to trade or must search, sometimes for years, if you happen to need a rare set or car to fill in a series. If you have the money there are very few coins and stamps that you cannot get, but I have found that certain scarce trains cannot be bought at almost any price. Because toy trains were mass-produced, not many trains are in that category of scarcity, but you'll find that many items don't come up for sale too often and when they do you'll wind up paying a stiff price to get them.

Large and elaborate train accessories can be fully appreciated only when properly displayed on a layout such as the one shown above.

44

Prices

This brings us to the unpopular subject of prices. For a number of years train prices have gone up on an average about twenty percent a year. While this may seem unusual to some, I have been told from antique firearms collectors that guns rise yearly from twenty to twenty-five percent. Certain key comic books have doubled in value year after year. In fact, we can generalize and say that practically all fields of collectibles have greatly appreciated in value over the last few years. Are trains then good as an investment? They probably are, for I have seen most items rise in price every year, with some trains doubling in six months' time. I must point out, however, that I do not recommend anyone entering this hobby with the idea of investing in it to "make a killing." There are very few investors within the hobby, although we have more than our share of hoarders, and then who's to say what is the difference between an investor and a hoarder? Train prices are high and they will more than likely get higher, until this for the most part "middle-class" hobby becomes dominated by the wealthy, like antique cars and guns, or mechanical banks for that matter.

How do I learn about prices? Most knowledge is passed on among collectors by word of mouth, which may account for the lack of substantial material available on toy train collecting. Books on prices tend to be highly inaccurate, and most prices are reached by consensus among the more knowledgeable collectors. Finding other collectors in your area and joining the various collector's clubs are probably the best and quickest ways to learn. Train collecting is similar to most other hobbies: prices reflect the supply and demand for a particular item, and condition is very important, with a restored or repainted train always bringing less money. (Since most parts are available, almost any engine can be made to run; therefore whether it runs or not is *not* an important factor in determining price.)

Model Numbers

One important thing that has made collecting easy to learn but that sometimes confuses the novice is that most trains are referred to by their model numbers. You'll hear collectors talk about a 400E locomotive or a 6464-825 boxcar, and unless you know the numbers you'll end up lost. Checklists and catalogs are available to help you know which is which, but in time most collectors learn the numbers by heart.

Variations are mentioned, such as a two-tone brown 408E, a white 215 tank car with the Sunoco decal, a 6464-100 boxcar with the blue feather, or perhaps a rubber-stamped 256. Always remember that while factory-made prototypes and handmade samples are legitimate collector's items, those models made by an individual for himself, no matter how finely made, cannot truly be called tinplate or tinplate-related therefore, giving such an item little if any value.

Tinplate

While tinplate is actually just steel that has been finely plated with a thin coat of tin, the word *tinplate* has always had a special meaning to collectors. Originally all mass-produced trains were considered tinplate, versus "scale" models, which are mostly handmade. Now the word has taken on a new meaning having nothing to do with mass production. Collectors today refer to any trains made entirely of metal that are not scale models as tinplate trains. Lionel Prewar O gauge is almost always referred to as O gauge tinplate. Which brings us to the question of just what is O gauge?

Gauge

O gauge simply defined has to do with the size of the track that the trains are made to run on. O gauge therefore is 1¼ inches between the rails, while Standard gauge trains are larger, having tracks which measure 2⅛ inches between the rails. It is important to note that these measurements come from the distance between the inside edges of the two outer rails and *not* from the center or the outside edges. This has in the past caused confusion, as some have incorrectly referred to O gauge as 1⅜ inches and Standard as 2¼ inches.

Although collecting trains isn't too different from other collecting hobbies and they are related in many ways, there is one major difference. Trains are beautiful, well made and durable, and can easily be run. Could you hand your child an antique gun to use? Can coins and stamps be handled easily without damaging their value, and can you display them and appreciate them from ten feet away? Can you buy a decent antique car for less than a few thousand dollars? These are some of the reasons why train collecting is one of the most popular collecting hobbies today. There is no doubt that train collecting will continue to be one of the fastest growing hobbies for many years to come.

4

POSTWAR O GAUGE

It may not come as a surprise to you but the majority of train collectors today collect post World War II Lionel trains. This chapter will deal mainly with Lionel items made between 1946 and 1969. I will purposely fail to mention anything substantial about Lionel-MPC, which started making trains in 1970 using some of the old Lionel dies. While Lionel-MPC products are collectible, they are not old enough to be considered legitimate collector's items yet. I hasten to write the word *yet*, for in time they will be as widely collected, studied, and revered as the postwar O gauge trains.

In order to limit this chapter and the following chapters, I will in no way attempt to publish a complete listing of all the items made within the time periods discussed, but will highlight some of the rarer variations, prototypes, and more popular pieces in most categories. To go into further detail and attempt to be complete and definitive would be impossible in a generalized book of this sort, simply for want of space. Perhaps by not mentioning a favorite engine or type of car that you collect I will be guilty of an error, the error of omission, a fact I wish to acknowledge early on. I believe, though, that you will find the facts straight.

Couplers

By 1946, Lionel Standard gauge had been discontinued for a number of years, and American Flyer was making S gauge trains. Lionel was the biggest and best-known company making electric trains, and since they hadn't made any trains during the war (except for a rare lithographed cardboard train set in 1943), there was tremendous demand for their new O gauge line. While some of the trains and cars and some of the accessories were carry-overs from before the war, Lionel did one important thing that dif-

ferentiated and clearly divided prewar trains from postwar. Lionel came out with their new knuckle coupler.

Previously their O gauge trains had either latch or box-type couplers (box couplers came first regular and then electrically controlled in the late 1930s) in the years before the war. Their new knuckle coupler was an improvement and an attempt at realism, although the coupler was still about five times scale size. The trucks were die-cast and the wheels had been changed to solid steel rather than the stamped tin and oversized journal boxes that characterized the trains made before the war. The first trucks made in 1946 are called "open-type trucks," for the slider shoe that activated the coupler was connected by a separate piece and the axles were exposed. Next came the same style of truck, except that the slider shoe was connected to a plate this time; this lasted from 1947 to 1949. These first trucks had a coil of copper wire wrapped around the yoke or neck of the coupler, hence the expression "coil couplers" used to describe them.

By 1950 Lionel's final and best-designed automatic coupler was issued. This coupler had no need for a coil and could be worked manually and also from a magnetic remote control track. This is the coupler used on most cars made in the 1950s; it was all metal. In the late 1950s and early 1960s Lionel produced plastic trucks, which signaled the decline in quality that marked the end for the Lionel company.

Operating Cars

In the late forties and early fifties many candy stores, discount houses, and especially hardware stores carried a stock of Lionel trains, for their popularity was at its height. Lionel could boast of many features, such as engines that smoked and whistled, operating

Postwar freight car trucks, from left to right:
Lionel open-type truck of 1946 and 1947,
regular coil coupler truck of 1947-1949,
plastic scout truck, regular metal truck
first issued in 1950, and poorly regarded
plastic truck first made about 1958 but
typically reminiscent of the 1960s.

accessories of all kinds, operating freight cars, illumi-nated passenger cars, remote-controlled switch tracks, and in 1950 they introduced Magne-Traction. This enabled their engines to pull more cars and to climb trestles and grades.

While people enjoyed watching their trains run around the track, few things could fascinate or grab their attention like the operating cars. These operating freight cars continue to delight many operators and runners, and some collectors have begun to collect the variations in this series. Most operating cars were made in such staggeringly large numbers that they couldn't be called anything other than extremely common, although there still are a few that are scarce and by comparison you might even say rare.

One car that is scarce and desirable is the 3854 operating merchandise car cataloged in 1946 and 1947. This car came in brown with black doors and was very similar in appearance to the 2954 scale boxcar made before the war. In 1947 only there was a smaller silver 3454 merchandise car, which is much easier to find today, probably because it sold for far less than the larger 3854 model.

The operating ore dump car or coal car No. 3459 and the later version 3469 are usually found in black. It is sometimes found in dark green. There also is a silver 3459 with blue lettering that is by far the scarcest. The 3451 operating lumber car and later version 3461 are also usually found in black. There is a variation of the 3461 that comes in green and is harder to find.

In 1947 Lionel introduced their 3462 operating milk car, which came with its own metal stand and set of milk cans. This is almost without a doubt Lionel's most famous operating car and was one of their biggest sellers for many years. The original versions had metal doors and were 027 size. They later went on to produce a larger and more attractive model in 1955. The larger car No. 3662 had a brown roof and brown ends and doors and the milk cans were no longer mag-netized but weighted.

In 1949 Lionel came out with another of their all-time favorites, the orange 3656 operating cattle car and platform. The cattle car worked on vibration and was second in popularity only to the milk car. Later in 1956 they made a larger version in green and called it their new horsecar. It was similar to the old cattle car idea but it was totally redesigned and was made to O gauge size. Their metal platform gave way to a new one made of plastic.

In 1949 they released their new 6520 searchlight car. Most are found with an orange generator in the middle, but it is also found with a maroon generator and a rare version is just as scarce as the 3549 silver dump, it cannot command the same price. Why not? It may be that fewer collectors are interested in searchlight cars than perhaps in coal cars, but the price difference still seems inconsistent. I feel that collectors haven't taken notice of the green search-light car and I would tend to call it a sleeper. In time it will probably rise in price to equal that of the silver dump car as collectors recognize its true rarity.

The basic appearance of the operating cars remained the same for a number of years, except for some mechanical changes. By the mid-fifties Lionel began to add new cars to the line. In 1954 they brought out the new barrel car No. 3562. The rarest variation is the all-black barrel car and next to it the black with the yellow trough. Following these relatively rare barrel cars are the orange, yellow, and gray colors, with the orange version harder to find than the extremely comman gray and yellow colors. The bodies of the barrel cars are plastic, signaling a switch from the all-metal construction found in the coal dump car and log car of earlier years. The higher cost of metal probably was the reason for the company's coming out with their twin-bin coal dump car No. 3359 in 1955. Lighter and mostly made of plastic, this car is always found in gray with a red undercarriage and is a lot longer than the old-style car.

In 1956 Lionel added their new 3530 GM generator car, the popular Wabash operating brakeman car No. 3424, and the 3650 searchlight extension car. None of these three cars ever came in any distinctive color variation, although the 3650 searchlight car is sometimes found with a dark gray base.

The year 1957 was a big one for Lionel; it marked the introduction of super O track. This new track had plastic ties that looked like the real thing and a small copper rail in the middle. The outside rails were flat "T" topped like the real railroads.

Lionel came out with the 3366 operating white and red circus car in 1959, using the same molds as the horsecar, although the circus car had white instead of black horses. In 1958 Lionel came out with the 3444 Erie cop and hobo gondola, which always comes in red with white lettering. In 1959 they introduced one of their rarest operating cars, the 3434 gray chicken sweeper car, which is highly underrated by most collectors. The 3672 yellow and brown Bosco car introduced the same year came complete with a matching stand and set of yellow Bosco cans. The Bosco car is more desirable and valuable than the chicken sweeper car, but from what I have seen it isn't rarer at all. Neither car has any distinctive variations.

Another desirable operating car is the 3435 aquarium car, which also came out in 1959. The rarest variation of this car comes with a hot-stamped gold Lionel "L" rather than the usual cut-out version. The 3376 giraffe car usually comes in blue, but there also is a rarer version that comes in green.

I have not mentioned every operating car made by Lionel, only the most important and the rarest. This brings us to another collecting category: Lionel's postwar steam engines.

Steam Engines

In their day Lionel's die-cast steam engines, especially those that smoked and whistled, were quite a sensation. Today there are very few collectors, in fact I would say only a handful, who try to collect all the many variations of these steamers. A group of serious postwar collectors corresponded and produced a list of the known variations of these engines, and to these men we are indebted. When I was in the Albany, New York, area I managed to visit Ron Niedhammer, who had compiled this list and personally owned most of the engines listed. There were 150 different variations accounted for, and probably even more are yet to be found. I have heard of a 2018 in blue and I have personally seen a 2037 in gray. Neither of these items was mentioned in this group of 150; they were probably factory samples and never produced in quantity. The variations mentioned in the list included rubber-stamped and hot-pressed lettering, engines with numbers on plates, wheel-type variations, and different colors. The variations sometimes seem endless.

Possibly because most steam engines are black and similar in design and therefore not as attractive as the more colorful diesels, there is not as much interest in them. Only a few postwar steamers create any excitement among collectors, and they are mostly the "top of the line" engines. The desirable items are the 1665 and 1656 bell switchers and the one-year-only 1625 engine, the early 726 Berkshires with the 2426w large metal tenders. (These are not to be confused with the 726rr. The *rr* stands for rerun. This engine was made in 1952 during the Korean War and came without Magne-Traction.) The 682 steam turbine, which, unlike the other turbines (681, 2020, and so on), came with a white stripe and an extra valve gear. There is also the popular 746 model of the Norfolk and Western's class J 4-8-4 steamer. The 746 comes in two variations, both concerning the stripe of the coal tender, with the long-stripe version considered harder to find than the short stripe.

The most valuable and desired postwar steam engine is the 1950 model 773 Hudson. This scale-size engine outclasses all the other postwar steamers, with its large 2426w die-cast tender, which has handrails, steps, and stanchions rather than cotter pins. The engine has a large motor geared down to run at slower speeds. A later-version 773, made in 1964, doesn't have the valve guide that was attached to the steam chest in the 1950 model. Also this '64 Hudson, as it is referred to by collectors, has larger white lettering on

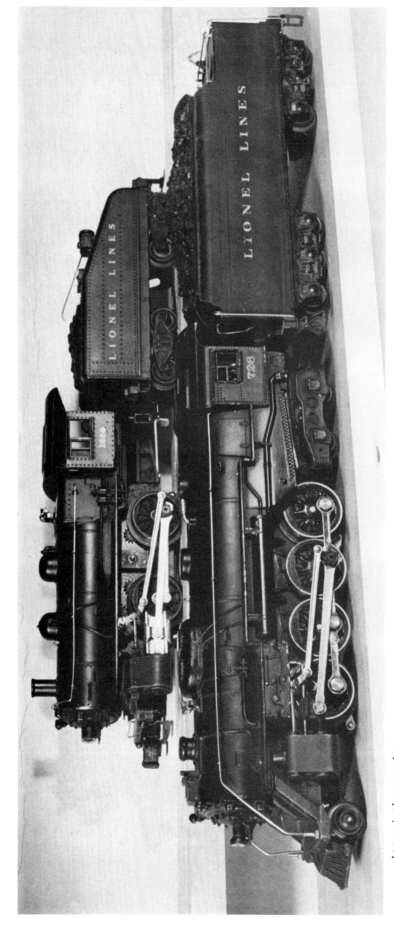

*At top is the popular
1656 bell-ringing switcher
and the 726 Berkshire
with its large, metal 2426W tender.*

The ever-popular 1950 model 773 Hudson locomotive, shown with two of the passenger cars from its original set. The passenger cars shown are the proper ones, having figures of people silhouetted in the windows.

the cab, and the coal tender is a far cry from the original 1950 tender. The later 64 tender is the short 2046w plastic tender (with plastic trucks) common to many postwar steamers.

The 736 Berkshire is a popular engine and probably would be valued today if it were not so common; it was made for many years. The 2037 in pink deserves mention for its rarity alone, not just for its desirability amongst collectors. Of course there is one other important type of steam engine not mentioned before: the Lionel Generals. There is the 1862 without smoke, referred to as the 027 General; the 1872, with smoke and a few little details added, is called the O gauge version. There is a particularly rare 1882 version, which is black and orange; it is sometimes called the "Macy special" General and is one of the few postwar department store specials ever made. It came in a set with an 1887 flatcar (the regular runs had an 1877 flatcar) with yellow fences instead of brown ones and a very rare 1885 blue and white passenger car. The baggage car of the set was the regular 1876 yellow and brown car.

Motorized Units and Switchers

Lionel also produced a number of interesting motorized units and tiny switchers, which are rapidly

becoming hard to find as collectors have begun to fully appreciate them. There is the No. 50 gang car, which usually comes in orange; a rare version comes in black. There are also the 52 fire fighting car, the 54 ballast tamper, and 55 tie-jector car. The 50 gang car is extremely common and is by far the easiest to obtain, although many cars are missing the three men they originally came with; children quickly broke off the little men, which weren't attached too securely. There was Lionel's 60 trolley, the first trolley issued in O gauge; it would have been more appreciated in 1935 rather than in 1955, the first year it was made. The trolley comes with two different types of bumpers and two types of lettering on the side. The black-lettering trolley is considered harder to find than the blue one. There is the 65 handcar issued in the mid-sixties and definitely one of the rarest of any postwar pieces ever made. Since most of the originals were poorly made, they melted after use and were thrown away. Lionel decided not to run off too many.

Lionel also made an executive inspection car No. 68 and a motorized maintenance car No. 69, both of which are fairly easy to come across. Within this category of motorized units I like to include the other small diesel switchers, which most collectors lump into this grouping. There is the 3360 burro crane, which has the number of an operating car, although it is still a motorized unit and should definitely be mentioned here. There's the 41 black army switcher, which is by far the most common of this group. There's also the relatively rare 42 Picatinny Arsenal engine in army green. The second most common switcher is the 51 blue U.S. Navy switcher. Of the snowplows there is the 53 Rio Grande and 58 Great Northern. While the 58 is considered rarer, I believe it actually

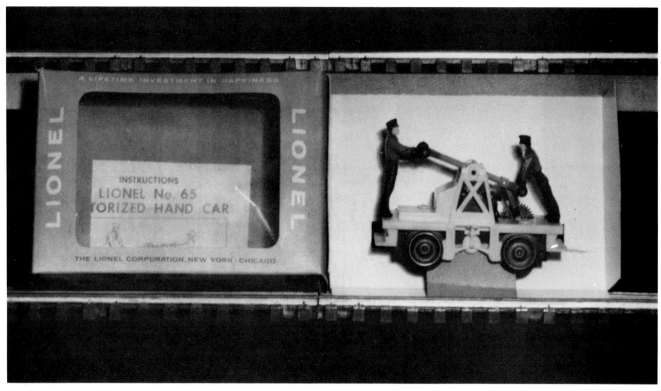

The Lionel No. 65 handcar
shown new with its original box.

to be about equal in scarcity to the 53 Rio Grande. The 56 red and white Minneapolis and St. Louis mining loco is one of the hardest of the series, as is the 57 Atomic Energy Commission switcher. Last but not least, the 59 U.S. Air Force Minuteman switcher completes the series and is also relatively scarce and hard to find.

The larger GM (General Motors) switchers are not sought after by most collectors and still remain a good buy for today's prices. Typified by the common 623 black A.T.&S.F. switcher, these Magne-Traction engines with their heavy die-cast frames are one of the best pulling and running engines Lionel ever made. Most operators can tell you that they rarely derail and can run for many hours straight problem-free. Slightly harder to find are those with a bell numbered 622 and 6220, both black with white lettering and otherwise identical. The only other road names of these switchers are the 624 blue and yellow C.&O. and the 6250 blue and orange Seaboard.

The last year for these high-quality engines was 1954 (they were first introduced in 1949 as the 622). In 1955 Lionel made a new version, which by comparison I would label junk. Though the 6250 was carried in the 1955 catalog, that year they introduced the 610 Erie and 600 MKT switchers in sets. While

these engines resemble the earlier switchers, their stamped steel frames, lighter motors, and less detailed plastic bodies marked a decline in quality that had already begun to occur in the mid-fifties. Of these later style switchers the 614 Alaska, 613 Union Pacific, and 611 Jersey Central are the most desirable of a group that included a few other numbers and variations.

There is also a scarce 645 all-yellow Union Pacific switcher unknown to many collectors, because it was made in 1969, a low production year. Also while talking about switchers I must mention the GE (General Electric) 44-ton center cab switchers made briefly between 1956 and 1958. The 628 Northern Pacific is the commonest, with the 625 and 627 Lehigh Valley slightly harder to find. The 626 B.&O. and the 629 silver Burlington are definitely rare by any standard, although they are not too valuable, for few collectors are interested in this series.

Road Diesels

One series of diesel engines that has always been popular comprises the GP-7 and GP-9 road switchers. Beginning in 1955 Lionel introduced their brown and gold Pennsylvania GP-7, the 2028. This was their first run GP-7, and even though it was pictured in the 1955 catalog for one year only, it was probably first made in 1954. The engine when found has a solid frame with no cutout for a battery, and it comes

missing the black horn cover that was designed to simulate fuel tanks underneath and cover the battery for the horn. It also came, originally, missing the ornamental metal horns, wire handrails, and lucite inserts for the headlight housing. Also the gold lettering was rubber-stamped rather than hot-pressed, and frequently like-new engines have lettering that is barely visible. On most of the originals I have seen, the lettering is always faint, and any found with excellent lettering have probably been redone by a collector.

In 1955 Lionel made a 2328 Burlington and a 2338 Milwaukee Road. There is a particularly rare variation of the Milwaukee Road that has an orange border on the bottom half of the cab. Later they made an attractive Wabash 2337 and 2339. The 2339 Wabash, while basically the same as the 2337, was designated O gauge; its only difference is the automatic couplers it has, versus fixed couplers on the 027 engine. The last GP-7 was the 2365 C&O made in 1962-63. There is a very rare version of the C&O numbered 2347 that contained a horn and was made especially for Sears, Roebuck & Co.

In 1958 Lionel first issued a GP-9; the only difference between it and the GP-7 is the addition of the dynamic brake housing that they glued to the top of the former GP-7 shell. The first two GP-9's made were the scarce red and white Minn. & St. Louis 2348 and the black and gold Northern Pacific 2349. Later in the sixties they issued two number versions of the Boston and Maine GP-9's, the 2346 and the 2359, both relatively easy to find. These engines painted in the Boston and Maine's "Bluejay" paint scheme are among the most attractive engines ever made by Lionel.

The most popular of the Lionel diesels are the

The 614 Alaska switcher shown above is a prototype as it has hand-cut decals, versus the hot-stamped lettering and solid plastic couplers found on the regular production engines.

double-motored F-3 units, most common of which is the red and silver Santa Fe. This engine, first made in 1948, sold for many years and was one of Lionel's biggest sellers. The numbers of the Santa Fe are 2333, 2343, 2353, and 2383, all designating technical changes in motors, body design and appearance. Next to the Santa Fe is the New York Central in availability, with the Nos. 2333, 2344, and 2354. In 1952 they introduced a third road-name AA F-3 diesel, the 2345 Western Pacific; it later became the 2355. All the early F-3's, such as the 2333's and 2343, 2344, and 2345, came with screen-top roofs. All the subsequent diesels came with the solid plastic vents on the roof. In 1950 "B" units were made available separately for the Santa Fe and New York Central engines. The only other B unit ever offered separately was for the Southern 2356 AA. The last and one of the rarest AA F-3's is the 2373 Canadian Pacific engine made in 1957.

In 1955 they introduced the first AB F-3's, the 2363 Illinois Central and the 2367 Wabash. In 1956 two of the rarest of the AB engines were made, the 2368 Baltimore and Ohio AB and the 2378 Milwaukee Road. There is a rare version of the Milwaukee Road AB that has a small yellow stripe running the length of the A&B units at the top. Later came the 2379 Rio Grande AB, the last double-motor AB issued.

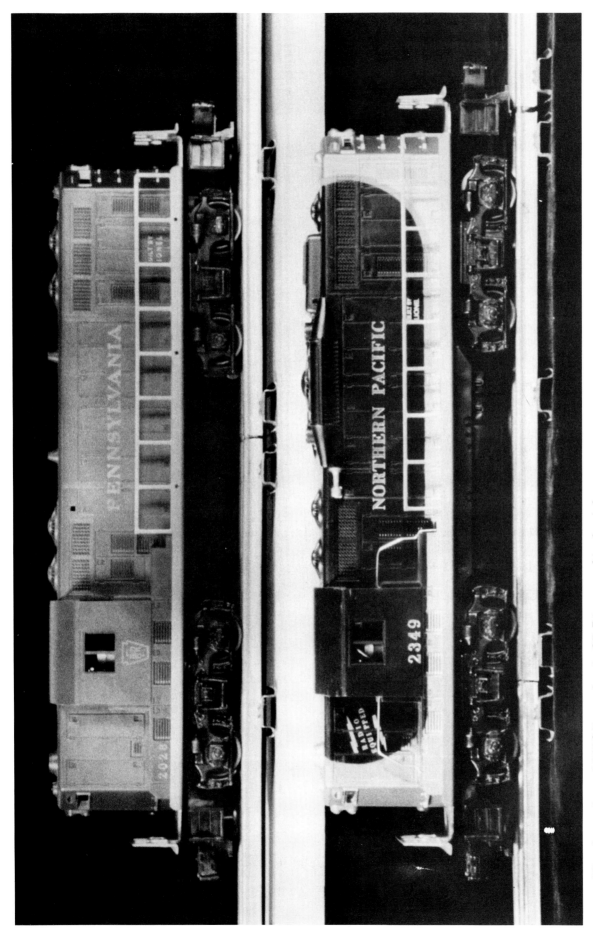

The above-pictured 2028 Pennsylvania GP-7 is unusual in that it has good original lettering. This was Lionel's first GP-7 and always came without the plastic battery box (it had no horn), wire handrails, and ornamental horn. The 2349 Northern Pacific GP-9 has the dynamic brake housing added to the engine roof.

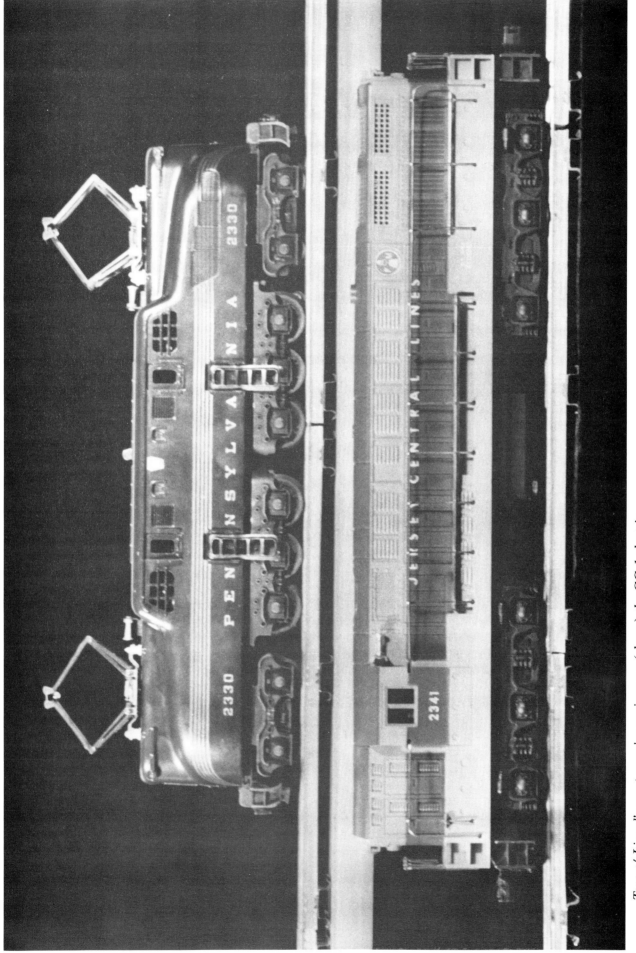

Two of Lionel's most popular engines are (above) the GG-1 electric and the Fairbanks-Morse diesel. The 2330 has unusually fine pinstriping, and 2341 Jersey Central is considered by many collectors to be the king of Lionel diesels. Both of these engines are double-motored.

In 1954 they came out with their new Texas Special AB, dubbed 027, even though it was the same size as the other AB's, for it had only one motor. It usually has silver trucks, but there is a version that comes with black trucks. Another version of the Texas Special 2245 comes with the MKT decals by the front of the engine rather than the side of the nose, where they are usually found. Lionel also made a 2240 single-motor Wabash AB and a 2243 (not to be confused with the 2343) Santa Fe AB. The rarest by far of the 027 AB's is the 2242 New Haven AB, which sells for more than many of the O gauge diesels.

Always a collector's favorites are the double-motored Fairbanks-Morse engines, referred to as the FM diesels. First introduced in 1954, the famous 2321 Lackawanna diesel was one of Lionel's best pullers. The brown roof Lackawanna rather than the all-gray engine is considered harder to find. The 2331 Virginian blue and yellow sometimes can be found black and yellow, which is much more difficult. One of the rarest and most attractive diesels was made in 1956 only: the 2341 Jersey Central in blue and orange. Also made was a 1966 version of the Virginian numbered 2322, and there is a rare version of the 2331 that comes in a very dark blue distinctly different from the usual Virginian's lighter shade of blue.

The GG-1

Undoubtedly when Lionel introduced their version of the famous Pennsylvania GG-1 they could never have imagined how high a standing this engine was to receive from collectors and runners alike when it first appeared back in 1947. The Lionel GG-1 is the only postwar engine other than a steamer to have a metal shell, for all the Lionel diesels have plastic shells. Lionel originally wanted to build their GG-1's to scale length, but, if they had, it would have never been able to negotiate the tight radius of their O gauge curves. Nonetheless Lionel's stubby version of the GG-1 is still greatly admired by collectors, and the double-motored versions are excellent pullers on any layout.

Collectors have traditionally considered eight different variations of the GG-1 as all there were, but, depending upon what you want to call a "variation," there are actually more. Here is a listing of the basic eight:

1. 2332 green
2. 2332 black

Note: the 2332 engines always come single-motored with steel-rimmed drive wheels. All the following engines have two motors.

3. 2330 green
4. 2340 green
5. 2340 tuscan

Note: Tuscan or tuscan red actually looks like a dark brown.

6. 2360 green
7. 2360 tuscan
8. 2360 tuscan solid-striped

All the other engines listed above have 5 pinstripes rather than one solid stripe.

The black 2332 is the rarest of the above group, while the 2340 and 2360 5-pinstripe tuscan engines (both originally pulled the Congressional set) are also difficult to find. The 2332 green and the 2360 tuscan solid stripe are probably the commonest of the basic eight. Since the GG-1 was one of Lionel's most popular engines and a big seller for more than ten years, naturally you can expect a few samples and special display pieces to have been made up using the GG-1 engine.

Outside of the basic eight I have seen and heard of some other variations. I know of two variations found in black 2332 GG-1's; one is the usual, which has gold pinstriping, and there is also a silver-striped version. I have seen the green 2332 come two ways, usually with a small decalled Pennsy herald located on the side above the stripes and also with a gold-stamped silhouette of the herald rather than a decal. I have personally seen a 2330 in brown, which was distinctly different from the usual tuscan red. This brown 5-pinstripe 2330 matched the paint of Lionel's Madison cars and may have been a sample made up before they decided in 1950 (the first year of the 2330) to have the Madison cars pulled by the 773 Hudson. There is a nickel-plated GG-1 in LaRue Shempp's collection given to him by Joshua Lionel Cowen himself. I have heard of chrome and copper-plated engines existing, but there is some doubt as to whether they were truly originals.

Fairly well known is the fact that the 2360 tuscan solid stripe comes with hot-stamped lettering and also with decal lettering. Not too well known is the fact that Bill Vagell, former owner of Treasure House trains in Garfield, New Jersey, had about twenty-five black 2360 solid stripe engines made up at the Lionel factory especially for his store; they were sold with a letter of authenticity stating the story behind them.

This is in no way a complete listing of every known variation, but it will illustrate how new variations are found. I expect newer variations to come to light as more and more trains are unearthed.

An important thing to mention also is the fact that many if not most of the GG-1's found in private homes will have their stripes worn off, especially in the middle, where people tend to pick them up. It seems that the striping was put on weakly so that it is hard to find GG-1's with perfect striping, as the striping wore off easily; this is also true of the lettering. Collectors prefer to collect excellent examples and tend to stay away from those engines found with their stripes worn off.

Lionel made a number of other electric design engines, one of which is distinctive and came in one road name only. I have in mind the Virginian rectifier 2329, which came out in 1958 in the same blue and yellow colors as their Virginian FM. All of these electrics were O gauge or super O and had one motor. The other four were of a different design from the rectifier and looked similar to the GG-1. The easiest to find are the 2350 New Haven, next the 2352 Pennsylvania, then in rarity comes the 2351 Milwaukee Road, and the rarest of the group is the 2358 Great Northern. There is a scarce variation of the New Haven with reverse color lettering in which the large letter "H" appears white and the "N" appears orange.

Freight Cars

Of all the many different kinds of freight cars made by Lionel the 6464 boxcars are without a doubt the favorite of collectors. A collection of 6464 boxcars and the other O-gauge-size cars, such as the 6468 automobile cars and the large 3484 operating cars, are a highlight of most postwar train collections. These boxcars, introduced in 1953, make an attractive display, because they were produced for many years in

a number of different road names that are colorful and interesting to look at.

Ask any collector how many cars make a complete series and you're likely to hear answers like forty, maybe fifty, or even sixty different ones. Well, depending on what detail you call a variation, there are a lot more. Exactly how many variations there are would be impossible to say, for new ones are being discovered periodically, but there are about 200 different types known. A handful of serious postwar collectors have gone to great lengths to list the many variations known, and detailed articles have been written by Charles Weber, Ernie Davis, and others, outlining the complete series.

Thanks to the outstanding research done by these and other interested collectors, they have discovered and listed variations that include rivet design and placement (or lack of rivet detail, as the case may be), different door designs, plastic mold coloring, the noticeable and not so noticeable color or shade differences, many lettering variations, different door types and colors, etc., etc. Most postwar collectors are not that "fanatical" and are content with trying to collect the different numbers from 6464-1 to 6464-900 and perhaps a few of the well-known variations, such as the 6464-150 Eagle with the striped door, the red door State of Maine 6464-275, or perhaps the 6468 tuscan red automobile car. The many variations that

An unusual Lionel experimental model made from a plaster mold shown below appears very similar to a French (S.N.C.F.) engine. Lionel made a number of experimental models that were never put into regular production.

The 6024 red Whirlpool boxcar is a promotional
car desired by some collectors. Other cars of
this type would be the Chun King boxcar, Wix filters
boxcar, Libby pineapple car, and so on and so forth.
Most of these cars are uncataloged.

exist are far too numerous and highly detailed for me
even to attempt to list them here. The rarest regular-
issue cars are 6464-100 orange Western Pacific with
the blue feather and the 6464-510 and 515 pastel cars
from the girl's set.

Now that I mentioned information that is "old
hat" to you, or if you are a new collector I have
gotten you interested in these cars, I must warn you
that the prices of some of the rare cars in the boxcar
series are quite high. The alternative is to collect
either 027 freight cars or specialize in some other O
gauge car, such as hopper cars, tank cars, or cabooses.

I have seen collections of 027 boxcars, milk cars, tank
cars, and flatcars. Most collectors will not collect 027
size cars, but there are still a few who do. Some cars,
like the uncataloged 6014 cars, which include the
rare Chun King, Whirlpool, and Wix Filters, can already command quite a price. Some freight cars will
always have a large following. Cabooses are a good
example and some are quite hard to find. The 6517-75
Erie bay window made in 1966 is the rarest of the
series. Some colorful road-name cabooses are still
modestly priced, such as the red and the brown 6059
Minn. & St. Louis cabooses and the 6167 yellow U.P.
caboose, which were made in the late sixties.

The rarest and the most desirable of the freight
cars are the prototypes and samples, some of which
were never put into production. While Larue Shempp
and others have some of these rare or one-of-a-kind

The 6361 log car,
although having plastic
trucks, used real branches
and metal chains and was
a creditable effort at
realism by Lionel.

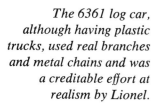

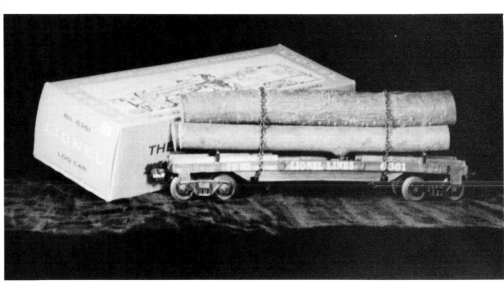

cars, there is one man in particular who has more prototypes, misnumbered and mislettered, and oddball cars than anyone I know. He is none other than Elliot Smith of Brooklyn, New York, who probably has the most comprehensive postwar Lionel collection in the country. Elliot accomplished this feat by specializing. He did not yield to temptation and collect everything and anything, but has specialized in postwar Lionel O gauge. His vast collection is a great credit to him, and it goes to show what time, perseverance, and lots of cash can do if you choose to limit yourself to a particular field of collecting.

Passenger Cars

Smaller in scope to collect but often harder to find than freight cars are the many different Lionel passenger cars. Even the smaller 027-size passenger cars are colorful and offer an opportunity to start a collection at a modest price. The only all-metal postwar passenger cars, the 2430 and 2440 series, come in three colors: blue and silver, green, and brown. Since the cars are 027 and undersized, most collectors do not bother with them and they can still be found quite

reasonably. Starting to gain in popularity are the 2400, 01, and 02 green with gray roof cars; the 2442, 44, 45, and 46 silver with red-striped cars, which are hard to find; and the continually popular yellow, red, and gray 2481, 82, and 83, which were pulled by a matching 2023 Alco diesel, as shown in the 1950 catalog.

In O gauge we have the long brown Pullmans with six-wheel trucks called "Madison" cars by collectors since one of the cars, No. 2627, has the name Madison written on its side. These cars, last produced in 1950, are beautiful and well made and are highly revered by collectors. In the aluminum O gauge passenger car category we have five basic types: the 2530 series Lionel Lines cars, the 2521 gold-striped Presidential series, the 2541 brown-striped Pennsy cars, the 2551 brown-striped Canadian Pacific series, and the 2561 red-striped Santa Fe series. The No. 2530 baggage

To postwar collectors one of Lionel's banner years was 1957, the year of the Canadian Pacific set and the 746 Norfork and Western steamer, to name a few. It was also the year they introduced Super O track.

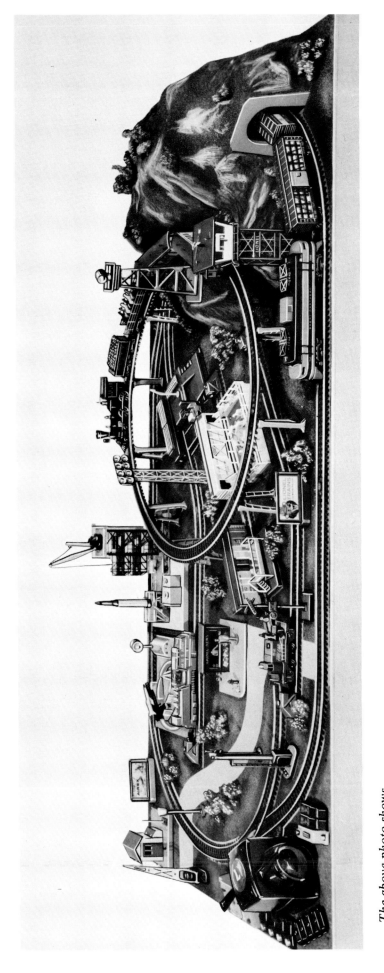

The above photo shows an artist's drawing of a possible dealer display layout. Lionel designed and built a number of promotional layouts over the years, all of them hard to find today.

Lionel made up a number of sets for Sears, Roebuck & Co. This factory memo details the equipment and price structure that went into a Sears "Allstate Special" and you'll notice just how inexpensive certain sets were. While 1060, 1061, and 1062 locomotives were cheaply made and are so common as to have virtually no collector value, any cars marked Allstate would be desirable as promotional cars and tend to be scarce.

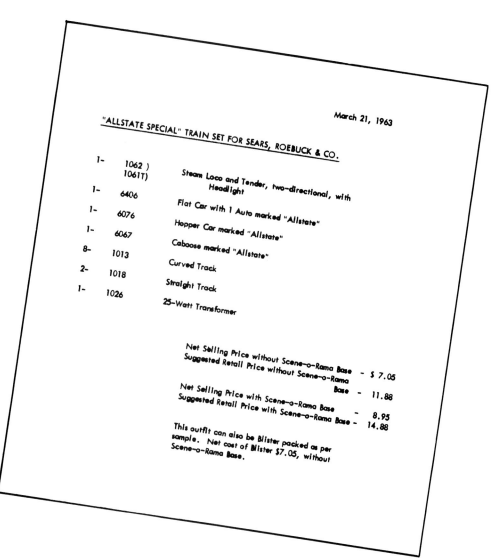

March 21, 1963

"ALLSTATE SPECIAL" TRAIN SET FOR SEARS, ROEBUCK & CO.

1-	1062) 1061T)	Steam Loco and Tender, two-directional, with Headlight
1-	6406	Flat Car with 1 Auto marked "Allstate"
1-	6076	Hopper Car marked "Allstate"
1-	6067	Caboose marked "Allstate"
8-	1013	Curved Track
2-	1018	Straight Track
1-	1026	25-Watt Transformer

Net Selling Price without Scene-o-Rama Base
Suggested Retail Price without Scene-o-Rama Base - $ 7.05

Net Selling Price with Scene-o-Rama Base - 11.88
Suggested Retail Price with Scene-o-Rama Base - 8.95
14.88

This outfit can also be Blister packed as per sample. Net cost of Blister $7.05, without Scene-o-Rama Base.

car was the only baggage car made in the aluminum series and comes commonly with the Lionel Lines plate at the top. There is a variation where there is no Lionel Lines plate and the R.E.A. plate is raised higher than usual, but the rarest baggage car, dubbed the "wide door," has a bigger door cut out of the aluminum side of the car. Both of these variation baggage cars can and have been easily faked by some unscrupulous collectors.

Lionel also made some fine O gauge models of the Budd rail diesel commuter cars dubbed simply "Budd" cars by collectors. There is a 400 motorized passenger car, a 404 motorized baggage-mail car, and two dummy (motorless) Budds: the 2559 dummy coach and the rare 2550 dummy baggage-mail. Interestingly enough, since Lionel used the same dies to make the motorized and the dummy bodies they both appear identical except for their different numbers. Most people purchased only the 400 or 404 motorized units,

causing the dummies to be quite scarce. Now in terms of price the dummy units command more than the motorized units from collectors, for they are well known to be far rarer!

While collectors try to own one of every engine and car, they still continue to arrange their shelves in orderly sets or matching trains of the same name. I am thinking of the many famous sets that form a postwar collection and are highly regarded by most collectors. The Canadian Pacific set is one of the most desirable, because Lionel made up not only a correctly painted diesel, the 2373, but a set of four cars to match; this consisted of three Vista Domes and one observation car. The Canadian Pacific Pullmans, the Blair Manor and Craig Manor cars did not come with the original set in 1957, made one year only, and so the Pullmans are scarce today. The Congressional set, made for two years, 1955 and 1956, is another prime set for any collection.

In 1950 there were two famous sets made in Lionel's golden anniversary year. One, appropriately dubbed the "anniversary" set by collectors, consists of the 2023 yellow and gray Union Pacific Alco pulling the matching 027 passenger cars, the other is the set that contains the 773 pulling the Madison cars—one of the best postwar sets you can own. There is the 1957 Lady Lionel set, referred to by collectors as the "girl's" sets which had to be included a second year in the 1958 catalog to sell off the unsold stock, since it was a flop and did very poorly. Just try and tell some collector that his precious girl's set with its pink steam engine and pastel cars is a flop and you're liable to be shown the door mighty quick! Since the girl's set didn't sell well it is genuinely rare and brings quite a healthy price from today's collectors.

The Alaska set is popular because it came with its own road-name cars. The Alaska engine has a special yellow superheater piece; there is a yellow gondola and a blue Alaskan caboose, and the other two cars, which did not come with the original set but which most collectors add to it, are the black Alaska hopper and the blue boxcar. The popular General set came both in O and 027 versions and in a number of different combinations for the few years it was made beginning in 1959. The O gauge set smokes, whistles, and the passenger cars are illuminated, while the 027 set does not have these added refinements. The special 1882 orange and black Macy special General set mentioned earlier is rarer by far than the other General sets.

Last but not least are the Lionel Scout sets made in the early fifties and late forties. Although these are not of any value to most collectors, we must remember that these are the trains that sold in the greatest number to the public and enabled kids from all walks of life to have and enjoy their very own electric trains. Who knows how many collectors started out in their youth with a Lionel Scout? With all due modesty, I must confess that I started out that way.

5

PREWAR
O GAUGE

Certainly there is much to be written about prewar O gauge trains. If we were to take any one major manufacturer, such as Marklin, Bing, Lionel, or Ives, we could easily devote an entire book to the many different models and variations made from the turn of the century to the thirties. Because I must contain my writing on these subjects to just one chapter, I will at times seem brief, for I could not possibly even try to mention every company that made O gauge trains in the years prior to World War II. While most of the present-day collector interest revolves mainly around Lionel prewar O and while some older collectors have specialized in Ives O, it would be practically criminal to fail to mention some of the fabulous models made by other manufacturers. One of the most notable of these was Marklin, which, in addition to making many famous models in 1 and 2 gauges, also pioneered in the early manufacture of O gauge trains.

Marklin

Marklin is a name familiar to most collectors regardless of their interest or specialty. It is no wonder, for they have been in business from 1859 to the present day. Marklin early developed a reputation for making quality trains and, as stated in some of their catalogs, they were makers of high-class metal toys. O gauge (1¼ inches between the rails) was first developed in Europe and then brought to this country in the 1890s. In these early years the first trains were all clockwork. Electric trains came to be in O gauge about ten years later. Most of the foreign-made trains were produced in Germany, which was the home of Marklin, Bing, and Carette and later Joseph Kraus (who made Fandor trains), Issamayer, and Karl Bub.

Trains were exported to the United States in great quantities in the years prior to World War I. Most of

these sets sold for about a dollar and were cheaply made. It is interesting to note that even these inexpensive sets were decorated in attractive lithography. Ives and later American Flyer and Dorfan were to use lithography to detail and decorate their equipment, but we must give credit to the foreign manufacturers who first introduced it here. The first foreign trains exported to this country were basically models of European locomotives and cars. Later, foreign manufacturers added on such American refinements as cowcatchers and locomotive headlights. Both before and after World War I foreign companies, most notably Marklin, Bing, and Fandor, made an elaborate array of American-type freight cars using lithography. These cars were made in different road names and designs, and the quality of the lithography was superb. American-made Ives trains had an extensive line of herald cars similar to the foreign manufacturers, and it has been said that many of the Ives designs were copied by the foreign companies, common practice in the early days of tinplate.

Many fabulous models were turned out by Marklin in O gauge. Marklin made an armored clockwork locomotive and they also had an armored gun car that fired caps; the smoke would rise from the gun barrels as if real! If this isn't impressive enough they made a small O gauge hospital car with a Red Cross insignia on its side. Inside it had stoves, chairs, beds, medicine cabinets, and wounded soldiers on stretchers. Even though these cars were made around 1906, a number of years before World War I, the wounded soldiers were still attired in blue French uniforms! Other Marklin goodies are items such as their Zeppelin rail car complete with its own propeller. The famous Marklin circus train was also made in O gauge, and it is believed that the circus wagons are the same used in the larger 1 gauge sets.

While Lionel and Flyer were boasting of their

A fine display of Marklin trains showing O, 1, and 2 gauge models as well as some interesting stations pictured on the top shelf.

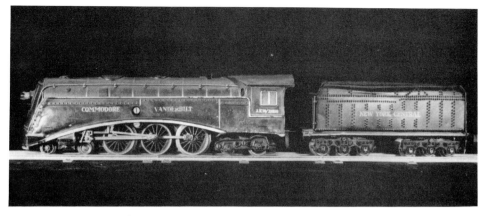

Scarce and desirable is this O gauge model of the Marklin Commodore Vanderbilt locomotive.

Hudson and Pacific engines, which came out in the late thirties, Marklin had, for a number of years, been exporting to the U.S. electric locomotives just as large as any Lionel was ever to make. In the Marklin 1934 catalog they had engines with wheel configurations of 4-6-0, 4-6-2, and even a 4-8-2, in addition to their famous "crocodile" electric engine and a host of other smaller models. Marklin also made, about the same time that they were making their armored locomotives, some passenger cars equipped with springs that on impact would break apart to simulate a train wreck. Another highly desired collector's item is the Marklin train introduced in 1935 called "Der Adler," which was modeled after the first train to run in Germany. Marklin also made a few models in live steam that were in O gauge. Last but not least is the American type scale-tinplate shrouded Hudson made in O gauge; it has been said that no more than fifty were produced, making it a very rare and desirable model.

Bing

When I think of Marklin I also think of Bing, a company similar to Marklin in quality, size, and significance. Years ago Bing was the largest toy manufacturer in the world. Bing, like Marklin, exported large quantities of clockwork train sets to the U.S. The general quality of these clockwork sets, from the boiler castings through to the clockwork mechanisms, was high. Bing also made as many as five different road names on their O gauge passenger cars. Bing also had quite an extensive line of finely lithographed box and refrigerator cars known to collectors as beer cars. An interesting variation among the beer cars is that during Prohibition, when advertising of alcoholic beverages became illegal, they continued to use the same car design, except that they blacked out the entire sentence or word *beer* with a black band.

Bing also made trains for the large British company Bassett-Lowke Ltd. Bassett-Lowke is chiefly known for their live-steam engines made in many different gauges, including O. Dating from the turn of the

Two interesting items made by Bing. The beautifully lithographed boxcar is one of many variations which were made by Bing in both O and No. 1 gauges. Many of these cars are highly sought after by collectors. The Bing clockwork handcar, made in O gauge, is completely detailed, right down to the expressions on the men's faces!

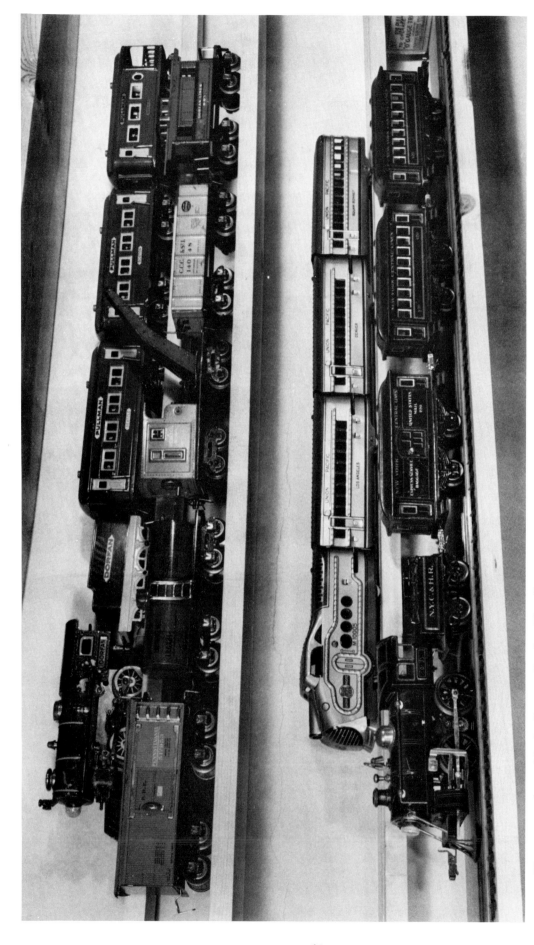

The top set pictured is the O gauge Dorfan Blue Comet passenger set; also shown are an assortment of their lithographed freight cars. Below is a Marx M-10005 electric streamliner set, which is very common and comes in a number of variations. On the bottom shelf is an unusual Karl Bub electric set made for the American market even though the engine has quite a European look to it.

*Two Dorfan die-cast take-apart locos
in O gauge. The 52 shown on top
is fairly common, while
the larger model 54 is scarce.*

century, they produced many fine live-steam models, but almost all were of British design. I do not believe they ever exported trains here in any substantial quantity. It's a shame, for they made some very finely crafted and highly detailed models of Britain's most famous trains. Many of the scale O Bassett-Lowke locomotives could be rivaled only by brass scale models, because their quality is above and beyond anything seen in tinplate.

Dorfan

Perhaps small among some of the bigger American manufacturers, yet important for its pioneering in die-castings, is the Dorfan Co. Famous for their take-apart design locomotives, Dorfan engines were well made, although the die-cast bodies of the engines rarely last. Originally Dorfan came out with a few versions of their mechanical locomotives, numbered 155, 156, and 157. Their most famous engines are their little 51 and 52 stubby little four-wheel electric. They also made a hard-to-find No. 54 box-type electric and a No. 53, which was a larger electric similar to the 51. Their No. 55 steam engine is usually found in black and also in a more attractive light blue. An interesting feature is that their more deluxe passenger cars have simulated people in the windows. The blue 55 steamer can be found with matching blue passenger cars in a set sometimes called the Dorfan Baby Blue Comet.

American Flyer

Of course I should not fail to mention American Flyer, which was making O gauge clockwork trains as far back as 1907. Originally a Chicago-based hardware company called Edmunds-Metzel it wasn't until 1910 that the name originated, when the company was renamed the American Flyer Manufacturing Company. American Flyer was very successful, for they limited themselves to mostly inexpensive lithographed clockwork sets in O gauge only and didn't undertake to go into Standard or Wide gauge until 1925, a number of years later. Basically limited to clockwork trains for many years, it wasn't until 1918 that they first came out with models of O gauge electric trains.

Most of the early Flyer sets were pulled by small cast iron locomotives with four-wheel tin tenders behind them. It took a few years before even rivet detail was added to the black boilers of these cute-looking engines. Freight and passenger cars were lithographed in an assortment of colors, but otherwise the line remained simple and small. In later years, when they were producing electric sets, their Champion line of trains was a big seller, for these small sets with their four-wheeled freight and passenger cars came in bright and attractive colors and appear similar to some of the Joy Line trains made about the same time.

In the twenties and thirties Flyer made an extensive array of different-herald freight cars similar to Ives of the same period. The only major **difference**

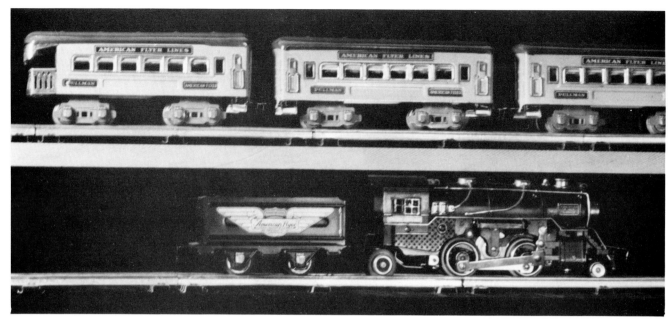

This attractive American Flyer passenger set is particularly nice because of the colorful winged decal on the tender.

is that Flyer failed to realize the selling potential of the different heralds available and so they never mentioned the different cars in their catalogs. Flyer O gauge is not as widely collected as are Lionel or Ives, yet they made almost as many models, and in fact much of what they made is even more prototypical than the work of their competitors. Certainly their 4-4-4 electric, the big 3020, is a good example of their better work. First appearing in 1922, this engine with its cast iron body topped anything available at

the time. With its matching set of long lithographed passenger cars it made an impressive sight and was far and away the best set Flyer had made to date.

Flyer then went on to produce a number of electric-type engines similar to those being made by Lionel. Because Ives had declared bankruptcy in 1928, Lionel became Flyer's chief competitor, and many of their train sets were alike. Flyer came out with their version of the City of Denver streamliner and they

Some more examples of American Flyer prewar O gauge. The large 3115 electric is found in the same two-tone blue colors as the Standard gauge President's Special set.

An interesting American Flyer freight set. While the caboose and tank car are decaled, the gondola and boxcar are rubber-stamped. These are generally hard to find, and most collectors are discouraged from trying to collect O gauge Flyer and instead choose to collect Lionel trains, which are far more common.

also modeled the Hiawatha passenger train, complete with an authentic "beaver tail" observation. They also produced an excellently proportioned model of the Burlington Zephyr in cast aluminum. One of their more interesting engines was their 9915 cast-aluminum 0-4-4 tank engine. This was made for one year only in 1935. Lou Hertz reports that only 500 passenger sets were said to have been manufactured, making them very rare. The set cannot command the same price as some easier-to-find Lionel items, for Flyer trains, in O gauge especially, do not have as large a following as Lionel and, while they may look similar and are as attractive, they are not as popular among collectors today.

Ives

One company that has never ceased to fascinate collectors is Ives. Originally they mainly sold tin clockwork trackless trains and pulltoys, but after the great fire that wiped out the factory in 1900 they decided to try something new. While clockwork track trains had been exported to the U.S. for years, in the 1890s it was a big decision to decide whether to make these "small" clockwork trains. After all, trains on tracks were merely a novelty at the turn of the century. Perhaps the fire was a blessing in disguise, because these new track trains became a sensation. Ives produced models in O gauge modeled after American design locomotives and they were an instant hit. People who marveled at the "trains on tracks" in store windows would never again purchase the trackless tin and iron engines that had once been king.

Ives was the first American company to produce O gauge trains here in 1901, and they immediately enjoyed phenomenal success. They began with their simple and petite No. 0 and its accompanying No. 1 four-wheel tender. The engine and tender were both made of tin rather than cast iron, and the first sets were hand-painted. They continued to produce their famous zero locomotive in tin until 1911, when they began to make them using cast iron bodies. Ives had an odd but simple numbering system that tends to confuse collectors, especially the uninitiated. Put simply, Ives would use the same number, some for the entire period from 1901 to 1930, to designate a particular item in the catalog, such as the number 0 for their smallest clockwork locomotive. Even though the engine would undergo many substantial changes, as it was made from 1901 to 1929, the number designation always remained the same, simply the No. 0. To make matters worse, they sold engines without tenders and you had to purchase tenders separately.

Tenders always had their own number because they came in different sizes. When cataloged, engines would be shown with a tender, and both had their own number, such as a 17 engine with an 11 tender.

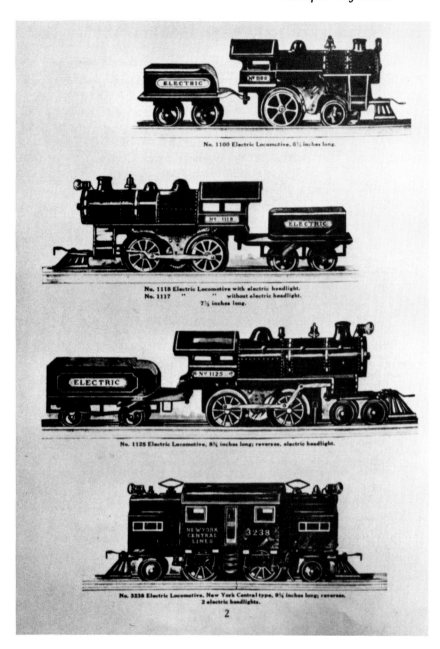

No. 1100 Electric Locomotive, 6¼ inches long.

No. 1118 Electric Locomotive with electric headlight.
No. 1117   "   "   without electric headlight.
7½ inches long.

No. 1125 Electric Locomotive, 8½ inches long; reverses, electric headlight.

No. 3238 Electric Locomotive, New York Central type, 9¼ inches long; reverses,
2 electric headlights.
2

*Page 2 of an Ives 1910 catalog shows
some of the O gauge electric engines
available at the time, among
them the deluxe 1125 and 3238
locomotives.*

A further dilemma is that, since all the early tenders were made of tin, many have been smashed and discarded over the years, and now collectors find themselves searching for a tender, any tender sometimes, let alone the correct one. Since Ives did not readily change a number even though a passenger car or engine underwent a particular change, within one number designation we find many variations to collect. Perhaps this is the reason for the popularity of O gauge Ives. The many variations to collect and the possibility of finding some new ones made Ives O gauge popular long before anyone started to collect postwar seriously.

Ives sold their clockwork sets in vast quantities and produced a number of finely made small engines.

The engines varied, and some of the differences found would be in the boiler design; some had rivet detail and others had boiler bands, some were partially painted and others weren't, some had side rods and some didn't, some had number plates while others had rubber-stamped lettering, and so on. Probably the most famous of all their clockwork engines is the No. 25, a large 4-4-0 locomotive, Ives' largest, which came in a number of variations. There are about eight different varieties, with the three-window cab version being the earliest. Tenders also varied, from the earlier four-wheel varieties to the later limited-vestibule express eight-wheel tenders.

In 1910 they introduced these same basic models, except that they were now available as electric trains, with the 17 becoming the 1117 and the 25 the new 1125, and so forth. Clockwork trains were still available, but soon afterward they were being outsold by the newer electric trains. While the first few years of O gauge production produced only hand-painted passenger cars, such as the small 50 and 51 series, Ives soon began to use the lithography that has made them famous among collectors. The designs varied, and many road names and colors were used as Ives expanded their series of cars, ranging from the small 50 series to the larger 60 series and their even bigger 120 and 130 series passenger cars. In 1912 in an effort to expand their line of available freight and passenger equipment they took some of their much larger No. 1 gauge cars and fitted them with O gauge trucks. These rare and odd-appearing cars were made in 1912 only.

Much of the interest in Ives freight cars centers around the O gauge boxcars, the 6½-inch 64 and the 9½-inch No. 125 cars. These finely lithographed cars came in a fabulous assortment of heralds of different railroads, and they were given a full page in the Ives catalogs so that prospective customers might choose those they liked best. Including the 68 and 124 refrigerator cars, there were about 16 different heralds made.

Ives also made some very beautiful lithographed trolley cars in O gauge. The original versions, numbered 800 and 801, were clockwork, and the commoner 809 and 810 were electric. They came in sets complete with trolley poles and overhead wires and the electric models could run off the overhead! Also highly desirable are the lithographed Harvard and Yale cars coming in four distinct color variations, not to mention any other sets of equivalent beauty.

It is sad to think that many of the finest and most elaborate Ives sets were made in the company's closing years. Many famous "named" sets came from this period. An example would be the Greyhound set, headed by the 3257 electric outline engine with the large deluxe 141 and 142 matching gray passenger cars. Then of course when Ives declared bankruptcy in 1928, Lionel and Flyer stepped in and continued production. In certain instances they used Lionel and Flyer bodies with Ives trucks and couplers. The years 1928, 1929, and 1930 are known as "Ives transition," for in 1928 Harry C. Ives left and the company was no longer run by the Ives family. The old Ives company was known to replace and repair items for free, and this and many other policies were kept as a tradition of Ives quality all the years that the company was run by the Ives family.

Lionel bodies were used on the 3260 and 3261 locomotives as well as some of the very last freight sets. The Ives 1122 steamer was more realistic and attractive than any other tinplate O gauge steamer available at the time. Heading the famous Black Diamond Junior with its 141 and 142 cars painted with black sides and red roofs, it was one of the finest-looking tinplate sets ever made. The same set, but copper-plated with nickel trim and titled the Major H.O.D. Seagrave Special Deluxe, sold for fifty dollars in 1929. While production figures are unavailable, probably fewer than fifty sets were ever made, and to this date collectors have managed to find only about six sets, most of which are incomplete. Another rare engine is the 1122, found painted red with gold trim and probably made just before the final closing of the Bridgeport factory.

In the years 1931 and 1932 all the so-called Ives trains were made by Lionel at their Irvington factory. Lionel put out a separate Ives catalog, which was mostly confined to the cheaper small electric train sets. The 1122 became a 1663 with a Lionel tender, and the Lionel 257 retained its number but was sold with Ives plates. In 1932 only they came out with the beautiful 4-4-4 electric 1694 engine and the long sleek 1695, 96, and 97 passenger cars with six-wheel trucks. While this set was made entirely by Lionel at Irvington, New Jersey, it is ironic that this set is the most sought-after "Ives" train and it also is very rare, as the production run is said to have been only 2,600 sets. In 1933 Lionel announced publicly that they had taken over Ives and they discontinued their separate Ives line. Ives trains became a memory.

Lionel

In prewar as in postwar, Lionel are the easiest to find and the most popularly collected trains. Although Lionel's history dates back to 1901, it was not until 1915 that they first went into the manufacture of O gauge electric trains. Lionel, unlike many other companies producing O gauge trains at that time, did not begin with clockwork models but started right in with electrics. While Lionel's O gauge trains were first cataloged in 1915 it is believed that some early sets and experimental models were made as early as 1913.

While size, shape, and body styles make it easy to date most of their trains, there are also differences in the couplers used. The first couplers, called "hook" couplers by collectors, were fairly simple affairs that consisted of a metal bar bent at a 90-degree angle and containing a slot. About 1925 what is called the combination latch coupler appeared, and after a few years this too was dropped; it became simply a latch coupler. Although called the "automatic" coupler in

*Lionel 700, 701, and 706
early period O gauge engines.*

the Lionel catalogs, it was far from that but was easier to use than the earlier hook couplers, which were difficult to uncouple. Latch couplers continued in use up until World War II, when production ceased in 1942. In 1935 box couplers first appeared, followed by the automatic box coupler, which was electrically activated and a true automatic coupler. Only the cheapest sets continued to use the latch coupler after the more advanced box coupler was introduced.

Early Lionel O gauge has little to offer in the way of body styles, and all of their first engines were electric outline models. They seem crude and simple when compared with the later classic design models made by Lionel. While there are many interesting variations to collect within early O gauge pertaining to various colors and lettering, perhaps their small

size and lack of detail have caused many O gauge collectors to overlook this category and not give it the proper attention it rightfully deserves. Perhaps another reason for few collectors taking a serious interest in early O is its scarcity when compared with most Classic period pieces. For whatever reasons, Lionel's first O gauge electric trains have never enjoyed great popularity among prewar O collectors. This situation, however, will not go on forever as more and more begin to realize that a prewar collection cannot be complete without the early period models being represented.

There are two basic engine series within early Lionel O. The very first and earliest are the 700 series and later the 150 series engines. While a number of models are shown and listed in the 1915 catalog, some are not known to have been made, although it must be admitted that they could have been produced in limited quantities. As an example, even Lou Hertz himself did not know that the 703 locomotive had been made, and it wasn't until recently that he found out to his surprise that it *had* been made, when a

*Variations abound
in early production,
as evidenced by these four
different early
800 boxcars.
(Ted Sommer collection)*

Possibly the rarest single set in O gauge prewar is the 703 set shown here. At present there are less than six known surviving examples.

local collector who owns two of them brought it to his attention. Those engines that probably weren't made (since no known example has yet been found) include the 702, 704, and the 710 steam-type locomotive.

All the 700 series engines came in dark green, although if you were to have a few to compare you probably would notice slight shade differences among them. They began with the small No. 700 four-wheeled electric, which was available between 1915 and 1917. Slightly larger but almost otherwise identical was the 701. The 706 was the same engine as the 701, except that it had a hand reverse. All of these engines are hard to find, but by far the rarest of these is the deluxe 4-4-4 electric No. 703.

All 703's found to date are twelve-wheeled electrics and all have spoked drive wheels. While all 703's are quite scarce and few examples are known, variations exist between the pony and trailing truck wheels.

The first versions have regular passenger car wheels, which are secured by hex nuts. Other versions have the car wheels secured by peening the axle ends. There is even one known in Lou Redman's collection that has regular die-cast wheels on one truck and peened car wheels on the other. Possibly as more trains are found and come to light even more variations will be found. Also, although the large baggage car is pictured in the catalog numbered 611, sets found contain two 610 Pullman cars and one 612 observation and there are no known examples of the 611 mail car.

The almost immediate predecessors to the 700 series engines were the 150 series, first appearing in

Working to further the hypothesis that no matter how rare an item is there are still variations to be found are these two 703 locomotives shown side by side, having two different types of lead and trailing trucks.

1917. The No. 150 engine was made in 1916, though, and can be found with early Lionel Mfg. markings. The 150 can be found in dark green, brown, maroon, wine, mojave, and peacock (meaning peacock blue). The 152, similar but slightly larger in size can be found in dark green, dark olive, light gray, dark gray, peacock, and an offshade of peacock that I would label aqua green, which appeared lighter than the usual peacock. The 153, the same as the 152 but having a reverse, can be found in the same colors that the 152 appears in. I must stress here and now that any of these early engines when found in bright shades such as peacock and mojave are rare, and it is believed that they were never made in these colors as part of a regular production run. These early engines found in these odd shades were probably sent in to the factory years later and, as part of their customer repair service, badly scratched engines were repainted using those colors available at the time. Also as Lionel experimented with new paints from time to time some of these "experimentals" may have been taken home by those people working for the factory.

In 1921 a No. 151 and 153 steamer was cataloged but none have yet been found. The 154 electric was slightly larger than the 153 and always came with a reverse. The 154 can be found in dark green and a dark olive shade. Another engine, which can only be described as "cute," is the tiny 158, which had tiny nickeled dummy headlights on each end. The 158 came without an ornamental bell and is found in gray and black.

Always popular is the 4-4-4 electric No. 156, which is the brother to the rare 703 mentioned before. The 156 can have solid and four-hole die-cast wheels on the trailing trucks and also regular peened car wheels. Usually found in dark green it is also known in light green, apple green, dark gray, and maroon. There also is a hard-to-find 156X, which is the same as the 156, but it had only four wheels rather than twelve. The 156X was made for only a few years and can be found in maroon and a light olive green. As desirable and scarce as any 156 is the No. 203 battleship gray armored locomotive and its matching gray 702 baggage car and the more common 900 four-wheeled boxcar. This set has always been a favorite among collectors, but few survive in excellent condition, as this set was a natural target for any kid who owned an air rifle or sling shot. Although a novelty in its day it lasted only from 1917 to 1920. While many variations exist in the early four-wheel freight cars, I feel the subject to be too detailed and not within the interest of most collectors.

Easier to find and obtain and chock-full of colors and varieties are those trains made in the Classic era of Lionel O gauge tinplate, a period stretching from approximately 1924 until 1942. Within this time span many trains were made, and popularity began to switch from the Standard gauge trains to the smaller and easier-to-work-with O gauge models. It would not be long before O gauge was king, and in a short time Lionel was to make their scale Hudson, for the first time a truly full-scale model.

In describing the Lionel electrics rather than go by year I think it would be easiest to list them according to size, from the smallest to the largest. The small boxlike 248 was Lionel's smallest and is usually found in orange and red. The 248 also is known in dark green, olive green, and terra cotta. Next in size is the 250, which has the same body as the 252, only without a reverse. The 250 in dark green is scarce and is

The scarce Lionel No. 203 armored locomotive, followed by a 900 gray four-wheel boxcar and the rare gray 702 baggage car. One of the most popular early sets among collectors, the armored train is difficult to find in good condition.

A boxed Macy Special 253 set. Not only is there a celluloid decal on the observation deck but the set box is also labeled. This set, which is found in red with cream trim, is not to be confused with the red 450 locomotive, which has its own special brass plates inscribed "Macy Special."

easier seen in yellow-orange with an E stamped on the door denoting a reverse. Far more common is the usually seen 252 in either olive green or peacock. The 252 or 252E can also be found in yellow orange and terra cotta.

The 253 is a slightly longer engine and is usually seen in peacock and dark green. The 253 also is found in maroon (scarce), mojave, apple green, terra cotta, pea green with an orange stripe, and also in red with orange, brass, or cream-painted windows. The 254 electric is found in pea green, olive green, dark green, mojave, orange, and red. The 254E is found in olive and apple green. The 254 is found in many different variations, and some of the colors mentioned come with and without stripes painted around the base, some have orange or red hatches painted on their

sides, some have orange inserts in the louvers, and. some are also found with an E rubber-stamped on the door.

Using the same basic body as the 254 are the two variations of the No. 4 Bild-A-Loco. Usually seen in orange it can be found with and without weights. All versions have O gauge Bild-A-Loco motors, but the rare version comes painted gray with apple green hatch covers. Both the orange and gray No. 4 locos are highly desirable and hard to find and are an important part of any prewar O collection.

Next in size is the 251 and 251E engine, which is hard to find and I believe underrated, for, while most of the common versions of the 253 and 254 are always available, the 251 is not that easy to find. It is found in gray and red, and the red version can

When Lionel added a reverse to their locomotives they usually changed the plates but, as shown with the 253 above, they sometimes just as easily rubber-stamped an "E" on its side. Other engines besides a 253 are known to come in this variation.

Not that often found is the short and stubby Lionel No. 257 locomotive. This one happens to have a scarce crackle-black four-wheel coal tender behind it.

sometimes be found with a cream stripe. Lastly, the largest and finest of Lionel's O gauge electrics is the famed double-motored 256. Always found in orange there are four variations of the 256. The first and most common version has rubber-stamped lettering, spoked wheels, and had a large nickel headlight and nickel trim. The second variation was rubber-stamped, the pantograph was nonoperating, it had brass trim and solid wheels. The third version, which I believe to be the hardest, although many I've heard say that the fourth version is the rarest, came with a brass plate that had no border, it had an operating pantograph (same as the 408E in Standard gauge), and the windows were painted pea green. The fourth version was the same as the third except that the brass plate had a double line border.

Lionel's O gauge steam type engines didn't appear until later, a number of years after the first Classic O electrics. First appearing in 1930 was the stubby-looking 257 engine without a reverse and coming with a four-wheel tender. This engine, looking very similar to the Standard gauge 384, had the same basic design and had a die-cast frame, as did all the first O gauge engines made in the early thirties. The 257 always comes in black and can be found with and without an orange stripe. There also is a rare black crackle tender, a four-wheel version that can be found with the 257 or the 258. The 258 is the same size as the 257 but is usually found with an eight-wheel tender and comes in the same variations.

While the 257 and 258 were simple 2-4-0 steamers, the next in size was the 2-4-2 No. 261 locomotive. The 261 comes in black with a four-wheel tender and has copper trim; its later counterpart, the 261E, has an eight-wheel tender and nickel trim. Probably the easiest to find of these early steamers is the 2-4-2 No. 262. The black 262 and 262E with copper trim came

The 262 locomotive is one of Lionel's most commonly found tinplate steamers. The one pictured is an unusual variation in that it has an orange stripe on the engine and tender. The common 262 is normally found all black without any stripe.

first and is a common engine, but the later version having nickel trim is harder to find. The 262E can also be found in a black satin finish, and there is a rare variation that has an orange stripe on the engine and tender.

Another one of the first steamers, which first appeared in 1930, is the long 2-4-2 engine No. 260E. The 260E was Lionel's first deluxe O gauge steamer. Coming with an eight-wheel Vanderbilt-type oil tender, it can also be found having twelve wheels in some later sets. Commonly it is seen in black with copper trim, and the engine has a green frame. It is slightly harder to find with a cream stripe on the engine and tender. The last versions were made in a dark gray and have nickel trim, but most originals when found have broken frames and steam chests, probably due to an incorrect mixture of the metals that went into the die-casting process. Die-cast materials when they are mixed incorrectly tend to crystalize after a certain period of time and become brittle, causing them to break rather easily.

While most gray nickel-trim 260E's are found with broken frames, the similar-appearing 255E locomotive is usually seen with a perfect frame. The 255E engine is identical to the 260E except for the addition of a chugger mechanism. The 255E is considered hard to find and always comes in gray with nickel trim and the Vanderbilt oil tender.

Another tinplate steamer which appeared later in 1936 is the 2-4-2 No. 249. The 249 is usually seen in gray with nickel trim, but it also can be found in black. One of the very commonest of the Lionel steamers is the 259 and 259E, which was made for a number of years and came in many different sets. The 259 was a small engine and did not have a die-cast frame but had a stamped metal body. Coming in a host of variations it can be found in a number of combinations with nickel and copper trim and a few different size tenders in black, gray, and a late flat black color.

Another popular Lionel loco is the 264E and 265E Commodore Vanderbilt 2-4-2 streamlined locomotive. This engine always came with nickel trim and is found in four basic colors. Usually seen in black, it was also made in a gunmetal gray color. The two other colors have always been collector favorites, the easier being the red color of the Red Comet set, which came with the streamlined tender and a harder-to-find coal tender and the sky blue color of Lionel's famous Blue Streak set.

One of Lionel's largest tinplate engines using the boiler of the 260E is the large 2-4-2 No. 263E loco. Always using the twelve-wheel Vanderbilt tender (the same one used by the gray 260E), it comes with

nickel trim and later-style wheels in gunmetal. It also is found in two-tone blue similar to the Standard gauge Blue Comet and it was used to pull Lionel's O gauge Blue Comet set, which is a favorite among collectors.

This list of tinplate steamers is not complete, nor was it intended to be, for while Lionel made a number of other steamers they would fall into another category, that of the later die-cast steamers. While I don't think it's necessary to delve into the various 027 engines, I will lump the later die-cast and scale engines into the collector category usually referred to as Lionel 072, which I'll get to later.

Passenger Cars

Lionel made a wealth of passenger cars, from the tiny four-wheel 529, 530 to the large deluxe 710, 712 in a host of major and minor variations. For those of you interested in knowing every known variation of every car, the answer would be to get a copy of the Train Collectors Association's fine Lionel number list. Since most collector interest surrounds the more deluxe passenger sets, I feel it necessary to mention a few of the more desirable items.

The 605, 606 passenger cars came in Lionel's better sets in a number of different colors. Usually found in gray in sets with a gray 251 loco, they are also known to come in gray with an off-white clerestory stripe and also with an apple green stripe. They also are found in both orange and red and having cream trim. The rarest versions are the olive green 605, 606 cars.

Appearing similar to the 605 cars are the slightly larger 710, 712 passenger cars. They come in a number of minor variations as to different door colors, New York Central or Lionel Lines lettering, and some cars come interchangeably with either four- or six-wheel trucks. They are usually seen in red, also orange, and slightly harder to find and always having six-wheel trucks are the more desirable two-tone blue 710 cars.

Probably the nicest-proportioned tinplate O passenger cars are the 613, 614, and 615. These cars are all hard to find and come in terra cotta and maroon, two-tone blue, and the rare red with aluminum roofs sometimes called red and silver. The 2613, 2614, and 2615 cars are the same, except that they always come with the automatic box couplers and are found in two-tone blue and a scarce two-tone green. Variations abound in all the Lionel passenger cars, and these are no exceptions, as some sets are found with vestibules and some later sets without. The two-tone green 2613 cars, which are rare to begin with, are known with two different observation decks; one is found painted

Some of the trains from the Ted Sommer collection. The large steamer pictured at top is a gray 260E and its appropriate oil tender.

a matching dark green, and the other is found painted a flat black to match the cars' underbellies.

Always collector favorites are the Lionel uncataloged passenger cars numbered 1685, 1686, and 1687, which were once part of the short-lived Lionel-Ives line. These cars were made for a number of years and came with a number of different engines, although most are found with a 262E. These cars are usually found in red with a maroon roof and are also seen in a bright vermillion shade with a maroon roof. Slightly harder to find are the beige or gray with a maroon roof (ex-Ives colors same as the 1694 set), and the rarest set is that with the blue and silver (or aluminum) cars.

Freight Cars

The many different sizes and variations of Lionel tinplate freight cars offer the collector an opportunity for a long, interesting, and intriguing search to try and obtain them. Of course it can also end in insanity, as you'll find the variations sometimes seeming endless. Well, relax, the easiest thing to do is what most collectors have done and that is to take one series of freight car at a time. The 800 series latch coupler cars are fairly common and so are the 650 series

freights. Slightly harder are the attractive 800 series box coupler freights, which are found in many of the later colors. The 2800 series freights always come with the box automatic couplers and are somewhat hard to find.

Most collectors sooner or later find themselves wishing to complete a set of the 800 and 2800 rubber-stamped freights. These were the very last O gauge tinplate freights made by Lionel, and they have some interesting features, such as the fact that their ladders, brakewheels, and trucks are completely painted a flat black. These cars are completely rubber-stamped and all are hard to find, while some of the harder ones border on the impossible. The red and brown caboose, the orange gondola, the black 2816 hopper, and the 3814 merchandiser are among the easier to find of the rubber-stamped series. The brown 813 cattle car, the dark orange and brown 2814 boxcar,

The highly desirable and scarce Macy Special 450 set. In addition to the engine having its own special brass plate and number, each of the passenger cars has the lettering "Macy Special" inscribed above the windows.

the 2812 black gondola, and the 814R and 2814R white and brown refrigerator cars are all rare and hard to find. There also are a few known 2800 series cars with nickel plates in the later rubber-stamp colors. These cars are so rare that many collectors do not even know they exist!

Name Sets

While many sets are desirable, the specially named sets by Lionel have always been very popular. The Red Comet set was one of the less expensive cataloged sets, but it is nevertheless one of the most attractive. Consisting of a red streamlined 264E, 261T or 265T tender, two matching 603 Pullmans and 604 observation, the set was even equipped with an enameled red transformer. The Blue Streak set in its rich blue and white would be a natural counterpart to the Red Comet. With its 265E engine and tender and its matching 617, 618, and 619 streamlined cars, the Blue Streak is one of Lionel's most beautiful sets; it also is hard to find in nice original condition. There also is a rare variation of the Blue Streak that is all blue without the usual white trim.

The O gauge Blue Comet is another natural favorite, with its two-tone blue 263E, oil tender and matching 613, 614, and 615 and later 2613, 2614, 2615 passenger cars. Always a favorite too is the O gauge work train set with its gray 263E engine and vandy tender, an 812 gondola car with barrels and an 812T tool set, the operating 810 derrick car, the 820 floodlight car, and an 817 caboose.

Highly desired amongst collectors too are the various department store specials. These were sets especially made up by Lionel for a particular store or chain and were usually different in some way from the regular cataloged sets. Lionel would simply add on a car, paint on a stripe, use a different engine, or use the store's name to make these sets in some way different so that they could be sold to the stores at a special price. While this practice was carried on for a number of stores and chains, most collectors are familiar only with the Macy specials, because Macy's probably did the most business with Lionel along these lines. Some of their sets had the Macy name inscribed right on the trains themselves rather than just on the set boxes.

An example of one of these Macy specials would be the 252 in maroon with a cream stripe, two 607 cars and a 608 observation in maroon with the name Macy Special on the cars, and the 608 car having a Macy Special brass plate attached to the deck. Another set would be a red 450 (that's a red 253 with a special brass plate with its own number) pulling 610, 610, 612 cars and the name Macy Special rubber-stamped in script above the windows. One other rare set consists of an orange 254 and the regular 605, 605, 606 cars identified as a special when there is a brass Macy Special plate on the observation platform. There are others but these are among the most desirable sets. Who knows, maybe one day you'll pick up a set from an original owner in its original set box and you'll have found another department store special when the seemingly normal set box is examined closely and you discover the name of a local store stamped or labeled right on the box!

Belonging to a special category unto themselves are the famous Lionel Disney handcars. While Lionel made very few windup trains, these handcars, first introduced in 1935, were one of Lionel's biggest sellers ever. Certainly it's no wonder, for who could pass up such a bargain? These beautiful clockwork hand-painted toys sold with a circle of track for one dollar! There was the 1100 Mickey and Minnie Mouse handcar, the uncataloged 1103 Peter Rabbit Chick-Mobile, the 1105 Santa Claus handcar, and the 1107 Donald Duck Rail Car. Always a collector's favorite is the famous Mickey Mouse Circus Train Outfit, consisting of a red windup Commodore Vanderbilt engine and Mickey Mouse complete with a shovel standing in the tender; the engine pulled three beautifully lithographed circus cars. The set also came with a cardboard circus tent, cardboard gas station, signs, an

auto, circus tickets, and a molded Mickey Mouse barker—all for only two dollars complete! Even though these sets were sold in enormous quantities, few survive, especially complete, as people tended to take less care of a less expensive set, and cardboard in the hands of a child is not known to last too long.

072

One of the hottest collector categories of all would certainly have to be those trains we lump into the group labeled Lionel 072. The 072 trains made in the latter part of the thirties and the very early forties are a far cry from some of the trains mentioned before, because many 072 models are almost completely scale models, and some are full-scale models. They nevertheless are part of the overall picture of prewar O gauge trains. The 072 wide radius track was available as early as 1934, and a year later, in 1935, Lionel introduced 072 switches and solid T-rail track. The real development of 072 trains began later. Pictured on the front cover of the 1936 catalog is what seems to be the front of a Lionel scale Hudson, but it was not introduced until 1937. From that period forward Lionel went on to produce some of their finest made trains ever.

I do not regard only those trains designated by Lionel as part of their 072 series as being the only 072, but some of what Lionel referred to as O gauge I think deserves to be classified among the Lionel Hudsons. Certainly the Lionel scale and semiscale

Two Lionel 0-6-0 switchers. The 203 at top is smaller and comes with the shorter Lionel Lines tender. The semiscale 8976 (correct number 227) is made to scale size and length but has tinplate trucks and couplers.

The 2350 New Haven electric (above) and the 0000 Alaska GP-9 diesel (center) are both prototypes. While the New Haven was put into regular production, minus the large LIONEL lettering on its side, the Alaskan engine was not. Only four sample Alaskan engines were made by Lionel.

Two variations of the Milwaukee Road 2338 GP-7 diesel. The bottom engine, known as the orange all-around Milwaukee, is considered scarce.

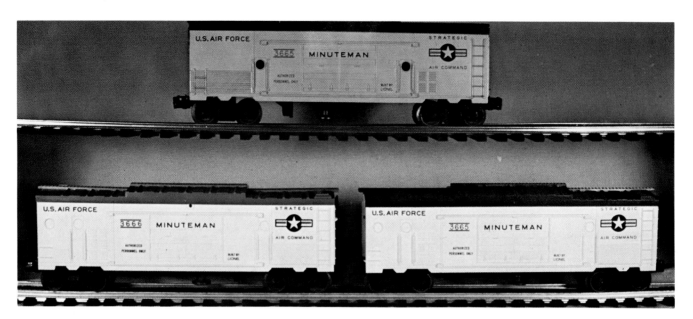

Three different variations of the Lionel Minuteman Car.

*The 6516 bay window caboose pictured on top is an experimental model with
Santa Fe markings. The 6517-60 Erie caboose is rare as it was a short-run
service station special. The 6517 Lionel Lines caboose
shown has the double lines variation.*

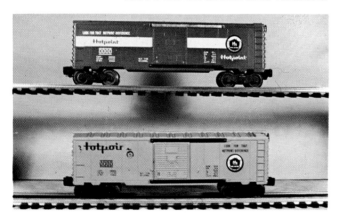

*Two versions of the Hotpoint 0000 prototypes.
(Courtesy of the Elliot Smith collection)*

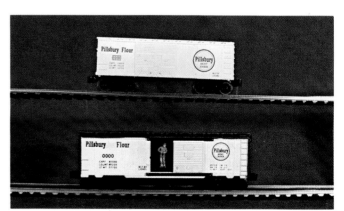

*Two Pillsbury 0000 promotional prototypes
shown both as an 027 boxcar (top) and
O gauge version.*

Two 6464-300 solid-shield Rutland boxcars. While all solid-shield Rutlands are rare, the one pictured below is even more unusual as it also has the scarce striped door.

Two pink 2037 locomotives from the Lionel girl's train. The one pictured below is extremely rare because of the unusual square-type tender. (Elliot Smith collection)

Four scarce 6464 boxcars. The green 6464-50 Minneapolis & St. Louis is a one of a kind. Pictured next to it is a 6464-375 red (not maroon) Central of Georgia, while below we have a 1954 (not 6464-100) Western Pacific boxcar with the blue feather. The dark blue 6464 Western Pacific is also extremely rare. These 6464's are all from the Elliot Smith collection.

The top row from right to left shows
an orange Lionel 256, a gray 251E,
and a pea green 254E. The bottom
pictures a two-tone green 253E,
an olive 252, a dark green 250,
and the small red 248.

Two rare early Ives O gauge sets
in unusually fine condition.
A No. 17 passenger set and No. 20
freight set. Note the rare
inboard trucks on the
merchandise car and the stock car.

An early and rare Ives 25 engine
(made about 1903) with an
orange 50 baggage car and
51 coach (both missing roofs).
The passenger cars are handpainted
as well as the early short tender, and
the engine has six boiler bands and
its headlight set back.

The Lionel blue 710 series passenger cars (above) are always found with
six-wheel trucks. The 617, 618, and 619 solid blue, passenger cars
of the Lionel Blue Streak set are very rare. On the end of one of the
original boxes are stamped the letters SB, which probably stand for solid blue
or special blue as these cars are usually found
in a lighter blue and white combination.

Two Lionel 4U Bild-A-Loco sets compared. Orange sets are
hard to find but gray sets are even rarer.
Note the large curved hand reverse on these engines.

Four nines compared.

Three scarce No. 10's (from left to right): *The peacock Bild-A-Loco, the red 10, and the brown or tan variation.* (From the Tom Sage collection)

A Lionel 385 crackle gray tender. Believed to have come with a number of different engines, among them a 385 and a 392, the engines came in the usual gunmetal gray and are not known to ever have come in the crackle gray finish.

Probably the first-run colors of the 218 dump car or possibly an experimental paint scheme is this extremely rare freight car found in the hands of its original owners by Ed Prendeville.

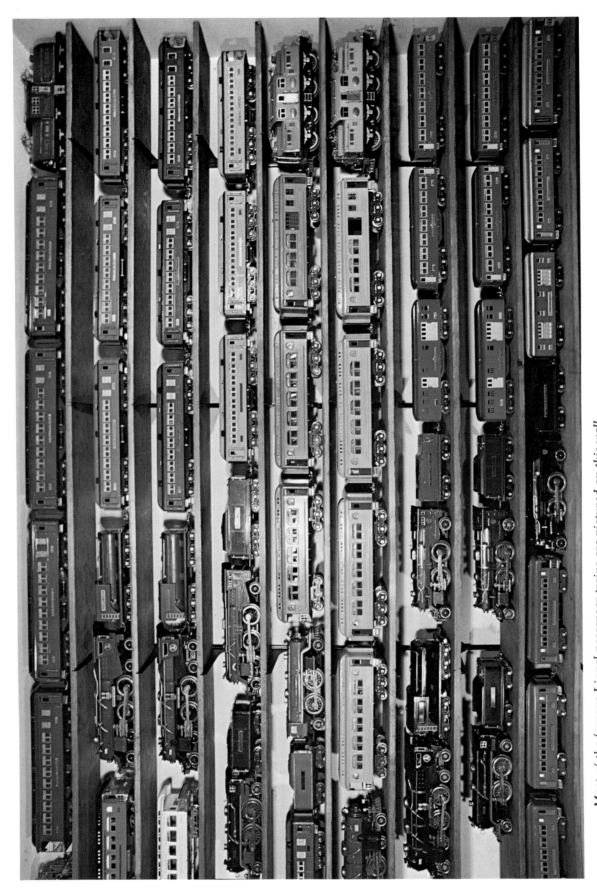

Most of the famous Lionel passenger trains are pictured on this wall (from top to bottom). We have the four-car 381E green State Set, a gray nickel-trim 400E pulling the full nickel Blue Comet cars, a 400E Blue Comet set, a 392 Girard set, two 408 sets, and two 385 transition sets, and so on and so forth.

The three basic versions of the763E semiscale Hudson. At top is a black 763E, below it the more commonly found gray 763E with the Vanderbilt tender, and on the bottom shelf is another gray 763E Hudson shown with the rare gunmetal gray coal tender.

B6 0-6-0 switchers are more than just what we would think of as an O gauge engine. I feel the 226, with its long black die-cast coal tender, is one of Lionel's best-running engines and although not scale it still is quite a fine-looking loco.

Though small and not to scale size, the 0-6-0 switchers numbered 201 and 203 are not so easy to find, and their geared-down motors are better than anything made postwar. The 201 with its magic electrol is harder to find. Of course when one mentions 0-6-0 switchers, most collectors think of the fabulous 8976 scale model switchers. There are a number of variations among these engines that consist mainly of a different number on the boiler front, in conjunction with a corresponding different coupler on the engine and its tender. While these engines are cataloged as the 900, 901B, 902B, and so on, most collectors know them as the semiscale switchers; they are referred to by the number shown on the boiler front,

because all of these engines (including the full-scale model) have the same number 8976 on the side of the engine cab.

The numbers 227 and 228 are the commonest of an otherwise hard-to-get series. Some of the other numbers are 230, 231, 232, 233, and a blank boiler front engine. These engines all have tinplate trucks and various different box couplers. The most valuable engine and also rather rare is the full-scale 8976 switcher, which comes with scale flanges, trucks, and couplers and is made to run on solid T-rail track only. Only the full-scale switcher has the number 8976 on its boiler front.

In addition to two types of switchers there are two kinds of Hudsons. The commoner semiscale version is typified by the beautiful 763E gunmetal gray Hudson with its Vanderbilt oil tender. Sometimes referred to as the modified scale Hudson, it can also be found in black with a long die-cast coal tender. A rare variation is the gray 763E, sometimes found with a 2226W coal tender in a matching gunmetal gray.

Last but not least is the Lionel scale Hudson 700E locomotive. The full-scale model made to run on T-rail track only could be purchased with a display board, for Lionel knew when they built this engine that they had a masterpiece. Also available in kit form numbered 700K, the kit model can be identified

Two of Lionel's most famous and popular steamers are the No. 250E Hiawatha (above) and the 700E (5344) full-scale Hudson.

The Lionel scale Hudson was available fully built, or you could buy it as a six-piece kit (700K). Either way it remains the king to those who collect Lionel 072.

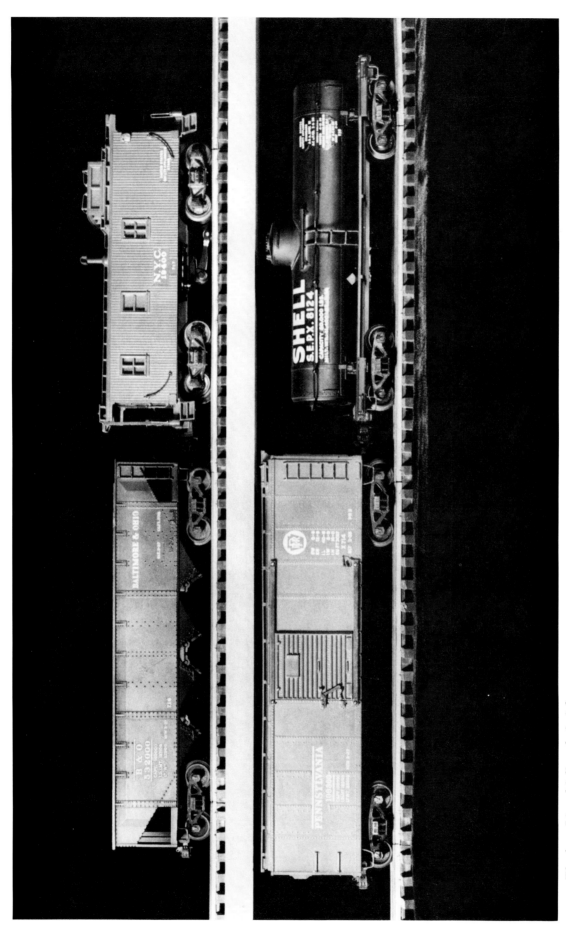

The four Lionel full-scale freight cars.

by checking the plate underneath the engine and seeing if it has the inscription "Built By——." The scale Hudson did not sell as well as Lionel intended, and many of these die-cast engines have warped, cracked, and broken through the years, but those in excellent condition command a price worthy of Lionel's greatest model.

Also I must mention the many fine streamlined trains made by Lionel, from their common chrome-plated Flying Yankee and Union Pacific City of Denver to their larger streamlined City of Portland. One of Lionel's most famous sets is their famous Hiawatha passenger set. The 250E Hiawatha engine had specially made drive wheels and the correct colors of the Milwaukee Road's great train. These same streamlined passenger cars were painted red and made to go with the scale Hudson in a set Lionel called the Rail Chief. While there are no distinctive variations of the Hiawatha and Rail Chief sets the 752E Lionel City of Portland streamliner is found in three- and four-car sets in both yellow, brown and in all silver. Some sets can also be found having the word *gauge* misspelled on the pickup plate as GUAGE.

The only other distinctive passenger cars made for 072 equipment are the 2623 prewar Irvington cars complete with six-wheel trucks and automatic box-type couplers. These long brown Pullman cars are usually found lettered Irvington, but are harder to find lettered as Manhattan. Although a 2624 Manhattan observation was cataloged in 1941, none were ever made. Most prewar Irvington cars are found in four-car sets pulled by Lionel's beautiful black 763E.

Lionel also created a special set of scale and semi-scale freight cars considered by many collectors to be the epitome of Lionel freight cars. The 2900 series freights are the same as the 700 series full-scale freights, except for their automatic box couplers, tin-plate trucks, and their different numbers. Consisting of the 2954 boxcar, the 2955 Shell tank, the 2956 hopper, and the popular 2957 caboose, these cars were made by Lionel to go with many of their better engines, such as their 227 switcher, the 226E, and the black 763E semiscale Hudson. The 2956 hopper, not included in many cataloged sets, is the hardest of the series, except for the rare 2955 tank car, which usually has Shell decals but is harder to find with the Sunoco motif.

The Lionel 700 series scale freights are full-scale cars and come complete with scale trucks and couplers. All of the 700 series cars are hard to find, if not outright rare; they consist of the 714 boxcar, 715 tank car, 716 hopper, and 717 caboose. The 715 tank car, similar to the 2955, usually comes labeled Shell but is very rare when found lettered Sunoco. In general the 717 caboose is the hardest individual car to find of the group. The full-scale cars were made to go with 708 (8976) scale 0-6-0 and the 700E (5344) full-scale Hudson. These cars were also available in kit form and when found are numbered 714K, 715K, etc., etc.

6

LIONEL CLASSIC PERIOD
STANDARD GAUGE

Many companies produced Standard gauge trains in the years prior to World War II. Some were better made and more beautiful than Lionel's models but few were as popular. So it remains today, because most collectors of Standard gauge concentrate on Lionel, and many will collect only Lionel, disregarding other makes as if they had never existed. There are many reasons for this. Perhaps such collectors never saw or were never exposed to other makes; perhaps they feel Lionel is the most attractive and the best-made choice. Because most collectors started out with their own Lionels, naturally they might tend toward the familiar. The likeliest explanation is that Lionel outsold its competition and is therefore the easiest to find and collect today. If many of these diehard Lionel Standard collectors manage to collect long enough, they will undoubtedly move on to other makes, for better or for worse. The fact remains that most Standard gauge collectors collect Lionel, almost exclusively, and the trains they like the most are the later or last period of time in which these trains were made. Lionel "Classic Period" Standard is the most popular. We can define it as an approximate period of time between 1925 and 1940.

The word *classic* is appropriate, for the designs of many of the models made in this period are far removed from earlier designs. They are distinctive, such as the Lionel Blue Comet set, and they are elaborate, with their copper and nickel trims, brass fittings, and baked-enamel paints. From their quality design and construction to their graceful lines they in many ways resemble antique classic cars and look similar in style to many Art Nouveau collectibles of the thirties and late twenties, the exact era in which these trains were born. Many of these trains were mass-produced for a number of years and even today are fairly common. If it were not for a continually growing collector in-

terest, they would end up thrown away in the garbage, as are most old toys when they are outgrown by the children who first owned them. Although some of the prices paid today for some of the better-made Standard gauge sets will seem too high for many new collectors, at least you can be assured that few of these trains will be thrown out by members of the public as they become increasingly aware of their collector interest. With luck for you, they may never learn their accurate value either, and you are just as likely to pick them up "for a song" as pay through the nose for them.

The 500 Series

The beginning collector usually tends to start out where prices are most reasonable. This makes Lionel 500 series freight cars an instant choice for the novice. These freight cars are very common and were pulled by a number of different engines, all of which marked the bottom of the line available at the time. Even the cheapest engines and cars had certain standard features and their level of quality was high. The 500 series freights were painted in bright colors, and they had finely etched brass plates, and copper and brass trim, such as journal boxes, ladders, and brakewheels. The later versions had nickel plates and nickel trim. All the cars had what Lionel called its automatic coupler, which is referred to by collectors as a "latch coupler." This is best coupled and uncoupled by hand as it is not truly automatic. These couplers are the same used on all of the Lionel Standard trains made in the classic era.

Beginning in sequence, we have the 511 flatcar, which was rubber-stamped "Lionel Lines" on the side and which always came with a wooden load. The 511 flatcar is usually dark green with brass stakes. A later

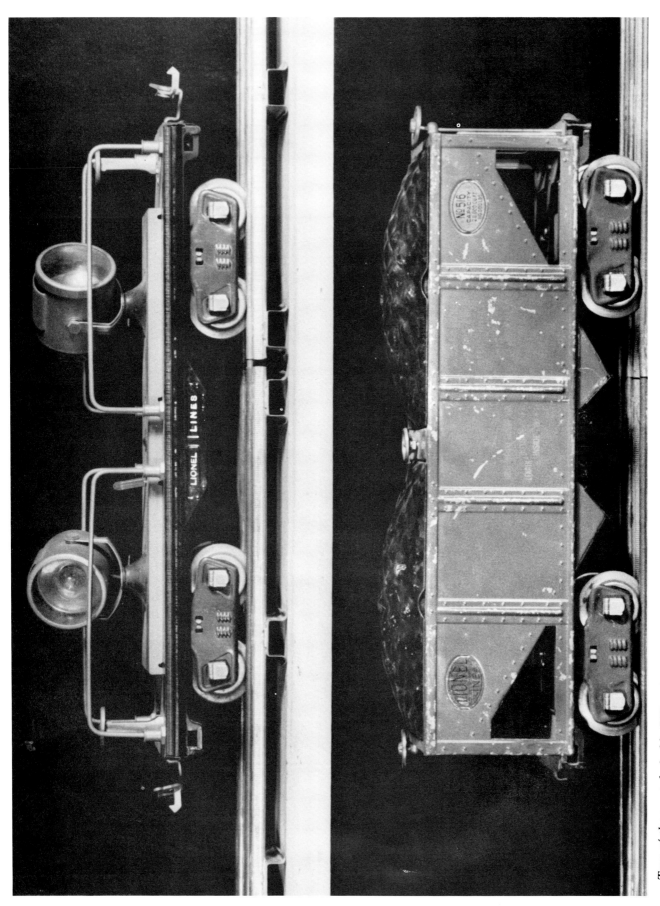

Two of the most desirable 500 series cars are the 520 floodlight car (above) and the 516 hopper with its coal piles.

version is found in light green with nickel trim. The 512 gondola comes in peacock blue, which is the Lionel designation for that color that appears as a sort of pale blue-green. The 512 gondola also comes in light green with nickel trim. The 513 cattle car generally has orange sides and a green roof and is also found in reverse colors, that is, with green sides and an orange roof. There is a nickel version of the 513 cattle car that has yellow sides and a maroon roof. This is definitely one of the hardest to find of all the 500 series freights.

The 514 boxcar comes in yellow with an orange roof, with the nickeled version having bright yellow sides and a brown roof. The 515 tank car is usually found in terra cotta, which appears as an orange-brown color. The 515 also is found in white, and there is an even scarcer white 515 that has a Sunoco decal. There are two versions of the nickel-trim 515 tank car, one being the common silver with Sunoco decal, and the other the rare orange Shell tank car. The 516 hopper is always found in red and it comes with or without the black coal piles that fit on the top. The 516 rubber-stamped car is harder to find, and the 516 with nickel trim and plates even harder. The 517 caboose, commonest car of the series, is usually found in green with a red roof, and the windows are either brass or painted orange. There is a scarce version that comes red and black with orange trim, and there also is a common all-red nickel trim 517. The 520 floodlight car comes with a terra cotta base and in nickel trim with a light green base. Last but not least, the 514R refrigerator car comes cream with a green roof. Sometimes the brass plate says 514 and omits the R; this car is slightly tougher to find. The 514R in nickel trim is even harder to find. It has a light blue roof and bright white sides instead of the usual green roof of the refrigerator car.

Sometimes the later-color freights, which usually come with all-nickel trim, can be found with brass plates and nickel journals and ladders; this marks something of a transition between all-nickel and the earlier brass-plate cars. In another chapter I mention the Ives transition freights, which used the basic 500 series Lionel cars but had an Ives number on the brass plate.

The 200 Series

In 1926 Lionel introduced its deluxe line of 200 series freights. Larger than 500 series, these cars had a larger truck with bigger wheels and were made to go with Lionel's better engines. The 211 flatcar always came in black and sometimes had round wood to simulate logs rather than the usual square-cut wood

load. The 212 gondola first came in gray. Later the common version came in maroon, with the light-green nickel version coming out last. The 213 cattle car came in gray with a maroon roof. It is usually found in terra cotta with a green roof. The rare nickel variation comes yellow with a maroon roof. The 214 boxcar is in terra cotta with a green roof in the early version. It is most often found in yellow with an orange roof. The nickel variation has bright yellow sides with a brown roof similar to the 500 series freights. The 214 boxcar is sometimes called an automobile or furniture car, because, unlike the 514 car, it has two doors on each side. The 214R refrigerator, always considered the rarest car of the series because it supposedly never came in any cataloged sets, is usually found in cream with a green roof, but there is also a rare version that comes white with a light blue roof, again similar to the 514R nickel variation.

The 215 tank car is usually found in green, but there is a harder-to-find version that comes in white. The white 215 also can be found with the Sunoco decal. There is a rare silver nickel-trimmed 215 tank car, and there is reported to exist an even rarer orange shell 215. The 216 hopper comes only in dark green, and the all-nickel trim hopper that has nickel plates is also quite a hard car to find. The 217 caboose comes in orange with maroon roof and rubber-stamped lettering instead of brass plates. The orange 217, considered slightly harder to obtain, can also be found with brass insert windows. The common 217 is found in red with a peacock roof. Some can be found with a completely solid peacock roof (rather than peacock and red). The nickel-trim 217 is found in red with cream trim and silver ends.

The 218 dump car commonly seen in mojave is very common. A 500 series dump car was never made, and anyone who wanted to purchase a "sand" or "gravel" car could purchase only the popular 200 series version. The earliest versions of this car are found with two rather than one of the brass turning knobs on the end, as well as a brass gearing mechanism, as compared with the later die-cast gears, which frequently have broken and cracked with age. Also they can be found with unpainted brass ends as well as with more commonly seen painted mojave ends. One extremely rare and unusual car recently found in the hands of its original owners is painted in pea green with maroon ends. This may have been an experimental or a display model or perhaps part of a very early run of which very few were made. While all kinds of minute variations are being discovered and noted by many astute and observing "variation buffs," there are a number of rare and unusually painted cars such as this one and others yet to be

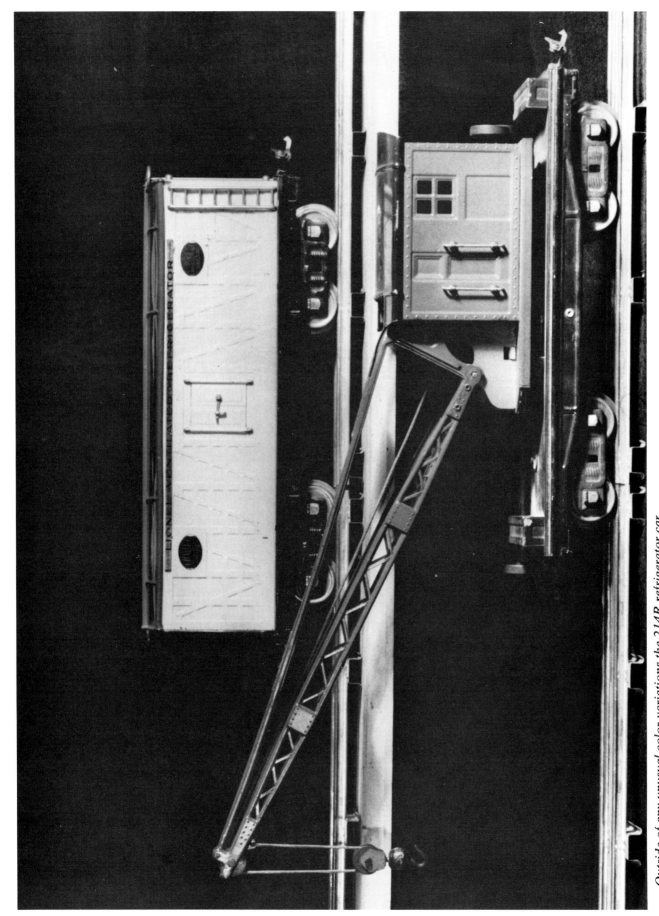

Outside of any unusual color variations the 214R refrigerator car is the scarcest 200 series freight car. The 219 derrick or crane is by far the commonest of the series.

found. I have been told of a gray 211 flatcar, a blue 219 crane and other cars painted in odd and unusual colors. The important thing to remember is that nobody has heard of "every" variation, so don't be surprised if you know of a few yourself that are not mentioned here, but please remember to pass the word around, for knowledge is useful only if it is shared.

Probably the most commonly found 200 series freight car yet still popular is the 219 derrick car usually seen in peacock blue with a dark green roof. Sometimes the red-painted window of the peacock crane can be found unpainted. In the nickel-trim variations the crane car can be found in white and yellow versions, both hard to find. The 220 floodlight car or searchlight car comes with a terra cotta base and brass trim, and the harder-to-find nickel trim version is found with a light-green base. As with the 500 series cars, some of the later-color freights that usually come with nickel plates and trim can be found with brass plates and nickel trim and are legitimate variations. The 200 series freights have a different coupler height than the 500's since they have larger-size wheels, so they do not readily couple to 500 series cars. I have tried to list all the major variations that I know of and have seen with my own eyes, but I am aware that this is by no means a complete listing; also new variations turn up from time to time as collectors are finding and uncovering new trains continually.

The 300 Series

Lionel naturally had a fairly wide assortment of passenger cars, ranging from the small and inexpensive to the elaborately detailed, larger, and more expensive passenger sets that came complete with interior fittings. Beginning in 1925 and 1926 Lionel first came out with its new 300 series passenger cars. These cars appeared in sets with locomotives numbered 8, 10, 318, 384, 390, and others and dominated the less expensive sets for many years. These cars all had four-wheel trucks, the same trucks used on Lionel's 500 series freights. Even these "bottom of the line" passenger cars had such features as ornamental air tanks, brass steps, removable roofs, doors that opened, and high quality baked-enamel paints.

There was the 337 Pullman and the 338 observation, usually coming with a No. 8, and the 339 Pullman and the 341 observation, usually paired with a No. 10 engine. There was also a 332 baggage that came in certain sets. The difference between the 337, 338 cars and the 339, 341 cars was that the latter had paired windows rather than the single windows of the 337, 338 cars. The 337 and 338 cars came in sets in

a number of different colors, such as red with cream trim, mojave with maroon trim, gray with maroon trim, and the very common olive with maroon trim. There also are two very rare sets, even though No. 8 sets are the cheapest and most common Standard sets. One is the peacock with orange trim 8 set, and the other is the apple green with yellow trim set. Both of these sets are rare and were made especially for Macy's as department store specials by Lionel. Collectors usually refer to them simply as "Macy special" sets.

The 339, 341 cars came in sets with the No. 10 engine in matching paints similar to the 8 sets. Some of the colors were the extremely common peacock with orange trim, peacock with green trim, mojave with maroon trim, and gray with maroon trim. The two rarest No. 10 sets are the red with cream trim No. 10 engine and the brown 10, which came with 339 and 341 cars in two-tone brown and is believed to have been a Macy special set. The 318 locomotive also pulled these cars, commonly coming in gray, mojave, and pea green sets. There is also a brown 318 that comes with a Bild-A-Loco motor (rather than the usually found Super motor). This came with the 309, 310, and 312 cars in two-tone brown. This is a particularly attractive set referred to as the "Baby State" set by collectors, because it resembles the deluxe brown State set pulled by the 408 double-motored engine.

The 309, 310, 312 cars were larger than 339, 341 cars and came in a wide variety of attractive colors, including light blue with dark blue roofs, usually appearing in sets with an 1835 loco, blue with silver roofs, apple green with dark green roofs pulled by a gunmetal No. 9E loco, and in a scarce set of two cars only in terra cotta and maroon pulled by a 384 engine. The same basic cars numbered 319, 320, and 322 came in maroon with 200 series trucks pulled by a maroon 380 locomotive. This is not a complete rundown on every color variation known that these 300 series passenger cars come in, but most of the basic ones have been mentioned.

The 418 Series

The larger 418, 419, 490 series passenger cars originally came with 10 series trucks, the same used on early 10 series freight cars. These early cars, which were painted in mojave to match the 402 loco, had simulated wood grain lithographed doors. Later these cars came with six-wheel trucks, as they are most often found, and Lionel added a 431 dining car to the series. These cars had individual seats inside, and the dining car came complete with tables, chairs, and a galley. These same bodied cars came numbered 428, 429, and

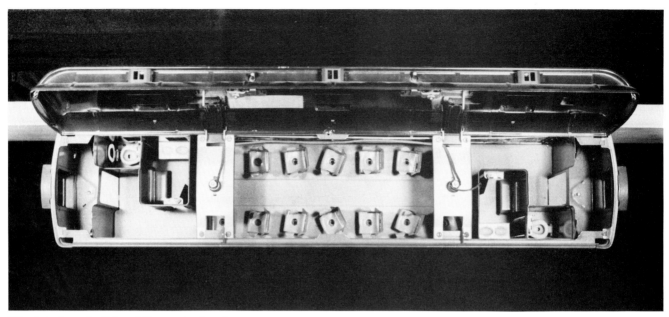

*The interior of a Lionel State car showing
its swivel seats, washrooms, vestibules,
and, yes—even toilets!*

430 with four-wheel 200 series trucks instead of the six-wheel trucks on the 418, 419, and 490 cars. These cars came in dark green with a matching dark green 380 engine and in a rare set with a dark green No. 9. They also came in orange with a matching 9E. The orange 428, 429, and 430 cars are considered the scarcest color in this series.

Among the odd balls there is reported to exist a 431 diner in orange and supposedly a diner rubber-stamped No. 427 rather than the usual 431. There also is a 431 diner in dark green that is very rare. The 418 cars come in apple green in sets with a matching 408. They are usually found in four-car sets with the dining car. Because some sets came without diners as three-car sets and because some three-car sets minus the diner were pulled by the 400E locomotive, the dining car is the rarest individual car of the 418, 419, 490, and 431 group. The mojave 408 set is considered easier to find than the apple green set.

Far different in appearance from the other large Lionel passenger cars were the 1766, 1767, and 1768, which were long, low, and less detailed than the other large series cars. Because these cars were first issued as Ives cars in 1932 and only in 1934 were they cataloged as Lionel and offered with Lionel Lines plates on the side, collectors refer to them as "Ives transition" cars. These cars, pulled by a 385 loco, came in two variations; one is terra cotta and brown and the other is red and maroon. These cars with low-slung six-wheel trucks did not come with interior fittings.

Girard and Blue Comet Sets

Probably the most important reasons for many O gauge train collectors jumping the track and coming over to Standard gauge collecting are the beautiful Lionel Girard, Blue Comet, and State cars. All of these cars came with six-wheel trucks, thick-etched name-plates, and colorful two-tone paint schemes. These are not only well made and durable cars but among the most beautiful designed passenger cars ever made.

The smallest of the sets, referred to as the "Stephen Girard," came in a bright light green with part of the roof painted in dark green; the windows had cream trim. Noted for their stubby appearance, they were numbered 424 Liberty Bell, 425 Stephen Girard, and the 426 Coral Isle observation. They came in sets with a 385, a 392, and a matching two-tone 9. The last sets made came with nickel trim and a nickeled observation deck, but the plates always came in brass. The only interior detail found in the Girard cars consists of long bench seats; otherwise their interiors are bare.

Possibly Lionel's most famous Standard gauge set but definitely one of their most popular was their "Blue Comet." Numbered 420 Faye, 421 Westphal, and 422 Tempel, these cars in light blue with dark blue roofs and cream trim are striking in appearance. For one year only, they were pulled by a blue 390 loco. Lionel then had them pulled by their biggest steam engine, the 400E, painted in matching two-tone blue. These cars came complete with swivel seats, toilets,

The three most desirable classic period passenger cars are the State car (top), *the Blue Comet car* (middle), *and the stubby Liberty Bell shown below.*

The scarce blue 400E locomotive shown below has an unusual cream stripe painted on the engine frame.

and washrooms in their interiors! Variations are minor, but I will list some anyway. There are die-cast journals on the first sets made, versus stamped journals on later sets; some cars have painted vestibule ends; some come in all-brass trim; some have brass plates but otherwise nickel steps and handrails, and so forth, and the last sets, which are said to be a slightly lighter shade of blue, have all-nickel trim and nickel plates.

State Sets

Similar to the Blue Comet cars with their interiors and bathrooms are the great and famous Lionel State cars, so named because the cars have the names of states written on their brass plates: numbered and named 412 California, 413 Colorado, 414 Illinois, and 416 New York. When these cars were first issued in 1929 they were pulled by the large 381E locomotive and came as a four-car set. Later it was found that the single-motored 381 could not adequately pull the four cars, so from then on it came as a three-car set in green, while the brown State set pulled by the double-motored 408 engine always came as a four-car set. Since the four-car set became a three-car set, one car was discontinued and is considered scarcest in green, that being the 414 Illinois car. Three-car green sets were also pulled by the 400E locomotive and billed in the catalog as the Twentieth Century Limited. These green State cars that came with 400 locos tend to have cream inserts in the windows rather than the usual light green trim, and these cars with the cream inserts also have rivet detail on their ends, which the regular run cars do not have.

Rarer and even more desirable than any green State set would be a State set in the two-tone brown colors. These sets were the most expensive Standard

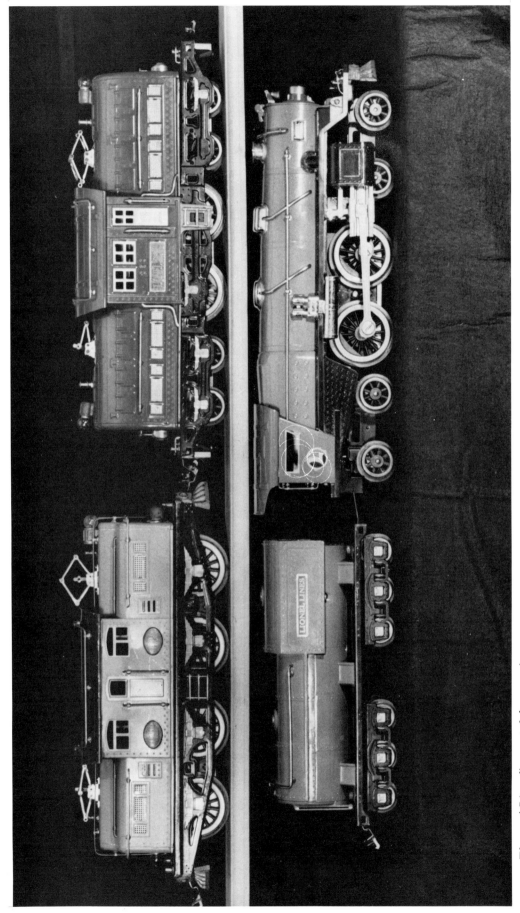

*Three of Lionel's most deluxe engines are
the double-motored 408E (top, left), twelve-wheeled 381E,
and (below) the 400E locomotive and tender.*

gauge set in the Lionel line at the time and were beautiful as well as big. The passenger cars are found having light and sometimes dark brown ventilators on their roofs. The brown 408 engines usually have two Bild-A-Loco motors rather than Super motors and there are two variations among them. The brown 408's come either all brown or brown with a dark brown roof, referred to by collectors as a two-tone 408 and considered more desirable than the all-brown version. Brown State cars are also known to come with cream doors, and some can also be found with rivet detail on the vestibule ends.

Lionel State cars were 21 inches long and were the top of the line in passenger equipment. Besides having more seats than the slightly smaller Blue Comet cars, the State cars have roofs hinged to the car body, making it easier to lift the roof to look inside at the car's interior. Highly regarded by Standard gauge collectors, they remain a prize, topping off many Standard gauge train collections. The desire to own a set of Girard cars, Blue Comet cars, and State cars has helped to launch many people into collecting Lionel Standard gauge. Certainly these passenger cars rank among the finest and most beautiful ever made.

Electric Engines

Lionel made a number of different electric outline engines in the era of Classic Standard gauge, ranging from the small No. 8 loco to the large 381 Olympian. The square and boxy-looking No. 8 engine was the smallest and least expensive Standard loco available and had only four wheels. Most of the smaller, less expensive engines of all the various manufacturers had only four wheels since they had to negotiate tight radius turns. Only the more elaborate and rather expensive engines had more than four wheels in the electric outline category. The 8 came also as an 8E with a sequence reverse unit, and so many were sold that even today this engine is considered extremely common by collectors. Even the relatively small No. 8 still had many prime features, such as headlights on both ends, large nickel journals and brass flag holders, and handrails. The No. 8 is found in a wide variety of colors, of which olive green is by far the commonest.

Next in size and similar to the 8 is the No. 10 loco, offered also as a 10E. The 10, also a four-wheel engine, was about the same size as an 8, although it was styled differently. Coming in an assortment of colors much like the No. 8, the No. 10 loco is most commonly found in Lionel's famous peacock blue shade. Both the 8 and 10 contained Super motors, as did most of Lionel's electric-type locomotives. There are, however, two versions of the 10E found with the

Lionel deluxe Bild-A-Loco motor. One is a peacock blue engine with an orange stripe that has an unusual dark green frame and is not too hard to find. The other Bild-A-Loco 10 is brown (sometimes called tan but not to be confused with the more common mojave color) with a cream stripe and dark green frame and is a rare variation, probably as tough to find as the scarce red No. 10 loco.

Slightly harder than the 8 and 10 yet still a common and reasonably priced engine is the 318 and 318E. Also a small four-wheeled engine the 318 is found containing the Lionel Super motor. It is commonly found in pea green, gray, and mojave. The rarest by far, though, is the black 318, which is found in sets as a coal train pulling three 516 rubber-stamped hopper cars and the hard-to-find red and black 517 caboose. Another version is the brown 318 loco that comes with and without the better Bild-A-Loco motor, and there is said to be a two-tone brown 318 similar to the larger 408 engine.

Next in caliber, size, and desirability is the 380 and 380E loco, looking much like a fat No. 10. The 380 commonly comes in maroon with a large metal step headlight rather than the usual diecast headlight common to the other electric-type engines. The 380 is also found in dark green and a hard-to-find mojave version. The 380 engine is also known to come with factory-installed lead weights so that the engine would have sufficient pulling power.

The next most desirable electric-type engine is the 402 and 402E. This engine was larger and longer and contained two rather than one of the Lionel Super motors. Because of the two motors the 402 engine is known as one of the finest pullers, and this eight-wheel engine is sought after by those who enjoy running and operating their Standard gauge equipment. The 402 is found commonly in mojave, and, while other colors of the 402 are known to exist, they are all quite scarce, such as the mustard yellow version.

Using the same basic body as the 402 is the deluxe model 408E engine. This engine is different from the 402 in that it contains such detailing as extra handrails, brass operating pantographs, and added marker lights on the ends. The 408E is found usually in mojave or apple green. The brown or tan 408E loco usually comes with Bild-A-Loco motors and can be found allbrown or a slightly harder variation in two-tone brown. The highly desirable brown 408's came in sets with the matching brown State cars, but they also were available separately and were sold in sets with 200 series freights. The rarest and most sought-after 408E is the all-dark-green engine matching the green Lionel State cars.

The story I have heard surrounding the rare dark

CRACK TRAIN OF THE LIONEL LINE—COPY OF A FAMOUS LIMITED

FOR "LIONEL STANDARD" TRACK

THE 400E Locomotive which pulls these two outfits is unquestionably the masterpiece of all model railroads. It is far ahead of its time and far ahead of any competition. Lionel engineers spent two years in studying, designing and constructing it. And you can spend years in enjoying its masterful appearance and powerful performance.

Outfit No. 358E consists of:

1—No. 400E Steam Type "Distant Control" Locomotive—With controlled headlight and illuminated firebox.

1—No. 400T Oil Tender—An exclusive Lionel model.

1—No. 212 Gondola Car—With eight barrels and set of tools.

1—No. 219 Derrick Car—With worm gear control.

1—No. 220 Floodlight Car—With adjustable reflectors. Throws powerful beams of light.

1—No. 217 Illuminated Caboose—Given true railroad atmosphere.

8—sections of C curved track.

8—sections of S straight track.

1—STC "Lockon" Connection—By means of which contact is made from transformer to track.

1—No. 81 Controlling Rheostat.

4—No. 28 and 1 No. 29A Lamps.

Loads of fun in this famous work train. Fill the barrels with a cargo of pebbles. Lift them with the derrick. Swing them on to the gondola. And away you go across the country with full speed ahead! When you consider the quality of workmanship, the painstaking details, and the fun in store for you, this De Luxe outfit is a real value. 88 inches long. Track forms oval 99½ by 45 inches.   **Price, $60.00**

Outfit No. 433E consists of:

1—No. 400E Steam Type "Distant Control" Locomotive—With concealed headlight and illuminated fire box.

1—No. 400T Oil Tender.

1—No. 412 Illuminated Pullman Car—33½ inches long, 6½ inches high. Has two six-wheel trucks with roller journal boxes.

1—No. 413 Illuminated Pullman Car—Like the other cars in this outfit, it has a patented hinged roof. Just press the nickeled clip and it's open!

1—No. 416 Illuminated Observation Car—The outfit on brass platform, illuminates the tail light and the transparent nameplate.

—section of C curved track.

10—sections of S straight track.

1—STC "Lockon" Connection—By means of which contact is made from transformer to track.

1—No. 81 Controlling Rheostat.

8—No. 28 and 1 No. 29A Lamps.

Copied after the famous "Twentieth Century Limited," this prize outfit is one of the finest ever built. Cars are illuminated and have removable roofs, disclosing completely detailed interiors. They are long and graceful and enameled by the famous Lionel baked process. The doors swing open. The windows are transparent, with stained glass effect in transoms. Never before have you seen such luxury. The boy who gets this outfit will be lucky. And may that boy be you! 98 inches long. Track forms oval 114 by 45 inches.

[Page Twenty-five]

35SE
$60.00

433E
$85.00

The famous Lionel work train set and 400E State set pictured as the Twentieth Century Limited.

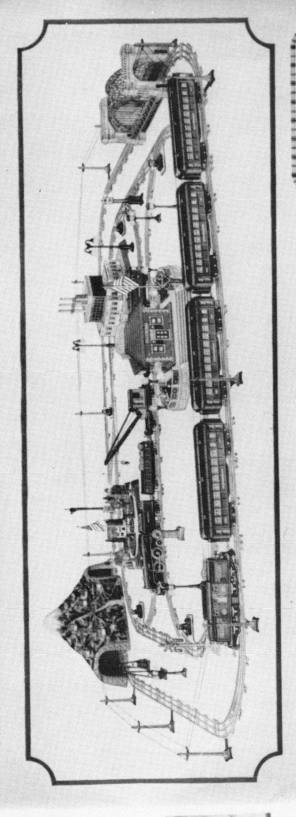

This is a plan of the track layout for the Lionel complete railroad.

[Page Twenty-Seven]

HERE is a real railroad. The finest gift that any boy can possibly receive. This is a complete Lionel "Distant-Control" Railroad including our two finest trains—work train with Steam Type Locomotive, and a gigantic twin-motor passenger train, as well as a large variety of electrically-controlled and illuminated accessories. Both of the trains have "Distant-Control" and can be started, stopped, reversed and operated at any speed at any distance from the track. The large power house is a central operating station from which you can control everything. This is a marvelous model railroad. Specifications are given below.

OUTFIT NO. 407E—Comprises:

1 No. 408E "Distant-Control" Locomotive	1 No. 218 Operating Dump Car	20 C Track	2 No. 77 Crossing Gates
1 No. 390E "Distant-Control" Locomotive	1 No. 219 Operating Derrick Car	2 1/2S Track	1 No. 69 Warning Signal
2 No. 81 Controlling Rheostats	1 Type K Transformer	1 No. 128 Station	1 No. 840 Power House
1 No. 412 Pullman Car	4 No. 222 Switches	1 No. 300 Bridge	2 No. 67 Lamp Posts
1 No. 413 Pullman Car	2 No. 23 Bumpers	1 No. 140L Tunnel	4 No. 56 Lamp Posts
1 No. 414 Pullman Car	1 Set 208 Tools	12 No. 85 Telegraph Posts	1 No. 87 Signal
1 No. 416 Observation Car	1 Set 209 Barrels	1 No. 78 Train Control	1 No. 79 Flashing Signal
1 No. 212 Gondola Car	47 S Track	1 No. 80 Semaphore	1 No. 195 Terrace
1 No. 217 Illuminated Caboose			16 STC "Lockon" Connections

Wires for making electrical connections, connecting ties for joining sections of track, lamps for headlights, interior of cars and all illuminated accessories are supplied with this outfit. Track layout is 12 feet long by 11 feet wide.
Code Word "ALLY."

Price $350.00

For a mere $350, at the height of the Great Depression, you could have purchased this wonderful 12-by-11-foot layout!

green 408E is that Lionel received complaints from owners who had purchased the four-car State set, cataloged as the Transcontinental Express in 1929, that was pulled by a single-motored 381E. It seems that these four large heavy passengers cars could not be properly pulled by a single-motor engine, so that many were sent in to the factory as irate customers thought there was something wrong with their 381E locomotives. Lionel quickly decided to paint up a batch of 408 engines in a matching dark green shade and supposedly sent these back to the customers, since the double-motored 408's could handle the four cars. While this story is credible and probably true, I have heard from collectors, and on one occasion from original owners of one of these engines, that they were purchased directly from a department store, so I think it is safe to assume that they probably also came in sets as an uncataloged special to one or more department stores at the time.

Rating high among collectors are Lionel's deluxe models, the 9, 9E, and 9U locos that look like a stretched-out No. 8. All of the different versions of the 9's came with the deluxe Bild-A-Loco motor, making it a fine operating engine. The 9's were quite expensive for single-motor engines and so were not as big sellers as the less expensive and smaller 8 and 10 locos. The commonest color is the gunmetal with nickel trim 9E loco. Next in rarity would be the orange 9U kit locomotive and the orange 9E loco. The two-tone green 9E engine, matching the same colors as the Girard passenger cars it came with, is hard to find. The rarest is the dark green 9 with the hand reverse knob that came in sets with the dark green 428, 429, and 430 passenger cars. Interestingly, all of the different color 9's have their own distinctive brass plate on the side rather than there being one standard number plate for all the different models.

Certainly one of the most beautiful, most well-liked, and most expensive engines would be the large 381E locomotive. Although it has only one Bild-A-Loco motor, this massive model of the Milwaukee Road's great Olympian engine is Lionel's only twelve-wheel electric engine. Always coming in its usual two-tone green color scheme to match the Lionel State cars, this engine, although more popular today, was originally priced below the 408E locomotive back in the early thirties. A rarer version of the 381 is the 381U with its hand reverse knob. The 381U comes with a plain 381 number plate rather than the usual 381E plate. Among the oddballs known to exist is a 381E in green but having a red frame. Although an all-red engine is pictured on the cover of the 1930 catalog, none are known to exist.

Basically I am concerned with production runs rather than samples, prototypes, and special display pieces within any particular category. I find these pieces interesting but limitless in that new oddballs are always turning up; sometimes their authenticity is questionable. Among these pieces are many odd-colored locomotives coming in every color under the sun, but since often only one specimen exists we could not call them collectible but rather only of interest, the interest being as to where they came from and why were they made. As examples I know of a crackle finish dark green 408E, a dark green two-tone 408E (darker green roof), a yellow 408E, and a reputed pink 408E (yes, pink!). These one-of-a-kinds or oddballs are not merely limited to 408's but can be found in all kinds of engines, freight cars, and passenger cars of every different manufacturer.

Classic Steamers

For a period of about five years Lionel produced only electric-type locomotives, even though steam engines were popular with the public and were certainly in demand. Possibly in this interim all-electric period Lionel was tooling up for their much improved and soon-to-be-introduced steam-type locos of the Lionel Classic period. Perhaps competition from Ives and Flyer had something to do with it, for these companies had heavy die-cast and cast iron steam locos in their line before Lionel introduced any at all. In 1929 Lionel introduced their 390 and 390E steam loco using a different design than their competitors. Lionel made the body of the loco out of rolled steel and equipped it with a die-cast frame and steam chest and their heavy Bild-A-Loco motor. Lionel never leaned too heavily on die-castings and so, unlike their competition, they never made a completely die-cast steamer.

All of Lionel's Classic period steam locos came with their Bild-A-Loco motors and all had die-cast frames, steam chests, and boiler fronts. Also all their coal tenders were die-cast, but they all had steel frames, and their coal piles were made of stamped sheet metal. Although the 390E was made only until 1931, a number of variations are found. Early 390's came in green with an apple green or light green stripe on the running board. Some also were said to have an orange stripe, and an all-green loco was reputedly also made. The 390E also came in blue with a cream stripe to match and pull the first Blue Comet sets. Both the green and blue versions are hard to find, compared with the common black 390E with the orange stripe on the engine and its tender. This engine can be found with brass sand domes and copper domes and stack. The 390 hand reverse is said to be harder to find than the 390E loco. There is also a legitimate 390E in black without an orange stripe that came with a 384 green-striped tender. Lionel also came out with a 390E, and the tender stamped 390-X came equipped with the larger 200 series trucks so that it could be used to pull the larger 200 series freight cars.

The next year Lionel introduced their smallest Standard gauge steamer, the 384 and 384E. The 384 was short and stubby in appearance but it had practically all the same features of the 390, except for one less set of wheels. All that I have seen have been painted black with a green stripe on the frame and the tender, but it is also said to come without the stripe.

Next in size we have Lionel's popular 385E, which came with a "Chugger" sound in the engine. The 385 engine came commonly in gray and gunmetal and in both copper and nickel trim. The nickel versions always have painted boiler bands and came with the ex-Ives design die-cast tenders. Most of the copper-trimmed 385's have solid pony wheels. There is also a scarce variation that came painted black in a dull matte finish, not to be confused with the common 1835 loco.

Lionel also came out with a less expensive engine that was identical to the 385E but numbered 1835E. Its only differences were that it came without the chugger, and the domes and stack atop the locomotive were painted over. 1835's are fairly common and are always found in black. Amazingly, almost all that you find either have a broken coal tender or the tender is bowed or warped, because the die-castings were made incorrectly when first produced. Both the 385E and 1835E are very common; they were cataloged and made for many years and came in many popular sets.

Similar in appearance to the 385E is the larger and more deluxe 392E locomotive having a 4-4-2 wheel configuration rather than the 385's 2-4-2 wheel arrangement. Coming with either a short four-wheel truck coal tender or a larger six-wheel truck version, it is much more desirable when found with the larger tender. The black 392E is usually found with a small tender usually stamped 384 and can be found with and without a green stripe on the tender sides. The large black 392 tender came with six-wheel trucks and has a distinctive Lionel Lines brass plate on the side unique to that tender. Contrary to popular opinion, it never came in black with nickel plates on the tender. The black engines always came with copper trim, and it is reported that some engines came with painted domes similar to an 1835E loco. Gray 392's are usually found with the larger coal tender and sometimes come with the smaller die-cast tender, always with

nickel trim. I have also been told that the last-run 392's had their sand domes chrome rather than nickel-plated, causing them to appear shinier than usual.

Lionel's biggest steam locomotive was their famous 4-4-4, the large 400E. Made for many years and coming in many different variations, the 400E loco pulled many of Lionel's most famous sets. It always came with an oil or Vanderbilt-type tender with six-wheel trucks that came only with the 400E engine. It is commonly found in black with copper trim, gray with copper trim, and gunmetal with nickel trim. The blue 400's, slightly harder to find and always more desirable because they came with the famous Blue Comet set, are found with copper trim, and the engines sometimes have painted boiler bands. The nickel blue 400's always have painted bands and black wheels and have always been hard engines to find. Definitely among the rarest of the 400E variations is the blue engine with the cream stripe on the running board. While not a major variation, some engines can be found with solid pony wheels rather than the usual spoked variety.

Other variations are the dark gray with painted bands. There also is a black engine with copper trim and nickel plates on the tender. Very rare is the black 400E found with a red stripe on the engine and tender. Almost a legend is the black crackle 400E, of which few originals are known but repaints and fakes are found aplenty. Odd and unusual variations are reported from time to time along the lines of a solid blue engine, an all-dark-green engine, gray engines with a factory-painted black stripe, and others. Most collectors would be happy to settle for just one.

Famous Sets

While practically everything Lionel made was offered individually in the catalogs, most people preferred to purchase a set as shown in the colorful and explicit catalog drawings. Many items sometimes seen in the catalog never were made, and engines such as the red 381E pictured on the cover of the 1930 catalog were never known to exist. Collectors usually display their trains in cataloged sets, never mixing later-color nickel-trimmed freights with an early engine such as a 390E, which was made years before and discontinued before the nickel-trimmed series began to appear.

The most sought-after sets are often the most attractive and in Lionel Classic Standard there are many. Certainly the two-tone brown State set is king among them, for in addition to being hard to find it was also Lionel's most expensive set and sold for $97.50 at the height of the Depression when twenty-

THE LIONEL SHOP   "STANDARD GUAGE"
                           300 Vail Ave.
                           Dunellen, N.J.

             These items will not last long. ORDER NOW!
Note:
        All prices F.O.B. Dunellen, N.J. Prices quoted on this sheet are
NET. Allow enough for postage or instruct us to ship postage collect.
We return any excess postage allowance. Shipments sent C.O.D. for
postage cost you 12¢ extra, for C.O.D. fee. As stocks are limited the
goods offered on this sheet are offered subject to prior sale. All
goods are new unless otherwise mentioned. Our guarantee is MONEY BACK
IF YOU ARE NOT SATISIFIED with your purchase. If you do not find what
you want on this sheet send us your order taken direct from the Lionel
catalog and take advantage of our liberal discounts.

Amt.	Cat. No.	Article	Type	No. of wheels	Reverse	Length	C	List Price	Our Price	Ship Wt.	Rmks
2	8	Locomotive	Elect	0-4-0	Hand	11"	R	9.75	5.00	6	
2	8E	"	"	"	Auto	11"	R	13.50	6.50	6	
1	9E	"	"	"	Auto	14½"	Y	16.50	10.25	8	
1	318	"	"	"	Hand	12"	G	10.75	6.85	9	
1	318E	"	"	"	Auto	12"	Br	12.50	8.00	9	
1	408E	Loco, twin mtrs	"	0-4-4-0	Auto	17"	LG	35.00	22.00	14	
2	381E	Locomotive	"	4-4-4	Auto	18"	G	30.00	19.00	14	
1	384	Loco & tender	Steam	2-4-0	Hand	21"	Bk	19.75	11.00	11	
2	384E	"	"	"	Auto	21"	Bk	23.50	12.50	11	
1	390	"	"	2-4-2	Hand	22¼"	Bk	30.00	8.00	12	Used
3	390E	"	"	"	Auto	22¼"	Bk	32.50	15.00	12	

Note: If #81 rehostat is wanted with E loco, add 75¢. For #88 add 35¢.

Amt.	Cat. No.	Article	Type	No. of wheels	Reverse	Length	C	List Price	Our Price	Ship Wt.	Rmks
1	Set #337-#338		Passgr	8	Lights	12"	R	8.25	4.25	5	2 cars
1	Set #332-#337-#338		"	8	"	12"	R	12.50	6.25	7	3 cars
2	Sets #424-#425-#426		"	12	"	16"	LG	22.50	15.00	14	3 cars
2	Sets #332-#339-#341		"	8	"	12"	Bl	10.00	6.70	7	3 cars
1	Set #309-#310-#312		"	8	"	13½"	LG	12.00	8.00	8	3 cars
1	Set #412-#413-#416		"	12	"	21½"	G	40.50	25.00	18	3 cars
1	Set #420-#421-"422		"	12	"	18"	Bl	29.00	20.00	16	3 cars
1	Set 418-419-431-490		"	12	"	18¼"	LG	38.75	18.00	18	4 cars
1	212	Gondola	Freight	8		12½"	R	3.25	2.00	3	
1	219	Derrick Car	"	8		"		9.00	6.00	6	
1	220	Floodlight Car	"	8		"	Bk	6.50	4.30	3	
1	217	Caboose	"	8	Lighted	"	R	5.00	3.00	3	
5	218	Dump Car	"	8		"	Br	5.00	3.60	5	

Colors: Black.Bk, Red.R, Yellow.Y, Brown.Br, Light Green.LG, Green.G,
Blue.Bl.

We can install an E unit in your Lionel loco. Send Loco # for price.
We carry a complete line of bulbs, trucks, parts, etc. for Lionel.
Items crossed off have been sold out & no more available.

*Believe it or not this is a copy of a price list
published on November 1, 1933. Notice that
the 408E sold for more than the 381E.*

five dollars a week could support a family in comfort. Things haven't really changed; you still need to be rich to afford a brown State set. Then of course you may rather have the Lionel Olympian set, which came with a 381E and three green State cars, or the Twentieth Century Limited set, which had the 400E pulling those cars instead. Maybe you like the colors of the two-tone green 9E pulling the matching Stephen Girard cars or an orange 9E set with the matching 428, 429, and 430 cars in orange. Not as large and elaborate is the coal train headed by a black 318E with three rubber-stamped 516 hopper cars and a matching black and red caboose that is not seen too often.

Believe it or not, two of Lionel's biggest sellers were both headed by the large 400E locomotive. One made up the set numbered 358E (later numbered 358W), the 400E work train set with its 217 caboose, 220 floodlight car, 219 derrick car, and a 212 gondola complete with eight barrels and a set of tools in a metal toolbox. Then there was the outfit numbered 396E (later 396W), which sold as the famed Blue Comet set with its three matching passenger cars. Both these sets were cataloged right up till 1939, when Standard gauge made its final showing in the catalog. I have heard it said that, although it was discontinued in the catalog, Standard gauge continued to be sold even in the late forties after the war, as there was still some unsold stock and sets were made up from existing supplies of parts. If not for the interest generated by collectors today, Standard gauge trains would be only a memory.

7

FLYER AND IVES
STANDARD GAUGE

I know what you're thinking. Ives and American Flyer cataloged their trains as Wide Gauge, so it is incorrect to call them Standard gauge. There are two reasons why I disagree: first, because Lionel introduced 2⅛-inch gauge track way back in 1906, naming it Standard gauge; it was soon to become the most established and popular of the larger gauges. So popular did Standard gauge become that it was not long before Ives, in 1921, and American Flyer, in 1925, got on the bandwagon and started making trains in this gauge; only they dubbed it "Wide" gauge instead of Standard. The second reason for referring to Ives and Flyer Standard gauge as such is because that this is the way most collectors refer to them. Whatever you decide to call them, you'll have to agree that these two great companies may have followed in the use of Standard gauge track but they were never Lionel imitators.

While Flyer Standard was short-lived in that it lasted only from 1925 to 1936, there were still many models made and a number of variations to collect. Flyer, which formerly produced nothing but O gauge models, was at this late date about to plunge headlong into competition with both Ives and Lionel. Flyer began with their lithographed passenger set named the "All American" and quickly went on to produce a more extensive line of trains. It was immediately apparent that these trains were not cheaply made; their quality and appearance were equivalent and at times even superior to their competitors.

Flyer Freights

In 1926 Flyer went to Lionel and purchased some 10 series freights so that they could add freight cars to their new Wide gauge line. These freights numbered 4005 cattle car, 4007 sand car, 4008 boxcar, and the 4011 caboose. These cars were painted by Lionel and are identical to the regular late 10 series freights except that they came with Flyer black flexible trucks, and underneath were stamped in yellow "American Flyer Lines." These unusual cars still retained their Lionel hook-type couplers and were sold by Flyer for one year only. Probably the only reason Flyer's competitor, Lionel, was willing to sell them the badly needed freights was that in 1926 Lionel had introduced their new advanced 200 series freights and felt the 10 series cars to be outdated.

Flyer introduced their own freights in 1927; they were big, distinctive, and very realistic in appearance. These first-run cars can be identified easily, because they come with the black rather than gray flex trucks. The freights come in bright colors, such as an orange boxcar, red gondola, and so forth, and are sometimes called pastel colors. The early ivory and tan 4011 caboose is usually found with six windows on the side, but there is a rare variation that is found with only five windows.

Later Flyer freights are found with gray flex trucks and come in a host of variations. These cars were first made with etched plates reading "six million happy owners," later giving way to seven million, and the last made reading eight million. Among the most desirable are the 4010 tank with the large air service decals, the highly sought-after blue tank car, and the hopper car introduced in 1931 and found in the "Grand Canyon" freight set.

Although most of the specials—that is, the specially painted or lettered sets or cars made for promotional display or for a department store chain—are passenger sets, I know of at least two Flyer special freight sets. One is a set lettered Burlington on the engine tender and freight cars. The lettering is rubber-stamped on the sides of the cars, and the set may have been made

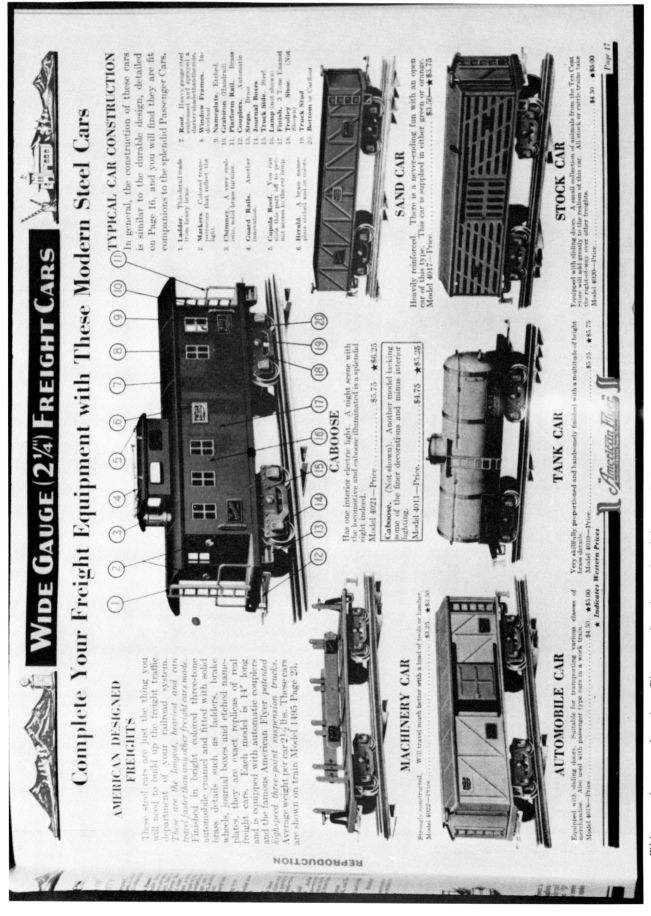

This page from an American Flyer catalog shows the elaborate design of the Flyer Standard gauge freight cars.

*This unusual American Flyer "Empire Express" uncataloged set
is believed to have been made as a department store special.*

for the Burlington Railroad. Another set believed to have been made for J.C. Penney stores came pulled by a small electric-type engine with three freight cars, all having brass etched plates reading "Nation Wide Lines."

Flyer Passenger Sets

American Flyer is well known among collectors for the many different lithographed passenger sets they made. Their smallest passenger cars were fourteen inches long and came in a variety of colors. Some examples of their smaller sets are the 4643 green "Eagle," the 4653 orange "Commander," and the 4667

red "American Legion Ltd.," all of which came with colorfully lithographed passenger cars. To brag about their wide variety of colors, Flyer dubbed themselves the "Rainbow Line" in 1927; it was an appropriate title.

In 1928 they first introduced two new passenger sets, both popular and well liked by collectors. The 4678 red Hamiltonian pulling the 4340 club, 4341 Pullman, and 4342 observation was one of the new offerings and can sometimes be found in four-car sets with a dining car. The other set is the 4637 Pocahontas pulling the same cars but cataloged as a four-car set with the 4343 diner. The Hamiltonian set came in a bright two-tone red, and the Pocahontas set came

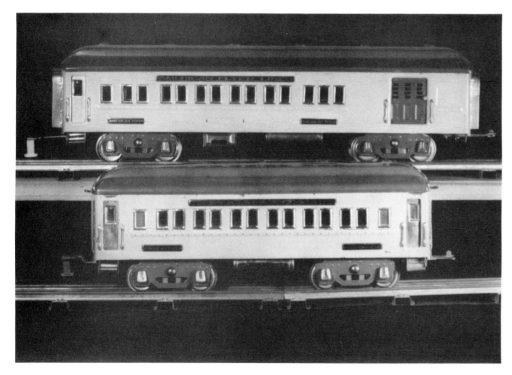

*American Flyer
Legionnaire* (top)
*passenger car
and Pocahontas car.
These finely made cars
had individual brass
window trim,
brass air tanks,
doors, steps,
and handrails.*

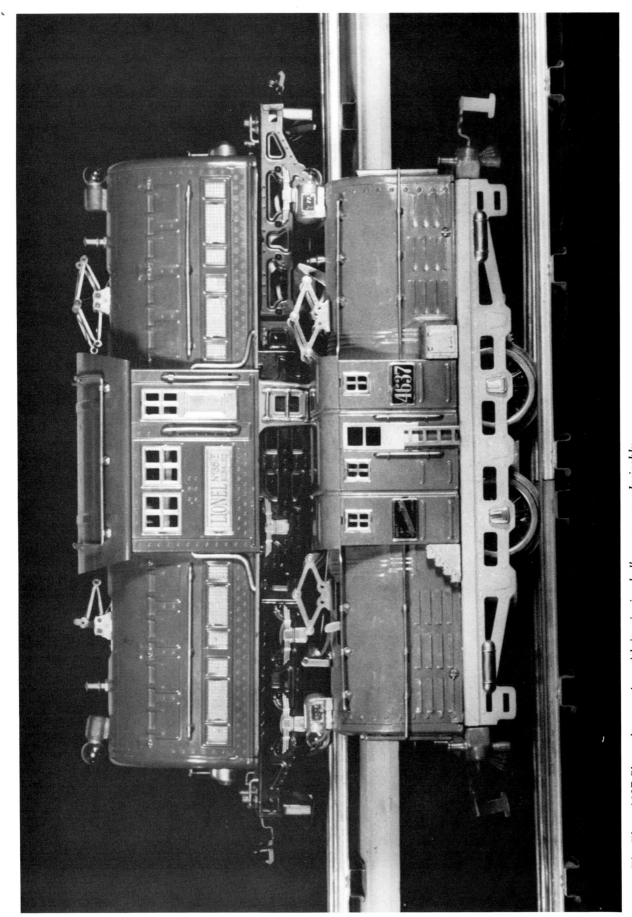

The Flyer 4637 Shasta locomotive with its ringing bell compares admirably with a Lionel 381, even though the Shasta today sells for less than one-fifth the price.

in what Flyer called "emerald green" roofs and "rookie tan" bodies. Both these sets had no lithography but came instead with full brass trim with brass insert windows.

While Flyer made many other passenger trains in their short yet distinguished career, they are most well known and famous for their President's Special passenger set. There are a number of different sets designated as the President's Special, but it is interesting to note that while Lionel considered lithography a cheap way to decorate trains and Lionel never used it on any of their better sets, Flyer never had this hangup, and so they even decorated their first few deluxe President Special sets with lithography.

The first set, made in 1926, came in a light brown color properly called Imperial Buff, with the 4039 engine and the 4080, 4081, and 4082 lithographed cars. This was a four-wheeled engine, virtually the same as the 4677. Appearing a year later in 1927 was the "Chief," which came with the 4677 and the same cars in the same color, except that more detail was added to the set, such as rivet detail on the engine cab; brass journals were added to the cars. While cataloged as the Chief, it is sometimes referred to by collectors as the fourth President Special.

In 1927 Flyer introduced their improved President's Special train. This set came with the blue 4687 4-4-4 electric modeled after the engine used on the famous Twentieth Century Limited. The cars had blue lithographed sides and six-wheel trucks instead of the previous four-wheel versions. The cars are numbered 4090, 4091, and 4092 observation.

The most prized and valued of the President Specials is the version painted in a Rolls-Royce blue enamel, which came with brass insert windows and trim and was first introduced in 1928. Pulled by the twelve-wheel 4689 and pulling the 4390 club car "West Point," 4391 Pullman "Academy," 4393 diner "Annapolis," and 4392 observation "Army Navy." This set, believed by many to be the most beautiful Standard gauge train ever made, continued in the catalogs through till 1934. The earlier versions are found with brass air tank and battery boxes, while later versions were simplified and came with truss rods underneath the passenger coaches.

Also introduced in 1928 and because of its scarcity at times commanding even more than the enameled President Special is the famous "Flying Colonel" set. This set came in a deep dark blue with the twelve-wheeled 4686 loco and the 4380, 4381, and the 4382 passenger cars. In 1928 the engine came with the brass "Ace" plate, and with the Ace inscription is the way most collectors like it. Always coming as a three-car set, it appeared without the Ace plate in 1929 and 1930.

The king of Flyer trains has always been and will continue to be the famous Mayflower set. First cataloged in 1928, this set used the same engine and four cars as the enameled 4689 President Special, except that it was finished in chrome plate with brass trim. The first sets turned out were cadmium-plated instead of chrome-plated, and there is reason to believe that some of the first sets made used steel passenger bodies rather than brass as usually assumed. I have heard from more than one source that some sets picked up from original owners came as mixed sets, that is, some cars were brass and some were steel. Many collectors refuse to believe that they came in anything other than all brass, but whatever you choose to believe probably no more than about a hundred sets (originals, that is!) were ever made.

Flyer Steam Engines

Flyer made a number of steam engines, all of which are numbered in such a way as to confuse collectors and anyone else trying to make sense out of them. Simply, Flyer numbered the individual tenders separately; the engine was also numbered separately, and together they had their own numbers as a combination. A perfect example would be the 4660 hand reverse loco alone, the 4693 tender having red data 4694 plates, together becoming the 4664 engine and tender. I feel the numbers are too lengthy and confusing to list. I would rather talk about the different engine styles.

It seems that Flyer had only electric-style engines in 1929, and they needed a steam loco to add to the line. Because Ives was already bankrupt and Flyer had a part interest in the Ives concern, they purchased the remaining 1134 (the old model with the exposed headlight) boiler castings and die-cast tenders and, with the tender bearing brass plates named "Golden State," they marketed it as their own. In 1930 they sold it with a Flyer Vanderbilt tender, but it always came, in both 1929 and 1930 with a Flyer motor.

In 1931 they came out with a cast iron rather than die-cast engine numbered 4670 with a short 4671 tender; together they were numbered 4672. In 1931 also, looking somewhat similar to the Ives 1134 was their new 4692 loco, which, when teamed with the 4671 tender, became the 4675. Some of their steamers, such as the 4681, 4695, and 4696, came with brass piping on the side, in addition to being deluxe engines with complete valve gear. Those engines with the extra piping and data plate tenders are the most desirable to own.

Flyer also made some uncataloged sets. One particular passenger set came with the 4743 or the 4753 engine with the matching litho 4141 "Henry

4380

INSP.
3

SOLD AS
SHOPWORN
AMERICAN FLYER M'FG. CO.

The bottom of an American Flyer passenger car shown with the markings of the Flyer retail outlet. This car can then be considered as a factory repaint, still original.

Hudson" Pullman and the 4142 "Knickerbocker" observation. Usually seen in tomato red, the cars come with the early black flex trucks without journal boxes. Flyer also produced their share of oddball and experimental models. Among them would be the blue 4637 Shasta matching the blue of the rare blue tank car and a brown Shasta (without number plates) that matches the color of the early 1926 President Special.

Flyer kept a factory retail outlet at the main Chicago factory from which they sold many test-run sets, experimentals, or imperfect models that they couldn't sell as new. Many people returned these items to the Flyer main office since they had imperfections and, when this was discovered, the factory decided to sell the items from the outlet with a marking. That is the reason that some sets have the inscription "Sold as Shop Worn" stamped underneath the cars. Because the factory outlet was a small retail store that, in effect, was able to handpick its own sets, many uncataloged and unusual combinations resulted, adding almost limitless variety to what may have been made and sold as sets. While Flyer Standard still maintains a certain level of popularity, very few collectors of American Flyer attempt to obtain "every" variation known. That kind of fanaticism is usually reserved to a certain breed of collector known as an "Ives fan."

Early Ives

The great Ives mystique is hard to define. Perhaps it has something to do with Ives's long and illustrious history, which dates back to the 1860s. Perhaps it's the Ives legend of quality toymaking that has enhanced everything Ives ever made. Possibly too it might have to do with the uniqueness of Ives, their tending to cast iron, the realism of a 3243, or the lithography they used. Maybe it was the catalogs that first inspired an interest with their personal approach to many a young Ives railroader, or the reputation of standing behind their products made famous by Harry Ives himself. For whatever reasons one chooses to collect Ives trains, many will agree with this quote from an Ives catalog: "Competition Strives, But Never Equals Ives."

Although this chapter is supposed to deal with only Standard gauge models, we must begin at the beginning. The first large Ives electric models were made in No. 1 gauge (1 gauge is 1¾ inches between the rails). At the turn of the century, No. 1 gauge was a popular gauge being made by a few different foreign manufacturers. Ives therefore undertook to compete with these companies when they introduced their own line of 1 gauge clockwork trains in 1904. These were

listed as mechanical train sets for No. 1 gauge track; it was not until 1912 that they began to make 1 gauge electric trains.

They began with their beautiful cast iron 4-4-0 locomotive, the No. 40. The engine came with a No. 40 tender, for Ives, like Flyer, had separate tender numbers. The 40 tender was always an eight-wheel version and it was tin and lithographed. Appearing in one-, two-, and three-car sets, it pulled the 70 baggage car, the 71 combination or buffet car, and the 72 parlor car. These cars always came attractively lithographed and in a variety of colors. They can be found in brown, white, and yellow litho sides and with gray and green roofs. These 70 series cars are scarce and are highly sought after by early Ives collectors.

The No. 40 clockwork made from 1904 to 1916 comes in a few different variations concerning the tender lettering, number plates, and early versions having nickel domes and stack rather than an all cast iron boiler. In 1908 Ives first made the 41 0-4-0 loco, which was the smaller brother to the 41. The 41 made until 1911 came with a No. 40 tender and is a very rare engine.

The first 1 gauge freight cars came along in 1910 and had cream-colored lithographed sides. There was the 73 refrigerator, 74 stock car, 75 caboose, 76 coal car (actually looking more like a gondola), and 77 lumber car. All of these 1 gauge freights are surprisingly scarce. The 75 caboose shown as a two-door version in the catalogs is always found as a four-door model, appearing much longer than it is shown.

In 1912 Ives introduced their first electric 1 gauge engine, the 3240, an eight-wheeled cast iron electric outline loco. The 3240 engine can be found in black and also in gray. In 1913 they first made the 3239, which is also an eight-wheel cast iron engine but slightly smaller than the 3240. Usually seen in black, the 3239 is also found in gray, brown, and a rare olive green. The fifth and last 1 gauge engine is the 1129, introduced in 1915. The 1129 was always sold with a 40 tender, because it was a 2-4-2 steam-type engine. The 1129 always came in black, as did the earlier 40 and 41 locos.

With the introduction of electric 1 gauge equipment in 1912 came the 180, 181, and 182 passenger cars, which are found in dark green with gray roofs. The 180 series cars are easier to find than the 70 series lithographed cars. Appearing in 1915 were the new freight cars, for 1 gauge this time, painted rather than lithographed and not as attractive as the earlier 70 series freights. A rare item produced from 1917 until the end of 1 gauge in 1920 is the odd-looking 73 observation car made to match the 70 series passenger cars. Although Ives made and sold 1 gauge

An interesting wall of Ives from the Ward Kimball collection, showing mostly a large array of No. 1 gauge sets.

equipment for a number of years, they never made very many different models and mainly sold O gauge train sets during this time. Lionel, which was Ives's chief American competitor, was doing well with their Standard gauge trains, and so the inevitable happened.

In 1921 Ives introduced their new wide gauge trains, which were coincidentally the same as Standard. Before they could tool up for new wider motors for this larger gauge, they took the remaining 1 gauge motors and altered them to accept longer axles. They then used these motors for their first Standard locomotives.

Ives Standard

The first Ives steam engine was the 1132, a four-wheel cast iron locomotive. The tender, although lettered differently, was still the same tin tender, the No. 40. The 1132 is usually seen in black, but it can also be seen in tan, green, and white, which are all very rare and hard to find. The only white 1132 I know of comes with gold trim and three matching passenger cars (the tender is missing) and is in the Tom Sage collection. Among the other early engines are the very commonly seen 3241 and 3242 four-wheel electrics. Both appearing in 1921, they are almost identical except that the 3242 has handrails and two headlights, while the 3241 comes with only one headlight. The 3241 is commonly seen in olive green, but it also comes in red and in maroon as a Wanamaker Special. The 3242 usually is seen in dark green but can also be found in red, gray, cadet blue, orange, pale green, and in a very rare black. The 3242 also is found in maroon as a Wanamaker Special and is extremely rare.

The Ives deluxe engine at this time, first introduced in 1921, is the twelve-wheel electric 3243. The 3243 is well known among Ives collectors and, in addition to being a very accurate model of a New York Central electric locomotive, it is an excellent operating engine. Usually found in orange and pale green, it also can be found in orange-yellow, yellow, red, maroon as a Wanamaker Special, and in a rare black. The 3243 also comes in white, which was a special display model and can be found with either gold trim and lettering or a combination of red and gray trim.

Ives patented their famous reverse mechanism in 1924, and they designated engines with a remote control reverse by the addition of the letter R to the number. As an example, the 1132 became the 1132R, the 3241 became the 3241R, the 3242 the 3242R, the 3243 the 3243R, and so forth. Ives continued to use this system on all their engines that came equipped with their automatic reverse. Also all of the early

electrics, such as the 3241, 3242, and so on, first came rubber-stamped but later, around 1926, they came with brass number and name plates.

In 1924 they first issued the small 0-4-0 numbered 3235. The 3235 is usually seen in light green and brown, and it is also found in red and in maroon as a Wanamaker Special. The very last versions came with steel rather than cast iron frames. Similar to the 3235 is the small 3236, usually seen in green, brown, or red but also known to come in cadet blue, orange, and light olive green. All of the engines mentioned before, such as the 3241, 3243, 3235, and so on, may be found in other colors that I may have failed to mention as many variations are known and new ones are sometimes discovered when collectors get together and compare notes as to what was made. Those train collectors fortunate enough to own large collections sometimes have rare variations that they're not even aware of, because the very size of their collection prevents them from displaying and being able to compare the different models they may own.

In 1926 Ives made a beautiful model of a Milwaukee Electric, numbered the 3237, a four-wheel engine. This engine came in the commonly seen cadet blue and green, but it can also be found in gray, orange, and an extremely rare black. The 3237 had the interesting feature of having the engine number inscribed on the brass headlight. The 3237 bodies were later used on some of Ives's rarest electrics, namely the 3245.

Long considered to be one of the rarest and finest-looking of any of the Ives engines is the 3245 twelve-wheel electric. First appearing in 1928 as a short-cab engine, it has a body that is virtually identical to that of the 3237. Because this was a very late production item for Ives, the frame is not entirely made out of cast iron, but the center section of the frame is made of stamped steel. This engine is a good example of an old rule that states, "No matter how rare an item is, there are still variations to be found." While very few original 3245 short-cabs are known, those that have turned up are seen in a number of different colors. Since any 3245 short-cab is very rare indeed, it would be hard to say just which colors are the rarest. It is known to come in cadet blue, gray (which may be the same as the cadet blue that some may have called gray), pale green, and orange.

The brother to the short-cab is naturally the Ives 3245 long-cab twelve-wheeled electric. While more long-cabs are known it is nonetheless also a rare engine. Most collectors find the long-cab 3245 to be more attractive, and so it is equivalent in desirability as well as price to its rarer short-cab brother. This engine was made in small quantities in 1929 and 1930

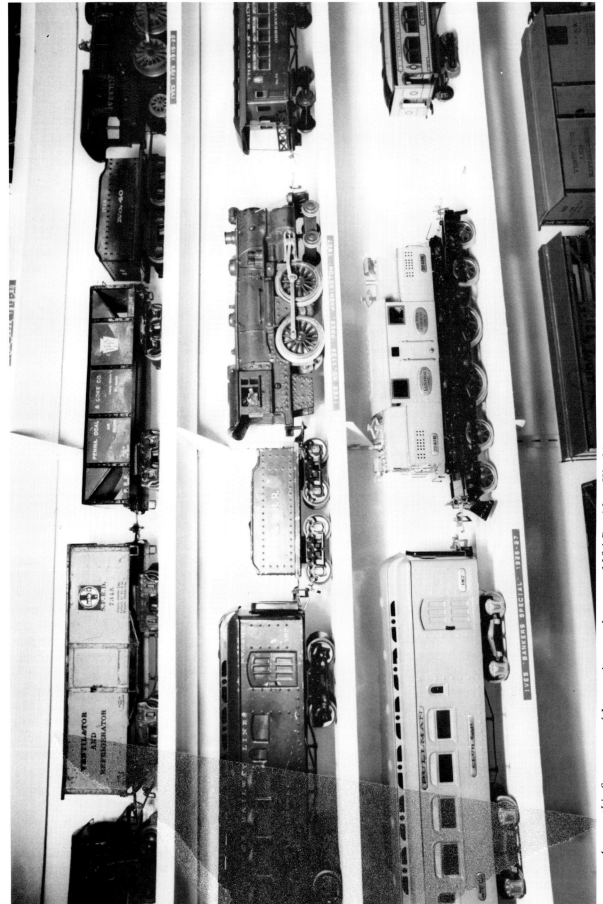

Among this fine group of Ives trains stands out an 1134 President Washington locomotive with its engineer in the cab window and a later 3243 electric engine with brass plates.

and is always found in black with an orange frame. Even this scarce engine is known to come with two types of trim, both brass and nickel (the nickel engine has a black stripe on the frame), creating two variations for those of you who have to own one of each. There also is reported to exist a black long-cab 3245 with a red instead of an orange frame that came with the red and black cars of the Chief set.

When Ives dropped the 1132 steamer from the catalog in 1927, they replaced it with another, even better cast iron locomotive, the 4-4-0 engine No. 1134. This engine, stamped "President Washington" on the engine cab, even had a little engineer at the window. While a beautifully proportioned model, it was to remain in the catalog for one year only, accounting for its scarcity today. Usually seen in olive green with a tin No. 40 tender lettered for the B.&O. R.R., it is often referred to as the B.&O. President Washington locomotive. It is also known to come in black with the later-made die-cast black 40 tender. Some versions of this engine can also be found lettered 1132, which is the number of the earlier 0-4-0 steamer.

Immediately hailed as a sensation in 1928 was Ives's new 1134 all-die-cast 4-4-2 steamer and tender. In 1928 this engine was very far advanced from any of Ives's contemporaries, and two companies openly purchased this finely proportioned locomotive and added it to their line. The two competitors were American Flyer and Dorfan, which probably would never have had the chance to buy this engine had Ives not been in financial difficulties in that year, which finally ended in Ives declaring bankruptcy. While the die-cast tenders remained the same, the 4-4-2 1134 underwent a change in 1930. In 1928 and 1929 they came with the usually seen high headlight, but in 1930 the headlight was placed in the center of the boiler front; it is often referred to as the concealed headlight version. By far most of the 1134's that you will see are black, but they also came in a few different and rare variations. Since the 1134 is a very well-liked engine among Ives fans, most of these engines are highly prized and difficult to obtain. Among these rare 1134's are the red engine of the National Limited, a green model, and a copper-plated engine made to go with the Prosperity Special set. There are also nickel-plated display models, also believed to have come with the Prosperity Special set one year.

Getting back to the rolling stock of Ives's first Standard models, we find that Ives took the old 1 gauge freight car bodies and placed Standard trucks on them. Later they gave these models their own numbers, such as 190 for the tank car, 192 boxcar, 193 stock car, and so forth. Variations exist among these cars, but the most interesting would be some of the later all Ives equipment, such as the two-window

caboose instead of the normal five-window 195 caboose or the special "Harmony Creamery" 196 tank car.

Ives Transition

Most collectors find the Ives transition period freight cars the most interesting to collect. The Ives transition period, which extends from 1928 to 1930, and those three years only, produced an interesting array of odd-looking freight cars using Lionel and Flyer bodies mounted on Ives trucks, with Ives couplers and Ives plates. All Ives transition period trains are hard to find, but among those seen more often are the Flyer-bodied 20-195 caboose, 20-198 gondola, and the 20-192 boxcar. The Flyer-bodied 20-193 cattle car is hard to find, but the 20-190 tank car is the rarest of all.

While these Flyers-Ives transition cars were probably made for one year only in 1929, there are still some distinct variations. The boxcar, usually seen in yellow with a cadet blue roof, can also be found in pea green with a dark red roof. The cattle car, usually found in orange with a dark red roof, can also be found in pea green with a dark red roof. If you don't already own a set of transition freight cars you'll probably be happy to settle for any you can find, but it's nice to know just what was made, even though you'll never be lucky enough to find them for sale.

Among the Lionel-bodied transition freights made in 1930 we have another hard group of cars to complete. While the 195 caboose and 198 gondola are not too hard, the 192 boxcar is a lot scarcer. Very rare is the modest-looking 197 lumber car and the 190 yellow tank car. All the freight cars come in colors very different from those regularly seen on the all Lionel 200 series freights, such as the 198 gondola coming in black and the 197 flatcar found in light green, etc., etc. Available separately but not in cataloged sets and also very scarce is the Ives crane using the Lionel 219 derrick body. Numbered 199, it is found in peacock blue with a maroon roof but having Lionel 200 series trucks and Ives couplers with bent shanks.

Going back to the earlier all-Ives period, we find that Ives made some special sets along the lines of the Lionel Macy Specials, except that these were for John Wanamaker & Co. Made in the early 1920s, these sets were all finished in a deep maroon and they all had gold-stamped lettering reading "Wanamaker Railway Lines" in a special script style. All of these sets are rare. There is a 3235 passenger set, a 3241 freight set, an even rarer 3242 freight train, and the 3243 passenger set, all of which come completely in the same special shade of maroon, freight cars included. Also made was an 1132 steam loco in black but stamped Wanamaker Railway Lines.

A detailed catalog description of the Ives Railway Circus.

*This page from the Ives 1930 catalog shows
a number of Ives transition sets, among them
the famous Chief set and below a freight set
with Ives Lionel-bodied freight cars.*

Ives also had been known to make up sets using special Southern Pacific nameplates, probably destined for a department store chain out West. All sets having these unusual plates are rare and desirable. It is believed that they may also have stamped some sets Illinois Central (not to be confused with Lionel, which also had some passenger cars similarly stamped) and possibly other railroads as well.

While Lionel Standard gauge trains are well known for their famous sets such as the Blue Comet and State Set, and while American Flyer is also well known for their beautiful President Specials and their fabulous Mayflower set, Ives had an even greater variety of large and beautiful sets, which are all highly sought-after collector's items and are priced accordingly. Amazingly, most of these large Ives sets were made after Ives declared bankruptcy in 1928. Therefore any of these sets using Lionel and Flyer bodies and made in the years 1928, 1929, and 1930 should technically

be referred to as Ives transition sets, since they were produced in that three-year transition period before Lionel completely took over Ives train production at their Irvington factory in 1931 and 1932.

Certainly one of the most well known and liked of famous Ives sets is the white Ives 3243 set. This set, painted all white, has a very striking appearance and no wonder, for it was always an uncataloged set and was especially made for store display models. Usually referred to as a "white Ives" set, it consists of an early 1920s 3243 engine with 187-1, 188-1, and 189-1 rubber-stamped passenger cars. All-white Ives 3243 sets are hard to find, and there are two variations among those found, with some sets having all-gold lettering and trim and others seen with red lettering and gray trim.

Another rare and desirable set is the Ives "Capitol City Special," consisting of the dark olive 4-4-0 numbered 1134 with the engineer in the window and the matching 187 club car, two 188 parlor cars, and a 189 observation car. This set, made in 1927 only, is a fine example of what Ives might have gone on to produce had they continued in business under the direction of Harry C. Ives. Sometimes called the B.&O. President

Washington set by collectors, it had an engine that was Ives's last cast iron steam-type locomotive.

One set that Ives competitors at the time could not boast of was a circus set. In 1928 Ives introduced their famous Ives Railway Circus, consisting of the new die-cast 1134 steamer and six cars. There was a 193C stock car, a 192C boxcar, two 196C flatcars with cages, one 196C flat with two tent wagons, and a 171 tan parlor car. The set also came with a large canvas tent with poles, two runways to load the wagons, twelve animals, including elephants, lions, bears, and horses, and a huge cardboard background depicting other tents, sideshows, and a musical band.

While all versions of the Ives circus train are hard to find, especially complete, the 1928 all-Ives circus set is particularly rare. Most circus sets are found incomplete, missing the tent, animals, and many of the circus cages. The usual version seen has two Flyer-body circus cars, the 20-193 stock car stamped "The Ives R.R. Circus," and the similarly stamped 20-192 boxcar, both cars having yellow sides and dark red roofs. These two cars replaced the earlier 193C and 192C Ives cars, but the rest of the set remained the same although some of the last sold in 1930 had the newer 1134 engine with the concealed headlight.

Among the rarest of the Ives transition sets was the "Northern Limited," cataloged in 1929. This set consisted of a pale green 3237 and matching 244 baggage, 245 parlor car, and 246 observation. These passenger cars in pale or, if you prefer, light green are possibly the scarcest Flyer-bodied cars made by Ives. They also have been known to come with a matching 3245 short-cab locomotive instead of the 3237. Although they are extremely scarce, of the two such sets that I have seen (I know of more), I found that while one set had its properly etched brass plates, the other set of passenger cars had some blank plates that evidently were never stamped at all. I can only hazard a guess that perhaps when the cars were made the dies had not been set up to stamp the plates, and so, in an effort to get the cars out in time, they may have allowed them to go through with the odd-appearing blank brass plates.

Without a doubt one of the most striking train sets ever made and one of the most expensive ever sold is the famous Ives Prosperity Special appearing in 1929. Ives timed this set perfectly; here was a train set selling for one hundred dollars in 1929 as the Great Depression was just beginning. This rare train consisted of a copper-plated 1134 and the 241, 242, and 243 Flyer-bodied passenger cars, similarly copper-plated with nickel-plated roofs. This beautiful but ill-fated set can also be found with the engine entirely nickel-plated instead of copper-plated as usually seen.

Appearing similar to the Prosperity Special and made available a year earlier in the 1928 catalog is the Ives Black Diamond Express Senior. Known by collectors simply as the Black Diamond, it came with a black 1134 and the 241, 242, and 243 passenger cars in black with red roofs. Known to come in both three- and four-car sets, the first sets in 1928 are said to come with an 1134 in a satin black finish different from the usually seen regular black 1134. This set, although highly desirable, is not as rare as some of the other Ives transition previously mentioned.

One of the most talked-about Ives sets is the well-liked long-cab 3245 Olympian set. Appearing in 1929 in black with an orange frame, the popular 3245 came teamed up with matching 241 series passenger cars with orange sides and black roofs. This set, while not the rarest Ives train made, is one of the most sought after by Ives collectors. Not as popular as the Flyer-body cars but definitely rarer are the Lionel-body cars of 1930, numbered 247, 248, and 249. While not cataloged, there are a few known 246 Lionel-bodied matching diners known to exist for this set. Interestingly, the orange paint of the 1930 set is exactly the same orange Lionel used on their orange 9E, leading me to speculate that these last 3245 sets may have been made or at least painted and assembled by Lionel.

Similar to the Black Diamond is the Chief set made in 1930, also using Lionel 418, 419 series bodies. Pulled by the 1930 1134 with the concealed headlight, it came with the 247, 248, and 249 cars painted in black with red roofs. There is also reported to exist a never-cataloged 246 diner in matching colors. All of these 247 series Lionel body passenger cars were decaled.

Even rarer than the Chief is the famous Ives National Limited. This set came with a scarce red with gold trim 1134, and it pulled the four different passenger cars, 246 diner, 247 club car, 248 chair car, and 249 observation. The cars were painted in an attractive blue with red roofs. The engine to this set, that is the red 1134 loco, is known to crack with age as the die-casting process was not perfected at the time. So even though these cars are rare, complete original engines are even rarer. The National Limited is just one more testament to why these rare trains of the Ives transition period are so sought after by collectors; they are beautiful and easily distinguished from commonly seen Lionel items.

In 1931 all the so-called Ives trains were made in the Lionel factory in Irvington. Trains of this period are actually entirely made by Lionel, and so, even though Lionel issued a separate Ives catalog and used the Ives names on these trains, they are actually nothing other than Lionel trains. Properly they should be called Lionel-Ives trains for the two years 1931 and 1932.

Among these items are a Lionel No. 10 engine with Ives plates, found in the common peacock color. Although the catalog drawing shows an 1134 as the engine 1760, it was actually a Lionel 384 with Ives plates and the 1760 number. Similar to this is the 1770 loco, which is a Lionel 390 with new Ives plates and number made in 1932. The 418, 419 series cars in apple green were also sold, having Ives decals in uncataloged sets with a regular Lionel 381E. These cars are even rarer when seen in mojave with the Ives decals. The common peacock with dark green roofs 332, 339, and 341 cars are also found in set with Ives decals. One extremely interesting car in the John Marron collection has Ives decals over Lionel rubber stamping and Lionel—yes, Lionel—decals over the Ives decals!

Lionel also took their smaller 500 series freights and made them part of their Ives line. Using regular Lionel colors they made the 512 gondola into the 1772, the 511 flat became the 1771, and the 517 caboose became the 1777. Other 500 series freights were shown separately in the back of the catalog, and a 1779 derrick car was shown using the body of the Lionel 219 crane.

In 1932 only, Lionel made a limited number of the Ives-designed 1764 twelve-wheel electric locomotive, in sets with the 1766, 67, and 68 passenger cars. These cars are different from the usually seen Lionel cars in that they have Ives plates using a lighter blue ink. The 1767 baggage car is also different in that it has flat doors rubber-stamped in red "Baggage, Mail," which regular production Lionel cars do not have. Also Lionel 1767 baggage cars have ribbed instead of the flat doors required for the rubber stamping.

While collectors may cherish the Lionel-Ives 1764 set it lasted only a year. In 1933 Lionel publicly announced that they had taken over Ives. The Ives saga of finely made trains had sadly come to an end.

8

EARLY PERIOD LIONEL

Perhaps I should restrict this chapter to that which the title refers, namely, early Lionel, but it would be far too easy a course to take. Wherever our collecting interest lies we must not forget to acknowledge the fine and noble efforts of the many companies that worked to produce the first toy trains in America. When electricity was merely a novelty known only to a few and was just beginning to find its way into the homes of the lower and middle classes, there were a number of early pioneers in the manufacture of electric toy trains. Perhaps the names of Carlisle and Finch, Knapp, Howard, and Voltamp conjure up visions of a remote Christmas past when the automobile and the airplane were startling new inventions.

Early Manufacturers

The first electric trains in America were made by none other than Carlisle and Finch in 1896. Their first models made used No. 2 gauge three-rail track, later giving way to the more commonly seen 2 gauge two-rail track. These early models of trolley cars were made in brass and were fairly simple four-wheel models. They literally had a rubber band belt drive to supply power to the wheels. Of course in these early days power was supplied by dry cell batteries.

Among the best-known Carlisle and Finch items are their coal mining locomotive and ore cars. There are at least five variations of the C&F mining loco, with the earliest versions having paper labels and coming in green, black, and red, and the later ones having the name "mining locomotive" stamped into the body. They also produced a number of steam-type engines, all having wooden frames which were always dyed green. C&F included a variety of freight and passenger equipment in their line and even went on to produce a 4-4-2 steamer in addition to a few four-wheel steam types.

Knapp started making trains about 1905 and lasted until 1913. Also using the early two-rail 2 gauge track, they produced at least two engines using cast iron bodies. The nicest model they made was the 221 steeple-cab locomotive, which was a small, excellently proportioned electric engine. They had a limited line of freight and passenger equipment, and all their engines had dummy headlights since the idea of an illuminated light hadn't caught on yet.

It was the Howard Miniature Lamp Company that first introduced the illuminated headlight on their engines, a feature quickly copied by their competitor, Lionel. Howard trains were made briefly between 1905 and 1910, yet they produced a wide array of engines and cars. Even rarer than C&F and Knapp, Howard also made a number of early trolleys. One had a removable top, which when taken off revealed a gondola car that could be used instead. An interesting feature is that all Howard locomotives have brass drive wheels, unlike many other early companies, which preferred cast iron engine wheels.

More well known and seen more often are Voltamp trains, first made back in 1903. From their cute four-wheel freight cars to their larger passenger sets, Voltamp produced a large variety of well-made train sets using the then-popular 2 gauge track. Voltamp made a beautiful 4-6-2 locomotive, the 2500, which was the largest engine of its kind at that time and could not be rivaled.

Lionel 2⅞

Very different from two-inch 2 gauge track was the kind first made by Lionel, measuring a very wide 2⅞ inches between the rails. While many collectors are familiar with Lional Standard, they have usually never seen 2⅞ gauge equipment. Lionel began producing trains in 1901 that were large and well made

Two variations of the scarce Lionel 2⅞ gauge gondola pictured inside the rare cast iron 2⅞ bridge. The B&O gondola shown at right is much rarer than the Lake Shore version.

and came with cast iron frames. The track was steel strip track that came with wooden ties. Switches, bumpers, a bridge, and even elevated pillars were available for use with these early models.

Their numbering began with the No. 100 locomotive, often called by collectors the B&O No. 5, since that is how it is lettered on its side. All the Lionel 2⅞ pieces came with sprung wheels and reversing controllers. The B&O electric locomotive was first made in an early light green and is very rare in that color. Most engines seen are found in maroon with a black roof.

The next model available was the 200 motorized gondola car. The first models lettered "Electric Express" were made with a wooden body. Simply referred to as the Lionel wooden gondola, two versions are known, one having brass corners and one without. Later they made steel gondola cars; the earliest ones were painted in light green and lettered "Lake Shore" and are as rare as the first wooden gondolas. Most motorized gondolas seen come in maroon and are similarly lettered "Lake Shore."

Lionel went to Converse and bought trolley bodies, which Converse was using for their trackless pulltoys.

Lionel added these new trolleys to their line, numbered 300, and equipped them with a motorized frame. The Converse trolley was an open summer car with reversible seats popular among collectors. What Lionel cataloged as their No. 400 trail car was simply the 200 gondola without its motor. Usually seen in maroon it probably is the single easiest-to-find item in 2⅞ gauge. Also made was a 309 trolley trailer identical to the motorized 300 Converse trolley, except that it naturally lacked a motor.

Probably the rarest single item is the 500 motorized derrick, usually just called the 2⅞ crane. It came motorized and had a manually operated hook and chain attached to its large cast iron boom. Even this extremely scarce item is known to come in the early light green and also the later maroon color. The derrick trailer numbered 600 is also known in both colors and, minus the motor, is otherwise identical.

Another popular 2⅞ piece is the 800 boxcar, referred to by collectors as it is lettered, simply the Metropolitan Express car. Part trolley and part boxcar, this Lionel invention is usually found in maroon with black trim. They also had a trailer car to the Metropolitan, numbered 900 and slightly harder to find. While it has always been the case that trailer cars in general are harder to find than motorized units, they do not tend to command higher prices than powered units. Since Lionel failed to stamp identifying numbers on their 2⅞ items one could easily convert any motorized unit into a trailer simply

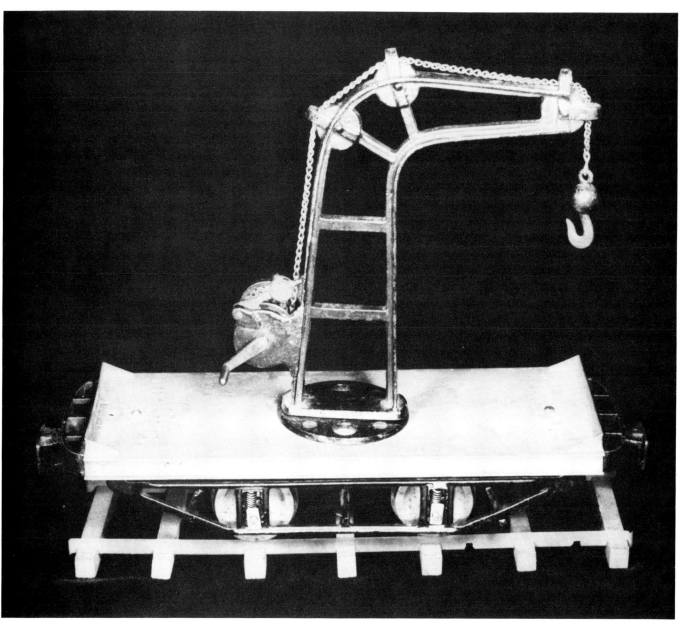

The single rarest piece
of 2⅞ equipment
is the No. 600 trailer crane.

A rare, B&O lettered No. 5 special pulling an incredibly rare No. 29 maroon knobby roof day coach from the Tom Sage collection.

by removing the motor; thus we find today that motorized units command higher prices than rarer trailers. Another reason for motorized pieces being more desirable might be that some collectors may wish to run their mighty 2⅞ items someday. While this is a fine idea, I think that those few collectors who do manage to run their 2⅞ trains are even rarer than the 2⅞ trains themselves.

Among the scarcer items made was the 1000 open-end trolley car cataloged in 1905. Found in maroon it is known to come with a few different letterings. Sometimes stamped "Metropolitan Express," the name usually associated with the 800 boxcar, it is also known to come stamped "Maryland St. Ry. Co.," and Philadelphia lettering also was used. It was probably made in at least half a dozen different designations, and undoubtedly more will be found in future years. It too came as a trailer car and was numbered 1050 in the 1905 catalog.

At this time 2⅞ production came to a close. After five years, from 1901 to 1905, Joshua Lionel Cowen, Lionel's founder, decided to switch to a smaller gauge of track, one that would allow him to make larger multiwheeled cars and engines. All the 2⅞ items were so large that every one had only four wheels so that they could safely stay on the track. Now, in order to keep up with competition, Lionel in 1906 first began to make Standard gauge trains using sectional tinplate track. Since the popular gauge at the time was No. 2 gauge (two inches wide) track and Lionel Standard was 2⅛ inches wide, it is safe to assume that Lionel probably had planned to make the more popular 2 gauge track. Also, as late as 1912 Lionel continued to state in their catalogs that the "gauge of track is 2 inches."

Early Period Standard

First, I must admit my partiality when discussing early period Lionel Standard, for not only is it one of my favorite train collecting subjects but I myself have been trying for years to put together a sampling of trains from this period. If I had to narrow down my collecting interest and specialize in one field, this would probably be it. I've always loved Lionel's early period models, characterized by thin-rim drive wheels, three-rivet trucks, early period electrics, knobby roof passenger cars, and of course the many trolley cars they made. While what we may define as early period Lionel Standard has a definite beginning in 1906, it extended for a number of years, until approximately 1925, when many of the new classic designs were first being introduced.

Lionel is credited with producing the first sec-

tional three-rail standard gauge track in America. Lionel's early models were large and distinctive. Lionel avoided the use of cast iron on their engines, they never used lithography on their cars, and they painted most of their equipment in dull flat shades, such as olive green and maroon. All of these Lionel practices were unusual, for most other manufacturers at the time relied heavily on cast iron engines, lithographed freight and passenger cars, and bright paints to sell their trains, but obviously Lionel knew what they were doing, for the company continued to grow and expand throughout this entire period. While Lionel catalogs continually boasted that their trains are "the best that money can buy" and that they were the "Standard Of The World," they kept up a certain standard of quality all through this entire period, and the public recognized this, for Lionel trains were soon to become world-famous.

Many variations exist among the trains made in this period, but especially among the earliest years from 1906 to about 1914, when many items were in an experimental stage and production runs were often done on a day-to-day basis in small lots. This perhaps would account for the overlapping of parts used and the fact that we cannot always date material made in this period to a particular year but rather to a few-year period when similar items are discovered. It is believed that the solid-side three-rivet freight truck came first, soon followed by the three-rivet open-sided truck and then the commonly seen large eyelet truck or single-rivet truck known to come in other minor variations.

It would be nice to say that we could easily date these early models according to the different coupler types used. Actually the couplers are known in a few variations and were often used interchangeably in early Lionel production. Basically we find that both the short and the long straight hook couplers are found on equipment made between 1906 to 1913 or 1914, the short and long crinkle hook coupler coming slightly later, from 1910 to 1918, and the commonly seen hook coupler with nibs at the bottom to prevent uncoupling appears from 1914 to 1925.

Early Steamers

Lionel's first and smallest Standard steamer was the No. 5, an 0-4-0 that was sold without a tender. The first versions made came with thin-rim drivers and dummy headlights, which were not illuminated until 1910. The No. 5 Special locomotive was made between 1907 and 1909 and was simply a thin-rim 5 with a single four-wheel truck slope back tender. The 51 engine is simply a 5 with an added eight-

*A thick-rim 51 with the Pennsylvania tender
(above) is not as rare as the thin-rim 6
Pennsylvania engine pictured at right. Note that
the lettering is different on both engines.*

wheel tender, which was first shown cataloged in
1910 but continued to be called a 5 Special, even
though it now came with the eight-wheel double
truck tender. It was dubbed the 51 engine beginning
in the 1912 catalog and continued to be made until
1923.

The No. 6 steam locomotive was a 4-4-0 first made
with a dummy headlight in 1906. It always came with
an eight-wheel double-truck tender and beginning in
1907 came with a working headlight. Like the 5 or
51, the earliest versions came with thin-rim drivers
and the tenders had solid or open-sided three-rivet
trucks. Both the 51 and 6 made for a number of years
can be found having a number of variations regarding
tender trucks, lettering, and headlights. The 5 and 6
are known with the lettering of the Pennsylvania, the
NYC&HRRR, and even the B&O railroads. There are
other variations, such as the missing "R" found on
NYC&HRR tenders and different styles of lettering
used, but the engines were always painted in black
with blued Russian iron boilers.

The third engine in the early steam category is
the 4-4-0 No. 7 locomotive, which is identical to the
6, except that it was made in brass and nickel-plated.
Originally advertised as a 4-6-0, it was never made;
the actual 7 was then introduced in 1908 as the No. 6
Special. It was not given the designation as the No. 7
until 1910, and it continued to be made until 1923.
The No. 7, offered in either brass or brass and nickel-
plated, came without lettering but had red trim
painted on the engine and tender wheels.

The thin-rim versions of the 5, 6, and 7 locomotives
are all difficult to obtain, with all versions of the No.
7 being harder to find. Since the early period steamers
were made for a long period of time, much longer
than the early square-cab electrics, they are not rare,
but most versions found are of the later thick-rim
variety. The thin-rim drivers, made between 1906 and
1912, are considered much more desirable, in addition
to the fact that they are rarer.

Early Electrics

It was in 1910 that Lionel first made their Standard gauge electric-type engines, all using the early
square-cab design. The engines were numbered 1910
(the year they were first issued), 1911, and 1912. The
1910 was an 0-6-0 rubber-stamped NYNH&H, always
seen in olive green and coming in sets with two early
shorty (only 7 inches long) 112 gondolas. The 1911
was an 0-4-0 coming with different lettering and
always found in olive green. The 1911 is unusual in
that the square-cab version is usually found with
thin-rim drivers; the thick-rim versions are harder to
find. It too came in sets with two early 116 dump
or ballast cars. Both the 1910 and 1911 locomotives
were made until the year 1912.

The 1912 engine made from 1910 to 1912 was a
large 0-4-4-0 square-cab electric type made in olive

*This boxed 1910 set with its shorty gondolas
is a rare example of an early period set
in superb condition.*
(From the author's collection)

*Besides the thin and thick rim variations
of the scarce 1911 locomotive there are at least
four different lettering variations as shown.
This is a prime example of the many different variations
that can be found in early Lionel Standard gauge.*

Two unusual 33's are the Penn R.R. six-wheeled 33 pictured at left and the C&O lettering 33 at right. Most 33 engines are found with the common New York Central Lines stamping.

green. It is found with the harder-to-find thin-rim wheels and later is found with the thick-rim drivers. Usually found stamped NYNH&H, it is also seen with NYC block lettering and is also known with the markings of a 42 engine referred to as a square-cab 42. Whether Lionel intended to rubber-stamp the 1912 body with 42 markings or whether the square-cab engine was accidentally rubber-stamped by a factory worker on an assembly line is something we may never know. Better yet it may be that when a 1912 was sent in for factory repairs it may have been repainted and stamped with the only markings that were available at the later date, that of the 42. Unsolved mysteries such as these have made collecting early Lionel fascinating for those collectors interested enough in learning the meaning of the many odd and unusual variations that come to light.

In 1911 Lionel introduced the 0-4-4-0 1911 Special, always found in maroon. Appearing with both solid and spoked cast iron wheels it is usually found with early 180, 181, and 182 passenger cars with solid clerestory roofs and was made until 1912. Also introduced in 1911 was the 1912 Special, which was virtually identical to the 1912 loco, except that it was made entirely of brass. While the 1912 Special loco-

motive is particularly scarce, it is known to come with either thin- or thick-rim drivers. In the year 1912 the 1911 Special became the 53 (sometimes called the eight-wheel 53) and the 1912 Special became the 54 (sometimes called the square-cab brass 54).

The eight-wheel 53 loco became a four-wheel engine by the year 1915, but it remained as the only square-cab electric until 1919. The four-wheel 53 in maroon is probably the easiest to find of the square-cab electric series, but it is also known to come in brown, mojave, and olive green.

It was in 1912 that Lionel introduced the six-wheel electric engine, the No. 34, to go with the new small 35 and 36 passenger cars, which came with ribbed sides, unlike the smooth sides of the later-made cars. The 34 was Lionel's first round-cab engine and was probably made to replace the earlier 1910 electric. Virtually identical to the six-wheel 34 was the six-wheel 33 introduced in 1913 and lasting as a six-wheel model until 1915. Most often seen are olive green six-wheel 33 engines, with the 34 being slightly harder to find. They also are known to come in black, and a few oddball lettering variations are known to exist.

It was in 1913 that Lionel began to switch over to the newer round-cab designs, which are commoner than the earlier square-edge electrics. Most collectors are familiar with these later-made engines, which were produced for a good number of years. Certainly the most common of these is the small four-wheel 33

The square-cab 42 locomotive pictured above is, other than its number, identical to the 1912 engine pictured below. The block lettering New York Central Lines is not typical of the 1912, as most are found with N.Y., N.H., & H. in script on the side.

Lionel No. 50 electric engine has transition-type latch couplers and the later "Super" motor.

locomotive, which made its debut in 1913 and lasted till 1925, the earliest models of which can be found with step headlights and cast iron wheels. The 33 is usually found in black or olive green but is also known to come in dark green, gray, pea green, maroon, mojave, red with cream trim, and midnight blue (especially painted for Montgomery-Ward).

Made to replace the early square-cab 1911 was the round-cab 1911 engine made for one year only in 1913. The 1911 round cab having the same body as the 38 had become the 38 loco by 1914. The 38 was slightly larger than the 33 and was made up until 1924. Usually seen in black it is also known to come in gray, olive green, dark green, maroon, pea green (sometimes called light green), mojave, and red. In 1920 Lionel used the 38 body in maroon and numbered it as a round-cab 53 engine, but it lasted for one year only and is therefore hard to find. They also used the 38 body in conjunction with their new Super motor in 1924 and 1925, but they now designated it

with a new number, the No. 50 locomotive. The 33 was also available those two years with the new Super motor but it was uncataloged and its number remained as the 33.

Larger and more desirable was the large eight-wheel 42 loco first made in 1913 and continued through until 1923. The 42 has long been a popular engine, for it remained the deluxe electric locomotive for many years. The earliest versions had sliding doors, and they all come with single motors, until after about 1920, when they came with two motors. There is a story behind the 42 that it was Joshua Lionel Cowen's favorite locomotive and that he liked it so much that it continued to be made after it was discontinued in the catalogs in 1923. Whether or not the story is true we may never be certain, but Lionel did paint the 42 in a wide array of colors, at least as many as the 33 or 38.

The 42 is usually found in black or gray, but it is also known in dark green, olive green, mojave, pea

This rare No. 3 enclosed trolley car (above) is particularly
scarce because of the unusual Bay Shore lettering,
specially done for a Baltimore, Maryland, company.
The No. 8 Pay As You Enter, pictured below, is the
largest and some say the most attractive
of the Lionel trolleys.

green, mouse gray (a distinctly lighter shade of gray), maroon, and peacock blue. Many of these odd colors, such as mojave, pea green, and peacock, are believed to be factory repaints. When engines were sent in to be repaired years later, Lionel often repainted the bodies in whatever paint they were using at the time, which accounts for the relative scarcity of these unusually colored engines.

Last but not least was the all-brass 54 locomotive, which was otherwise identical to the regular 42. The 54 was never lettered or numbered but, like the earlier 1912 Special, it had red-painted ventilators and red wheels. Like the 42 it was made from 1913 to 1923.

Trolleys

Always among the most popular train-collecting subjects are the many interesting Lionel trolley cars made between 1906 and 1915 and unrivaled by any of Lionel's competitors. All Lionel trolleys are hard to find if not outright rare, and they all are close matches to the real trolleys made in that period. The first models made did not have headlights, and it wasn't until 1910 that they came equipped with working lights, except for the No. 1 car. All of the trolleys (except for the 8 and 9) were sold as trailers without motors.

To simplify what was made, there are basically two types of trolleys: double-truck and single-truck (four-wheel or eight-wheel). The single-truck trolleys are in general easier to find and consist of the 1, 2, 100, 101, and 202, with their trailers numbered 111, 200, 1000, 1100, and 2200. The more difficult double-truck trolleys are the 3, 4, 8, 9, 10, and 303, with trailers numbered 300, 1010, and 3300. There were no trailers made for the large 8 and 9 trolleys. It is important to keep in mind that, although from 1910 on trailer cars were supposed to carry their own number, many trailers were probably sold using the number of the respective motor unit, so it cannot be expected that all trailers will come with their proper number as cataloged. Some trolleys cataloged were probably never made, and if made were issued in extremely small quantities. Among those cars that were doubtfully ever made are the double-motored 1011 interurban and 1012 trailer and the two-motored 404 summer car and the 4400 trailer.

The first trolleys made in 1906 and 1907 have plain window openings, usually referred to as flat-sided windows. Starting about 1908 they began to have embossed frames around the windows, as is usually seen. All the trolleys came with a reverse mechanism, except for the 1, 100, and the 101. Beginning in 1910 Lionel added vestibules to the 2, 3,

Lionel No. 10 interurban.

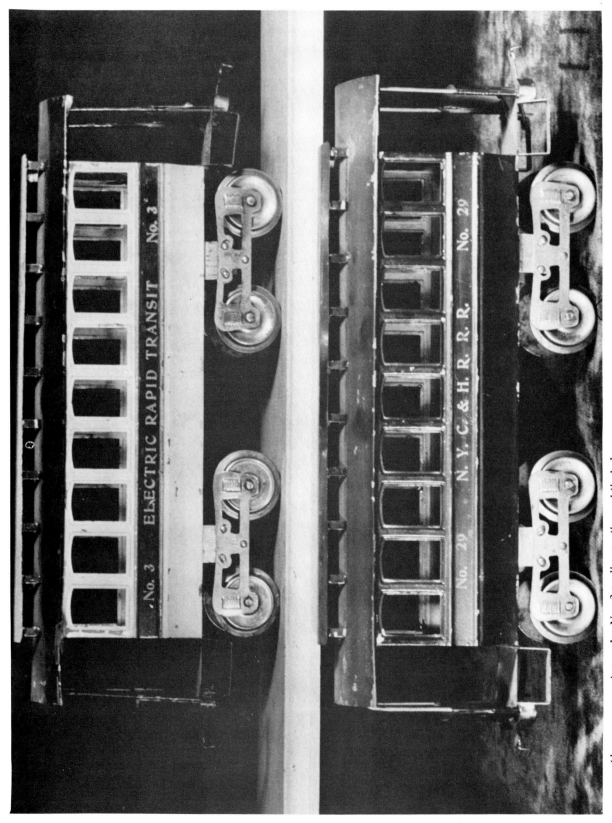

Above we see pictured a No. 3 trolley trailer, while below is Lionel's first 29 day coach. Except for the different paint and lettering these cars are otherwise identical.

and 4 trolley cars, and no longer were we seeing the earlier open-ended-style cars first made. In that year they also introduced their summer cars, the 101, 202, and the 303 trolleys with open-style bodies and reversible seats. The summer cars have always been highly sought after by collectors.

Always considered one of the most beautiful trolleys made is the No. 8 "Pay As You Enter." Although not one of the rarest cars it certainly is one of the most desirable. One of the rarest of the trolleys and perhaps even the single rarest trolley is the double-motored No. 9, which looks like a nine-window No. 8, except that it is found in orange with cream trim. Most No. 8 trolleys seen have eleven windows and are found in green and cream.

Mistakes and oddballs are known among the trolleys, such as a 202 summer car incorrectly stamped as a No. 1. Also Lionel did do special lettering on occasion for certain stores. One such company located in Baltimore, Maryland, had a list of street names available on the various Lionel trolleys, and I know of at least four actual examples that have come to light. Among them is a No. 1 lettered "Curtis Bay," a No. 3 lettered "Bay Shore," a set of 10 and 1010 interurbans lettered for the Washington, Baltimore, and Annapolis Railway (W.B.&A.), as well as a No. 100 trolley lettered "Linden Avenue."

Of the interurban cars made some interesting variations are known. Beginning in 1910 some cars came with knobby roofs (three painted knobs on the roof to simulate ventilators) and were painted in maroon. These maroon interurbans are rare, as are the other early interurbans in green with knobby roofs. Most interurbans seen are of the last variety, with the cut-out clerestory and the three-hole steps made between 1913 and 1915.

Passenger Cars

Lionel also made a few different types of passenger cars to go with their early engines. The first Standard gauge day coach was made in 1908 and is different from that pictured in the catalog. The first car actually made used a No. 3 trolley body painted over in dark green, numbered 29, the same as the later-made day coaches, and was lettered for the NYC&HRRR or the Pennsylvania. By 1910 this practice had stopped and the 29 day coach became an all-maroon car with a knobby roof. It further evolved into what we usually find today as a 29 coach in green with New York Central Lines lettering, but earlier versions can be found with rare Pennsylvania lettering and maroon trim and a maroon band across the windows; these are called maroon stripe day coaches.

Lionel's first passenger car, oddly enough, was stamped 1910 and was first made in 1907. The car was entirely enclosed, it had a knobby roof, and the three-rivet trucks were placed on the very ends of

This 190 observation car with three-rivet trucks, knobby roof, and straight-bar observation deck is probably the very first observation car ever made by Lionel. Needless to say it is quite scarce.

*Above is a No. 18 knobby roof Pullman while below is an almost
identical car but with different Pullman lettering and the number 1910.
This car should properly be numbered 18 and probably is a factory goof.*

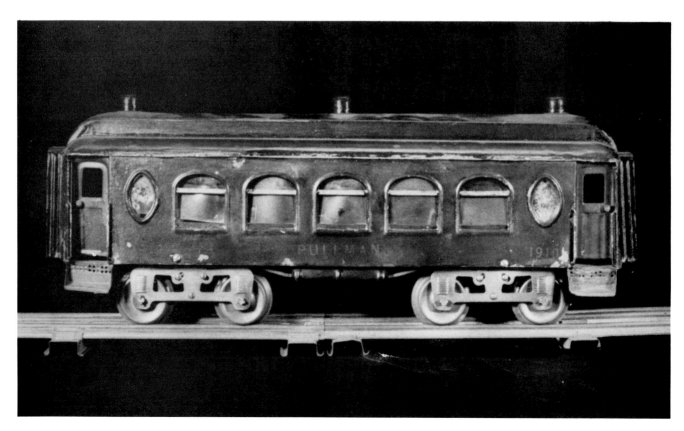

Above we see a regular knobby roof 1910 Pullman car, and you'll note that
it has no steps and that the trucks are situated at the extreme end.
Below is the properly numbered 1010 interurban trailer with the knobby roof.
While variations abound in these early period passenger cars,
any car found with a knobby roof is rare and hard to find.

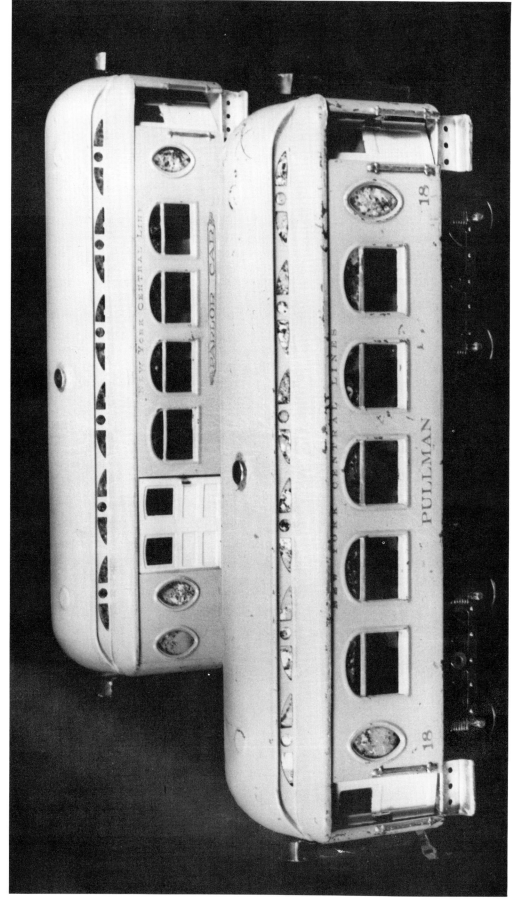

Lettering styles differ even on two passenger cars from the same set. The car in front has the earlier-style lettering with the number 18 on its side, while the combine behind it has the later small-size lettering. These are orange cars with the painted yellow doors.

the car, as it was made without steps. The body was entirely soldered together and no observation or combine was available to match the 1910 Pullman, which was made until approximately the year 1910. Lionel was soon to replace this car with the 18 Pullman and 19 combine car introduced in 1908. The 18 and 19 knobby roof passenger cars came with steps and wooden air tanks, and the bodies were attached to the floor of the car by screws, enabling the car bottoms to be dropped out for interior lighting first made available in 1911.

Two years later in 1910 an observation car was offered, numbered 190 to go with the 18 and 19 cars. The earliest versions of the 190 observation car are found with an unusual straight-bar observation deck looking almost like a jailhouse window. Later, probably around 1911 or 1912, they came with another round circle type of observation platform, but they still retained solid clerestory roofs and their simulated ventilators. While all knobby roof passenger cars are comparatively scarce, there are still other variations known, one of which is that there are two sizes in the knobs found on the cars, the earliest ones having high knobs and later giving way to the low knobs. After 1912 the 190 observation can be found with other types of observation deck platforms, and if all versions are counted there are at least five different types known. The very last cars made (the 190 was made until 1927) are found with a shortened platform known as the short-deck 190 car.

Interestingly, Lionel cataloged a set of 183, 184, and 185 passenger cars in 1911, which were said to be identical to the 18, 19, 190 cars, except that they were to come in brass and have a nickel-plated finish. Since none of these cars have come to light and since they are not mentioned in the following year catalog of 1912, they probably were never made. Needless to say if an original set is ever found the author would be very interested in purchasing it!

The 18, 19, 190 passenger cars are almost always found in dark olive green, a color that Lionel favored and used on many of their early period trains. They also can be found in an attractive yellow and also a similar orange color. These cars came later and do not feature knobby roofs or perforated steps as found on the very earliest cars, but the first ones made came with yellow doors, while the later orange cars came with maroon doors. These cars are generally scarce, but even rarer are these cars when found in mojave. Other interesting variations of these cars are the lettering styles used, which varied from the earliest versions with their larger printing and car numbers stamped on the sides rather than the ends. Sometimes they can be seen with unusual road names such as Pennsyl-

vania, instead of the commonly seen New York Central Lines lettering above the windows. Another oddity recently discovered is an 18 Pullman car in olive green and stamped as a dining car in the place where it is usually stamped "Pullman." The shorter 180 series Pullman car is also known to come lettered as a dining car, even though in both cases the interiors of each car are identical to those of the regularly made 18 or 180 Pullman.

In 1911 Lionel introduced their new medium-size passenger cars, numbered 180 Pullman, 181 combine, and 182 observation car. Made to go in sets with the 1911 Special electric or the 51 steam locomotive, these cars are usually seen in maroon. The 180 series cars are not known to come with knobby roofs, but the earliest versions made about 1911 or 1912 have solid clerestories. The cars were made until 1921, and the later-made cars, paired with the square-cab 53 electric, can be found in brown, maroon, and a reddish maroon appearing almost like a shade of red. The 180 series cars are also known to come in orange but are extremely scarce in that color.

In 1912 Lionel first introduced their small passenger cars, the 35 Pullman and the 36 observation. These two cars came teamed with a six-wheel 34 locomotive, and the first versions known are found with two horizontal ribs on the car sides underneath the windows. These cars are hard to find and are known as rib-sided 35 and 36 cars. Lettering variations are also found on these cars, such as New York, New Haven & Hartford, versus the usually seen New York Central Lines. In 1921 Lionel made a 31 combine and a 32 baggage car to add to the series, and they can be found in olive green and also a harder-to-find orange in four-car sets with a maroon 38.

Important to remember is that in 1918 the Lionel Manufacturing Company became the Lionel Corporation. Therefore Lionel, which before 1918 had embossed "Lionel Mfg. Comp." on the bottom of their passenger and freight cars, now left the cars plain or stamped the newer "Lionel Corp." underneath their equipment. Also on many of Lionel's engines, such as the bottoms of the coal tenders or on the ends of the 33, 38, or 42's, they changed the designation. This can be helpful when trying to date equipment of this period. Since Manufacturing equipment comes before the later Corporation trains, those trains marked Lionel Mfg. Comp. tend to be harder to find and more desirable.

Freight Cars

In 1907 Lionel first introduced their line of freight cars with the 11 flatcar, 12 gondola, 13 cattle, 14 boxcar, 15 oil car, 16 ballast or dump car, and the 17 caboose. These were Lionel's first large freights and are referred to as the 10 series freights. The very first cars made came with the first solid-side three-rivet trucks. The boxcar and caboose came with hand-painted vertical stripes, and the cattle car had extra-wide slats. The oil car had wood ends, and the first cabooses had awnings over the windows, with later versions having awnings just over the cupola windows. These cars gave way to the 10 series cars with the open three-rivet trucks and a flat yellow undercoat underneath the car bodies. Finally these cars yielded to the cars with the later-made large-hole eyelet trucks and continued to be made until 1926.

Many color variations and such exist among the 10 series freights as they were made for many years. The variations seem almost endless, and many cars are known in four or five different colors. The caboose is known with four different numbers stamped on the side, the boxcar too has four different numbers, and many cars, such as the gondola, are found lettered for different and varying road names. Lionel also had a similar-looking series of freights known as the 100 series, which were distinctly smaller. The 100 series freights are also known in many colors and variations, which are so detailed and minute as to go well beyond the scope of this chapter. I wish to add, though, that 100 series freights, which can be purchased at very modest prices from collectors, offer

a good opportunity to collect early period Standard gauge and to enjoy the fun of discovering the interesting variations to be found.

Special Sets

In the earliest years of Lionel Standard between 1906 and 1911, many people tended to purchase items individually rather than as sets, which helps account for the fact that many early thin-rim engines are often found with seemingly incomplete trains. Few collectors own matched sets of knobby roof passenger cars, more than one early 29 day coach, or a complete set of the very early 10 series freights. The only actual cataloged sets usually found are the 1911 Special with the early 180 series passenger cars, the square-cab 1910 with the 112 shorty gondolas, and the 1911 square- or round-cab engine with the early 116 hoppers or ballast cars. Other well-liked sets might be the No. 7 locomotive with the orange 18, 19, 190 passenger cars or those same cars pulled by the all-brass No. 54 engine. Also extremely desirable to early collectors would be trolley sets, that is, motorized trolleys with their correctly matching trailers. Needless to say because of the age of these early trains, many being far older than even Classic period Standard gauge, those sets found in original boxes or as complete boxed sets would be dearly cherished by anyone lucky enough to make such an unlikely find.

This 18 Pullman car just happens to be lettered as a dining car. The question is whether it was intentionally lettered that way or is it simply a factory error?

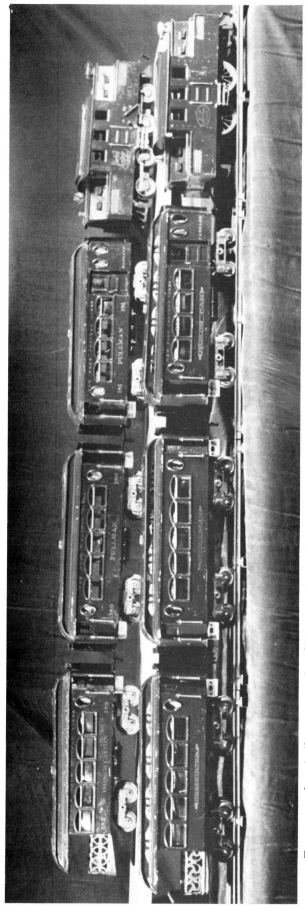

Two somewhat similar sets are the 1911 Special set (above) and the 53 square-cab set (below). Obvious differences are the eight wheels of the 1911 Special versus the four wheels of the 53, the different-style lettering of the passenger cars, and the solid clerestory roofs of the 1911 Special set passenger cars. The 1911 Special, predecessor of the square-cab 53, is also much rarer.

147

Interestingly, even in early period production we find that department store specials were made. Lionel especially stamped their black 42 for the F.A.O. Schwartz department store as the No. 61 with the abbreviation F.A.O.S. on the engine's side. Also similarly made and stamped for F.A.O. Schwartz were a 38 engine numbered 62 and a 33 numbered 60. All these engines are rare and unusual.

Another department store special was made for Montgomery-Ward and is an early set probably dating to about 1913. It consists of a midnight blue 33 engine with cast iron wheels and gold trim and matching 35 and 36 ribbed passenger cars. This set is unusual in that Lionel used an original color to paint this train not used on anything else at the time and so especially made up for the department store chain. This set too is extremely rare. It's items like these that make collecting early period trains interesting and fun. The only problem is that, with early period Lionel, especially the items made before 1913, you're dealing with mostly scarce items, and the volume encountered is quite small if compared to Classic Standard gauge, when Lionel was a much larger company and they knew how to mass-produce trains as never before. By the close of the early era, about 1925, few of Lionel's original competitors had survived, other than American Flyer and Ives, and even the great Ives company was soon to fall.

Dorfan

Two other train manufacturers that did manage to survive, but briefly, were Dorfan and Boucher. Something must be said in their behalf and it might as well be here in the early Lionel chapter as anywhere else. Dorfan first started making Standard gauge trains in 1926, and by 1934 production had almost completely ended, although remaining unsold stocks of trains were sold for another two or three years. Dorfan never remained in business long enough to produce an extensive line, but what they did make was made with quality always in mind. It is ironic that the Dorfan indestructible alloy would in time begin to expand and warp and what was initially considered an exceptional and advanced die-cast process become the broken and cracked remains so often found of many Dorfan locomotives.

While few good examples survive, the Dorfan twelve-wheel 3930 engine is as good an engine as a Lionel 381 or an Ives 3243. The Dorfan locomotive even came with ball bearings, and Dorfan engines were capable of hauling trains up a twenty-five-percent grade. To most collectors the most-noted Dorfan products are their large and beautiful lithographed freight cars made in Standard gauge. Six different cars were offered: the 800 gondola, 801 boxcar, 804 tank car,

The Boucher Blue Comet 2500 Pacific (4-6-2) locomotive.
This huge double-motored engine was the
only Standard gauge Pacific made, and it was made well.

805 coal car, 806 caboose, and 809 lumber car. These cars featured die-cast trucks, which unfortunately, like most Dorfan castings, have withered over the years, but luckily replacements are available.

Dorfan trains have not achieved a popular collecting status over the years. I can think of at least two reasons for this. One might be the lack of available models to collect, as Dorfan trains are comparatively scarce. Another factor is that when most Dorfan engines are found they cannot even sit properly on a shelf, let alone allow one to dream of running them. The Dorfan construction and features should not be underestimated. Who else can boast of a Take-Apart Standard gauge locomotive? No one had anything quite like the Dorfan Loco-Builder; both the smaller 3920 and the deluxe 3930 were far advanced over anything else available at the time.

Boucher

Boucher was also one of the last companies to produce Standard gauge trains. Their brief history started with the purchase of the Voltamp line in 1923, and Boucher immediately converted from the two-rail No. 2 gauge track to Standard gauge. They continued to produce trains until 1934, when it was no longer profitable because of the Depression years taking their toll. Boucher made only steam-type locomotives and avoided making any electric-type models, even though Voltamp, their predecessor, had made some. Their steam engines were finely made and well proportioned. Their line included everything from a short 4-4-0 Atlantic-type engine to a 4-6-0 and even a 4-6-2 Pacific-type engine.

Boucher made quality trains. Why, even their track came mounted on a wood base! While they made at least eight different freight cars and a variety of passenger cars, they are best known for one particular set—the Boucher Blue Comet. This magnificent set consisted of a blue 2500 4-6-2 locomotive and four matching passenger cars having the names New York, Washington, Chicago, and San Francisco. One of the most celebrated sets in train collecting, it is also one of the rarest. Many Boucher Blue Comets come with smaller 2222 4-6-0 locomotive, and many are also found in three-car sets instead of the complete train with four cars. This large set dwarfs anything put next to it and compares with any of the finer sets made by the other manufacturers, such as Lionel's State set or Blue Comet, the Ives 3243, or the Flyer President Special. All good things must come to an end, and so ended Boucher electric trains all too soon in 1934.

9

COLLECTING ACCESSORIES

Always an important collecting category in its own right is the collecting of accessories made to go with the trains and consisting of everything from a track bumper to a power station. Originally many collectors avoided collecting accessories, which were thought to be too large and bulky and a nuisance to store. This kind of thinking is rapidly changing as collectors have begun to appreciate fully the scarcity and beauty of the vast array of equipment made. Collectors now realize how accurately proportioned and designed many of these accessories are, from the lamp posts, railroad stations, and switch towers, through to the great variety of bridges and tunnels. Just a few years back, many collectors, upon picking up a train deal from a private home, would quickly look to sell off the accessories to pay for the trains, but now you are just as likely to see that same collector selling the train set to pay for the accessories he has decided to keep. At a train show you might hear the fellow exclaim to a friend, "I've seen plenty of 1835 sets around and I can buy them anytime, but this is the first Hellgate bridge I've ever picked up, let alone in the rare late colors."

Of course, not all accessories are rare or even hard to find, but it must be remembered that not everybody who bought a train set purchased accessories for it. Also, because many of the larger and more elaborate accessories were quite expensive, the only people who bought them were those who could afford the better train sets, as the cost of many of these accessories exceeded the price of some entire sets.

Early Accessories

It wasn't long after the first trains were made that the manufacturers began to see the need and potential of including various accessory items in their line.

Many early companies were too short-lived to have gone into accessory production, but those companies that lasted for more than a few years did start to make a few items and list them in their catalogs. Carlisle and Finch is one example of an early manufacturer. By 1915 they were offering a railroad station, two bridges, and their unique railway suspension bridge. Lionel also saw the potential in accessory items when they offered an iron bridge, a spring bumper, and elevated pillars for their early 2⅞ equipment.

Foreign manufacturers, such as Bing, Marklin, and Hornby as well as a few others, produced an extensive line of accessories that at times could not be rivaled. Their popularity would be great if not for the fact that in general many of these foreign accessories are genuinely rare. Some of the German-made stations were produced before the turn of the century and since they were made to go with clockwork train sets the stations were illuminated by candles. Likewise many early lamps and signals were illuminated by alcohol, complete with adjustable wicks. All sorts of fascinating stations and tunnels, many completely hand-painted in an assortment of colors, were made, as well as ringing signals and crossing gates, well before American companies began to produce these items. Many of these items are all but impossible to buy both here and abroad, since even Europe has its contingent of train collectors who scoop up everything nice they can lay their hands on; you can only hope to see occasionally a street lamp or something insignificant come up for sale. Marklin also made, in the twenties and thirties, a large if not gigantic passenger station in which trains can actually be stored inside. This beauty originally sold here for one hundred dollars!

Of course, America was not devoid of our own

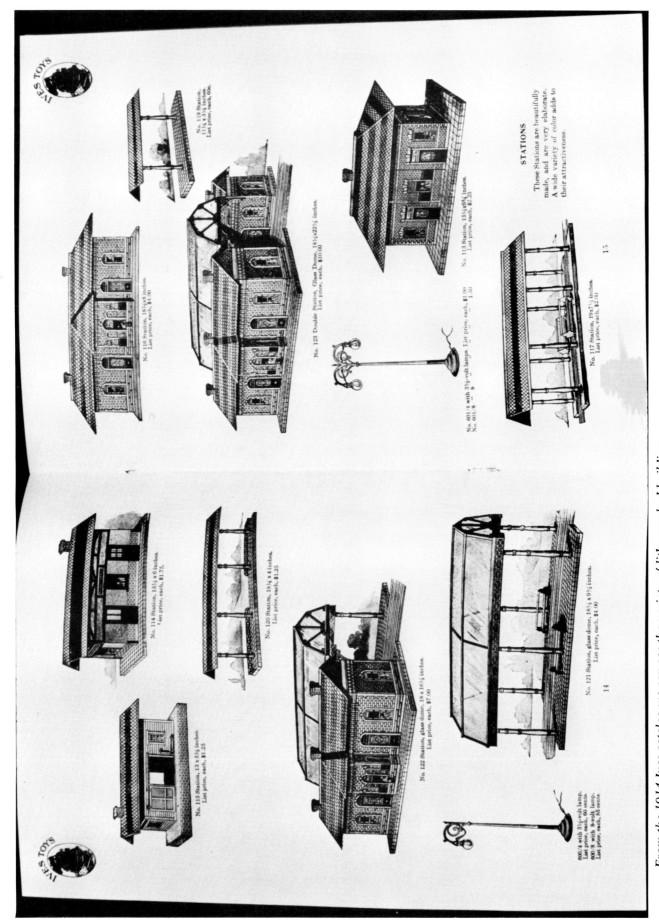

No. 119 Station.
11⅛ x 3⅛ inches.
List price, each, 60c.

No. 116 Station, 18⅝x8 inches.
List price, each, $4.00

No. 123 Double Station, Glass Dome, 18½x22½ inches.
List price, each, $10.00

STATIONS

These Stations are beautifully made, and are very elaborate. A wide variety of color adds to their attractiveness.

No. 113 Station, 13½x9¾ inches.
List price, each, $1.25

No. 601/4 with 3½-volt lamps List price, each, $1.00
No. 601/8 " 8 " " " " 1.50

No. 117 Station, 19x7½ inches.
List price, each, $2.00

15

No. 114 Station, 13⅛ x 6 inches.
List price, each, $1.75.

No. 120 Station, 13¾ x 4 inches.
List price, each, $1.25.

No. 115 Station, 13 x 5½ inches.
List price, each, $1.25.

No. 122 Station, glass dome, 18 x 16½ inches.
List price, each, $7.00.

No. 121 Station, glass dome, 18½ x 9½ inches.
List price, each, $4.00

14

600/4 with 3½-volt lamp.
List price, each, 60 cents.
600/8 with 8-volt lamp.
List price, each, 85 cents.

From the 1914 Ives catalog we can see the variety of lithographed buildings and stations offered. Some of the more deluxe buildings have actual glass domes.

interesting accessories. Even Dorfan had a fairly complete line of accessories, many of which are quite scarce today, ranging from various die-cast lamp posts and signals and a few different-size stations. Probably the most famous as well as the most desirable Dorfan item is the No. 70 large automatic electric crane. This crane was a full 20 inches high and weighed eleven pounds, as it was all die-cast construction. It came with an electric motor, double clutch, and worm gear and was a testament to Dorfan quality.

Flyer

American Flyer had a more extensive line of accessories to go with both their O and Standard equipment. They had a complete line of signals, street lights, and telegraph poles, which were distinctive from those offered by Lionel and Ives at the time. Flyer also made a few different models of their unique wooden trestle bridge. These bridges were long and well proportioned and usually are seen in red. One of these bridges was 70½ inches long, almost six feet from end to end. Flyer also made an array of stations, many of which were colorfully and realistically lithographed. One of the nicest single items Flyer made was their model 108 switch tower, which was a very accurate model of a real tower. It came with brass-trim windows and six knife switches in the back and of course was illuminated from the inside.

The most desirable Flyer station is their beautiful model of the Union Station made in 1928 only; naturally it is quite hard to find. American Flyer also sold a completely equipped layout, calling it Colonial City; it featured most of their major accessories. It came with their famous President's Special and a Shasta freight set and included their largest lighted bridge, their largest papier-mâché tunnel, various lamps and signals, and of course a few stations too. It came with a complete blueprint to set it up, and cost for the complete system was close to two hundred and fifty dollars! It is perhaps the dream of every collector someday to purchase a set such as this intact from its original owner, a dream not likely to be fulfilled.

Ives

Ives made a great number of accessories too, many of them quite original in their day. They made an interesting turntable of either manual or clockwork design for O gauge as early as 1909. Ives also made a rather unique roller lift bridge in the early 1900s; it automatically dropped into position as the clock-

work train approached! They even had a manually controlled swing drawbridge just like the real thing. Of course, their line included various and sundry signals, regular bridges, and tunnels, in addition to an array of finely lithographed stations.

Probably the most famous and sought-after of the Ives accessories are the various models of the glass-dome station. These elaborate stations came with clear and colored leaded glass set into cast iron frames. Ives made a single model supported by wooden poles numbered 121, which a train could run underneath. The 122 station consisted of the glass dome attached to a large lithographed station. The particular station when sold by itself was the No. 116. The largest of these models was the 123 double station, which had the glass dome mounted between the two metal stations. These stations were made for a number of years, so naturally there are a few different known variations among them. The earliest stations, which are a little harder to find, had the glass dome attached to the roof of the metal station with brackets, while later versions come with the wooden poles to support the glass domes.

Ives also made Struktiron construction sets, which were similar to the Meccano or Gilbert Erector sets of the period. A number of railroad and signal bridges could be constructed using these sets to go with the Ives train sets. Ives also produced a number of interesting little stations, such as their 115 freight station, the 113 passenger station, the 200 freight station, and others. Ives also made an almost scale-appearing water tank, No. 89, which is distinctively Ives, as well as their interesting 331 target signals. Ives produced all sort of signals and lights, which are of interest only to those endeavoring to collect them all. Ives trains are popularly collected, but their accessories do not enjoy an equally popular status.

What is particularly interesting are the Ives accessories made in the Ives transition years of 1928, 29, and 30. While some all-Ives (100% Ives) stations and signals continued through until 1930, many items were dropped and replaced with items from Lionel. Lionel took many of their accessories and replaced them with a new Ives brass nameplate, while others were transformed and given new colors too. All the accessories from this period using Lionel bodies and Ives paints and plates are, needless to say, quite scarce and interesting, particularly to those collectors wishing to collect transition period Ives.

An unusual item cataloged in 1930 is the Ives Treasure Chest. Made for either O gauge or Standard gauge trains, it was a complete railroad built into a chest that came complete with stations, signals, track, transformer—everything, except for the train. It is

IVES STATIONS AND HOUSES

IVES TOYS
SINCE 1868
MAKE HAPPY BOYS

No. 255 Signal Tower—Equipped with double throw switches on the back for operating various lights, connecting and disconnecting signals. Has cement type platform, steel beam support and beautiful signal tower house, lighted. Price, ✦ $5.00 * $5.50.

No. 251 Village House, Dutch Colonial Type—Electrically lighted. Much larger than No. 250. Price, ✦ $3.35 *$3.70.

No. 250 Village House, English Cottage Type—Very pretty. Price, ✦ $1.75 * $1.95.

No. 252 Village House Suburban Type—A very complete electrically lighted house with sun parlor, open fireplace, etc. Price, ✦ $3.50 * $3.85.

IVES automatic couplers are patented and an exclusive IVES product.
Long make track pull couplers O Gauge, 40¢ per pair.
Long make track pull couplers, 2¼ Gauge, 40¢ per pair.
IVES short couplers O Gauge, 25¢ per pair.
IVES short couplers 2¼ Gauge, 25¢ per pair.

No. 220 Freight Station, 9" Long — Lithographed sides, painted roof. Price, ✦ $1.25 * $1.40.

No. 226 Suburban Station, 10½" Long — Lighted, double waiting room, doors, double chimney. Price, ✦ $4.75 * $5.25.

No. 225 Way Station—A very well made, well finished station with a lot of interesting details on it. 8½" long, electrically lighted inside. Price, ✦ $3.10 * $3.40.

No. 221 Passenger Station, 9" Long — Lithographed sides, painted roof and platform. Price, ✦ $1.25 * $1.40.

No. 230—Town Station. Large, steel, lighted station with swinging doors, double chimney and cement type platform. 14" long.
Price, ✦ $6.75 * $7.45.
No. 230-3—Same as No. 230, but with 2 outside lights as well as inside light. Price, ✦ $9.75 * $10.75.

No. 253 Power House, 3½" Square—For use with No. 203 and 204 transformers. Completely houses transformer and adds considerable attraction to your railway equipment. Price, ✦ $2.75 * $3.05.

No. 228 Station Shed—Can be used separately or attached as shelter to other stations. Has cement type base, 6 wooden supports, red tile type roof, and 4 movable benches. 19¼" long. Price, ✦ $3.75 * $4.15.

Prices East of Missouri River * *Prices West of Missouri River*

Page Nineteen

REPRODUCTION

REPRODUCTION

Extremely rare are the Ives transition accessories shown here in an Ives 1930 catalog. Most of the structures are Lionel items having the Ives numbering and nameplates.

154

shown with many of the transition period accessories on it and an interesting paper background. I have not seen any examples of this Ives Treasure Chest, and I'm not sure it was actually made. It goes without saying that if one should be found the author stands waiting, an anxious and hungry buyer.

Since Lionel continued to perpetuate the Ives name and even made separate Ives catalogs in the Lionel period of 1931 and 1932, there probably exist even further variations among some of this equipment. Lionel took their 184 bungalow and their 189 and 191 villas and renumbered them 1868, 1869, and 1870. Lionel also gave new numbers to their other stations, such as 1867 signal tower, 1872 little station, and 1876 powerhouse, and added their 155 freight shed with the new 1875 Ives number. Many of these items are otherwise identical to the regular Lionel production items of the period; the only difference between many of these pieces is the addition of an Ives number plate or simply the lack of any Lionel

number stamp, which was usually found on the bottom of the bungalows or villas, as an example.

Lionel

Since Lionel trains are the most popularly collected, so are the many accessories made by Lionel. Many interesting and original designs went into many of the pieces made by Lionel, especially in the thirties, but early in Lionel's career they produced very few items at all. In fact, Lionel sold Ives accessories as their own beginning in 1908 and lasting right up until 1914. Lionel included in their catalog the Ives 113 passenger station with the Lionel number 121, the Ives large 123 glass-dome station as the Lionel 28, and the 116 passenger station as the Lionel 127. It is interesting if not perplexing to consider why Ives agreed to sell their accessories to Lionel, which was their competitor. Perhaps if Ives had sold only one or two very simple and small pieces I could under-

Even the boxes are attractive and colorfully designed, as can be seen from this set of Lionel telegraph poles.

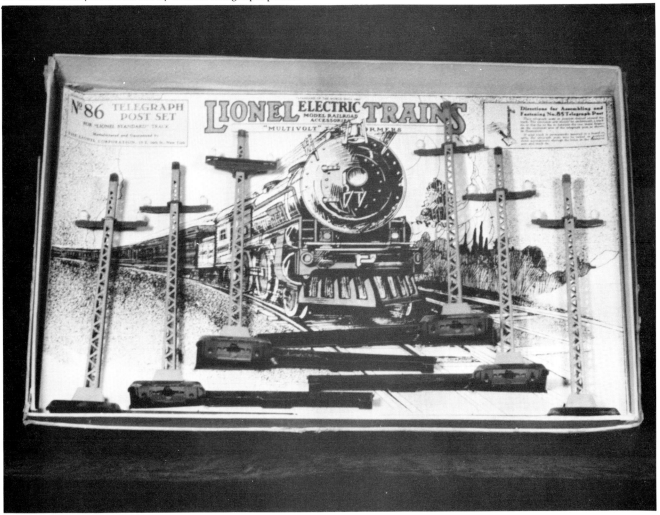

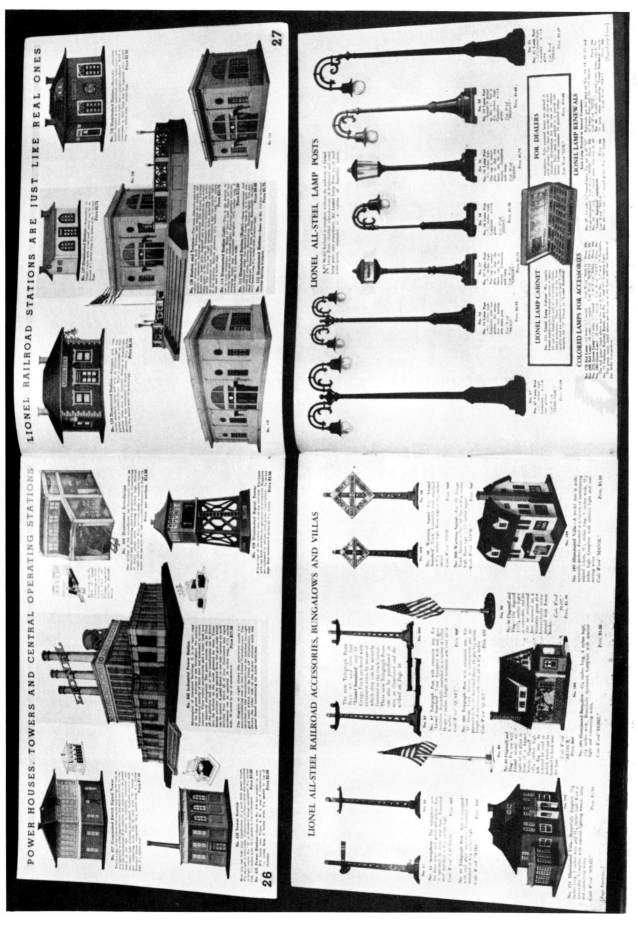

A wide variety of towers, buildings, stations, and houses were available from Lionel. They even devoted a full page to their assortment of lamp posts. These large and colorful Lionel accessories have become valuable collector's items in their own right.

stand, but Ives allowed Lionel to catalog the large glass-dome station as their own, perhaps feeling that Lionel was not a serious threat to Ives at the time. By 1914 we were to see the last year of Lionel cataloging the glass dome station, and only the small Ives design 121 remained until Lionel introduced their own model of the 121 station in 1920.

By the mid-twenties and the dawning of the Classic period trains, Lionel was beginning to make an extensive line of everything from houses, bungalows, stations, and signals to various-sized tunnels and street lamps. Lionel was beginning to realize the full sales potential in making train accessories, and from the twenties right up until 1942 they cataloged and sold many accessories that would today be described as made for Standard gauge. Interestingly, Lionel did make items strictly for O or Standard, such as different sizes of telegraph poles and tunnels, but most accessories made were to be used for either gauge.

As in train collecting, collecting accessories generally divides itself into two time periods. Most collectors choose to collect either prewar or postwar accessories; few try to collect both. Basically a lot has to do with the large size of many of the items and the incredible amount of space needed to display these items properly; space is a crucial problem to most collectors.

Because most Lionel accessories were made for many years, a number of color variations arise, all of which are eagerly sought after by most collectors. Some stations, for instance, are known in as many as four distinctly different color variations. As in Lionel prewar trains, the colors changed from the earliest items, made in duller shades such as gray and maroon, tending to give way to the later cream, terra cotta, and green shades, all found with brass plates. The last and generally considered hardest-to-find series has red, silver, and white coloring with nickel trim. Rather than attempt to describe every street lamp, signal, and station made and rather than go into describing every minute variation, I'll try to touch upon the more important and desirable items and give a general overview as to the variety of items available to collect.

Lionel made a number of different signals, such as the 80, 82, and 84 semaphores and 78 block signal, which are fairly common. They also made a 69 ringing signal, 83 traffic signal, 77 crossing gate, 87 railroad crossing signal, and 79 flashing signal. Most of these signals are easy to find, and there is more than one color variation known of each one. Lionel also made a large and popular 92 floodlight tower, usually found in green and terra cotta, with the later versions found in red and silver.

Lionel also produced an array of street lamps,

which are surprisingly well liked and collected. Probably the 58, 56, and 59 lamp posts are the easiest to find of the group. Some small lamps are deceivingly hard to find, such as the 53 or the even rarer 52 lamp, which looks like a straight silver pipe simply crowned by an opal-shaped frosted bulb. The 57 Broadway lamp has always been a collector's favorite and, while usually found in orange, it is also known in yellow and also gray. The Broadway lamp has four sides, all having the names of different streets, such as Main St. or 42 St., but there are many variations known among the combinations of the different names. The most desirable one is that which has the name of four different streets on the top; it is rather rare.

Lionel also made other larger street lamps, such as the tall 13-inch-high 61 lamp and the double 67 lamp post. Lionel also made a 54 double street lamp, also hard to find. The single rarest street lamp, which is all silver and very hard to find, is the 63 double-light lamp post, which came with two of the opal-shaped bulbs.

Lionel also made two interesting models of switch signal towers. They made a 437 tower, which had numerous windows like its real-life counterpart, but Lionel added six knife switches in the back and a bracket to attach the electric switch controllers. The 438 tower was taller and very attractive with its curving roof; it is known in three variations. Lionel also used the top section of the 438 tower to make their small and stubby 092 tower, which was recommended for O gauge use.

Lionel also made some power stations that were hollow and made to fit the Lionel Multivolt transformers; they came equipped with easily removable skylights. Few people used these stations to house or hide their transformers, because the power stations were such fine models themselves that most people used them for ornamentation, as they would a passenger station. Most commonly found is the 436 station, followed by the harder-to-find 435, which is slightly smaller. Both these models have one large smokestack and are known in a few color variations. Lionel made a much larger model of a powerhouse, numbered 840, which came with three large smokestacks with the name Lionel attached to the stacks and having numerous windows all about it. Since this gigantic model came with many individual parts, such as the steps, smokestacks, water tank, skylights, and the large green base, it is often found incomplete and having a few parts missing. The 840 power station was a very expensive item, cataloged some years at $17.50 and other years at a healthy $22.50; today it represents one of the most sought-after and expensive of any of the Lionel accessories.

Among the many bridges Lionel made was the

very common 101 simple three-piece bridge and its O gauge counterpart 106. Later Lionel made a simpler single-span 280 bridge and a 270 O gauge model, both of which are fairly common. These bridges do not generate much attention by most collectors, but one larger model in particular, the No. 300 model of the Hell Gate bridge, is tremendously popular among most collectors. Made to accommodate either O or Standard gauge track, the Hell Gate bridge is a very accurate model copied after the real railroad bridge, which still stands over the East River in New York. Usually seen in cream and green, it is also found in a later red and silver with white combination.

Lionel also produced quite an array of tunnels for their trains. Common and relatively small are the 118, 119, and 120 tunnels, simply constructed of sheet steel. Far bigger is the scarce and desirable 140L huge curved tunnel, which stood 20 inches high and was 37 inches long. The 140L is probably the most sought-after of any of Lionel's tunnels. Lionel made a few different models of their felt tunnels, which were all rather large. There was the 916, 915, 923, and 924,

all decorated with little houses, trees, and shrubbery, and much of the work done entirely by hand. The largest of these mammoth tunnels, the 915, was 65 inches long and almost two feet high!

Always popular are the innumerable variations of the 184 bungalow, 189 and 191 illuminated villas. These models are pretty accurately scaled to O gauge, even though they are often found with many Standard gauge train sets. Often referred to simply as the "little Lionel houses," these buildings were used on a number of Lionel made landscaped plots, all highly desired by collectors. The first one made was the 195 Terrace, usually called the "Lionel Village" by collectors and having the three different buildings set on a decorated board surrounding a flagpole, with two 56 lamp posts on opposing corners. Lionel also made a number of restangular plots numbered 911, 912, and 913, having one each of the different houses. They also made a 910 grove of trees that had no houses, and a 914 park landscape of oval design and a smaller 922 illuminated lamp terrace.

Among the other scarce items within this category

A Lionel O gauge pressed felt tunnel.
These tunnels were put together and painted by hand.

are the 917 and 918 models of the Lionel mountains, one being 30 inches long and the other 34 inches. The rarest and most sought-after items in the series of landscaped plots are the large and unusual Lionel scenic parks often called the "large Lionel Villages." Available as the two-section 920 or the three-section 921, it was a complete village mounted on boards and fully landscaped and detailed. It makes an impressive sight on any model railroad.

The most commonly seen Lionel station is the 122 (virtually the same as the 121) and the deluxe version 124. Also commonly seen are the 126 and 127 small passenger stations. Slightly harder to find is the 113 station sold as the 112 without outside light brackets and changed to the 115 with the addition of the automatic stop control. Even harder is the 114 station, often called the double-city station and basically a larger model of the 113. The 114 became the 116 with the addition of the automatic stop, and both stations are found in an early cream and green and a later red and white, considered to be slightly harder to find. One of the most elaborate and well-liked Lionel accessory is the 128 station and terrace combination. Lionel modeled a large station platform, numbering it by itself as the 129 and sold in combination with a station as the 128. While shown in 1930 and earlier with a 124 station, it was later sold with the more attractive 113 passenger station. The large metal terrace with its large flagpole, six lamp posts, and simulated greenery is known in two variations. The earliest ones come in a shade of gray looking similar to mojave, while later versions come in a much brighter white shade.

The single most valuable Lionel accessory and certainly one of the rarest is the 444 roundhouse. Made briefly between 1932 and 1934, it was large and bulky yet not made long enough to accept even a medium-sized steam locomotive and tender. It was made in individual sections so that one or more could be purchased at a time. Many collectors dream of owning the magic number of four sections, for that is how many are needed to complete a half circle. A very interesting fact was recently discovered when one of my friends was carefully examining one of his sections and noticed on the edge near the top "Made in Italy" stamped into the metal. After checking with others he found them all to have this marking. Why these sections were made in Italy probably had a lot to do with production costs, and, since the head production manager was Mario Caruso, he may have known certain firms that he gave the work to. It is doubtful whether they were actually completed there, and more than likely they were painted and assembled at Lionel in Irvington. Certainly it would be safe to

assume that, if Lionel contracted out the production of the roundhouse sections, they probably had other items made by other companies also. It is known that after the war Lionel had some items and parts also made by other outside companies.

Lionel also made a number 200 manual turntable for Standard gauge trains. While you may assume it was made for the roundhouse sections, it was available for a few years before and after the production of the roundhouses. As a result it is much easier to find and also is found in two different color variations, one being the usually seen green and red, and the other harder-to-find red and black variation.

Another interesting Standard gauge item is the 441 weighing scale. It actually worked and came with a little set of brass weights, which are usually missing when you find the scale today. The arm of the scale was die-cast. Few originals have survived intact, as most have warped and cracked over the years. Another fabulous accessory item, which is hard to find, is the 94 high tension tower. Lionel made an extremely accurate model of the real thing when they made the tall towers eagerly sought after by collectors. They are found in an early gray and maroon combination; later versions come in the popular red and silver colors.

Easy to find is the Lionel model of the freight shed numbered 155. It is seen in the early yellow, maroon, and green combination or the later red and gray colors. Many collectors decorate their freight sheds with some of the other interesting items of the period. Extremely popular and cute are the little 157 hand truck, 161 baggage truck, and 162 dump truck of the 163 freight accessory set. The red hand truck is the most commonly found individually, and even these items are found in a number of different shades and colors.

Many other small accessory items were made, such as the 208 tool chest with its miniature pick, hoe, rake, axe, sledge, and shovel. Tool chests are hard to find complete and nice, and even they are found in an early gray color and a later silver paint. Lionel also made barrels that were sold separately in sets of four, such as the 209 larger barrels; the smaller ones were probably made for O gauge use, such as the 0209 set, which included six of the smaller barrels. Extremely popular are the sets of the 205 merchandise containers referred to by collectors as the "L.C.L. containers," standing for "less than carload" railroad shipments. Made to fit into either the 512 of 212 gondolas, these small containers extract a price greater than that of many of the larger 200 series freight cars.

Just as American Flyer had their impressive Colonial City layout, so Lionel in 1931 cataloged their famous 407E railroad outfit. Consisting of their deluxe two-tone brown State set and a 400E work train, it included the 140L tunnel, 128 station and terrace, 300 Hell Gate bridge, 195 village, and the 840 power station, in addition to other odds and ends. You could own all of this sheer magnificence in 1931 in the midst of the Great Depression for a "mere" $350!

Lionel Operating Accessories

By the end of the thirties, with Standard gauge on the way out and O gauge trains firmly entrenched as number one, we find many of these elaborate and large accessories discontinued forever. Lionel had begun to develop a new line of accessories geared to the O gauge trains that were made with an emphasis on operation rather than simply being just pretty and ornamental. Some items associated with postwar trains were actually first made before the war, although Lionel's entry into wartime production cut short the amount of these items that were first made.

The 96 hand crank coal elevator and the 97 remote control coal loader were first made in 1938, but only the 97 continued in production after the war being made until 1950. The 97 was a large, metal, and impressive coal loader that both loaded and unloaded the coal into Lionel's coal or hopper cars. Similarly made and constructed was the 164 log loader, first made in 1940 and also continued until 1950. The 165 electric crane made between 1940 and 1942 gave way to the 182 crane made from 1946 to 1949. These cranes were remote-controlled, as were both the coal and log loaders. Cataloged as triple-action magnetic cranes, they could turn, raise, and lower the winch, and the magnet could be energized by remote control.

Last but certainly not least was the impressive 313 Bascule bridge made between 1940 and 1949. The Bascule bridge is a realistic metal working bridge that actually raises and lowers by remote control and is probably the single most valuable and desirable of the postwar period accessories. All of these items mentioned represent Lionel's first attempt at large operating accessories. Because of their fine metal construction and high cost, they did not last into the 1950s.

In 1950, Lionel's golden anniversary year, they cataloged the infamous No. 213 lift bridge. Some say it was made and others say it was never made; now who is right? Actually both opinions are correct, because at least one mockup model of the lift bridge was made, which still survives, although it is known that it was never put into actual production.

One particularly scarce item of the early postwar accessory group is the 38 water tower, made in 1946 and 1947 only. Sometimes called the drinking water tower, this unusual item appears to empty the water into the coal tender while it actually is just an illusion rigged up with a pump inside the water tank. Lionel then made a simpler No. 30 water tank, which had a spout that could be raised and lowered but did not include the illusionary device. The 30 water tower, which is easier to find, was made from 1947 to 1950 and came with a metal base. Lionel then went on to make a cheaper all-plastic water tank, numbered 138 and made from 1953 to 1957. These three different models of the water tank illustrate perfectly how Lionel quality progressed downward from the tremendous use of metal in the forties to the increased use of more and more plastic substitutes in the fifties.

Lionel introduced the 397 operating coal loader in 1948. Possibly issued as a less expensive substitute for the larger 97 coal elevator, the 397 coal loader was made until 1957 and is a very common accessory. Pictured in the 1948 catalog with a yellow motor housing and a small light, it actually was made that way, although that version of the 397 loader is particularly hard to find. Most 397 loaders come with the blue diesel housing and without any kind of light.

Another very common accessory introduced in 1948 is the 364 lumber loader, which was a long, gray, all-metal affair that continued to be made till 1954. Lionel also made a number of different kinds of lamp posts, most of which are fairly easy to find, such as the 64, 35, 56, 58, and 71 models, all of basically similar design. The No. 70 small swivel lamp is probably the hardest of the group and, appearing like a small spotlight, was first made in 1949.

A popular accessory first made in 1950 is the 455 oil derrick. This wonderful item, which has a little pump and a tube with a simulated oil flow, is usually found with the Sunoco oil sign missing; the four aluminum oil drums that came with the accessory are even tougher to find. Also made that year was the 456 operating coal ramp and hopper car, made to use in conjunction with the 397 coal loader. The 456 coal ramp set always came with the 3456 operating hopper car.

By 1952 Lionel had made their new 362 barrel loader, which is an extremely common accessory and was made to use with a plain 6462 gondola car, as the operating 3562 barrel car wasn't made until 1954. Most of the major stations were also made that year, such as the popular 445 switch tower, which has a man seemingly run down the stairs as a train approaches. There was also the 356 operating freight station, which has men on baggage carts that vibrate in and out of the station realistically. These buildings,

A wall of Ives. On the top we see the Lionel-Ives 418 passenger cars, and on the very bottom there is a dark green 3237 set. The various 3243 sets speak for themselves.

Here is the beautiful and famous white Ives 3243 set, shown here with gray and red trim.

Another Ives Standard gauge beauty is this closeup of a 3245 long-cab engine. (Herb Morley collection)

The similarities are obvious when one compares this 3237, with its black body and stamped orange frame, to its bigger brother, the 3245. (Photo taken by Peter Tilp)

This spectacular picture shows
a boxed 3245 long-cab passenger
set with the rare Lionel-bodied
cars. (From the
Ed Prendeville collection)

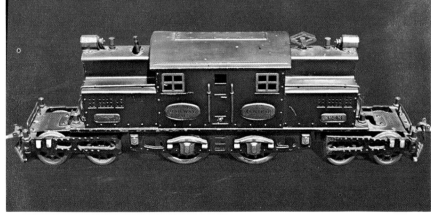

The rare black 3243 shown here
also has an unusual and perhaps
questionable stamped frame.
Most black 3243 locos have
cast iron frames.

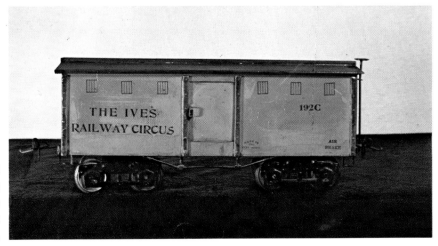

This 1928 All-Ives (100% Ives)
Circus boxcar No. 192C is
extremely rare. Most Ives Circus
boxcars utilize American
Flyer freight car bodies.

163

A fine example of an early Ives trackless, clockwork set. Named the "Lion," this set could also have been used as a tin pulltoy. The blue passenger car lettered for the Boston and Albany is extremely rare, as the few that are found are usually painted red and lettered for the Union Pacific. Rare items such as this set, which dates from the 1870s or the 1880s, are virtually impossible to collect today as few can be found for sale.

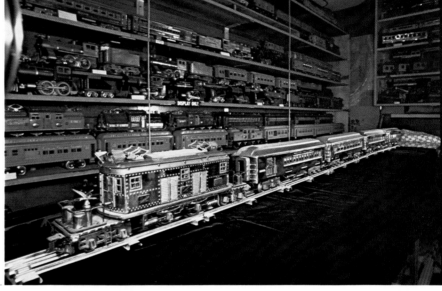

The king of American Flyer Wide (Standard) gauge is the chrome-plated Mayflower set. (Herb Morley collection)

Some of the rare Lionel 2⅞ gauge trains are pictured here. Among them the Converse trolley, the Metropolitan Express car, and the B&O tunnel locomotive.

Part of the Herb Morley collection showing at top some Ives No. 1 gauge with the rest consisting of a huge assortment of scarce Carlisle and Finch No. 2 gauge trains.

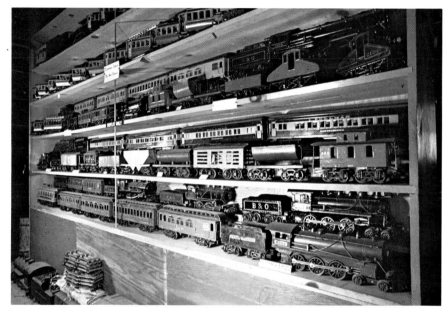

Pictured here are some assorted Voltamp trains as well as the famous Boucher Blue Comet.

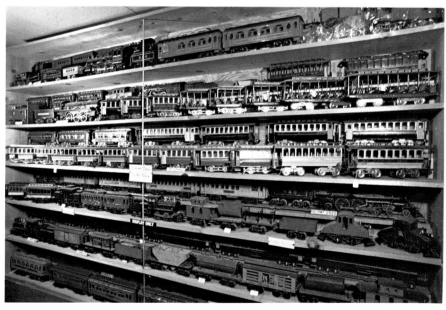

Many collectors would be happy to own just one Lionel trolley car, but Herb Morley is more than happy to own almost thirty!

Another mind-boggling assortment, this time from the Tom Sage collection, shows an array of trolleys beautifully displayed, from the little No. 1 to the large open 303 summer trolley.

A host of 42's and a brass 54.
(Tom Sage collection)

Behind are pictured a mojave, pea green, and red 38, while up front we find a maroon, a red, and a peacock 33. Needless to say all are scarce.

A most realistic view of the Lionel 920 scenic park, showing the large and scarce 915 tunnel mountain in the background.

Two variations of the Lionel 437 switch and signal tower. The one on the left having peacock and terra cotta colors is easily found, while the orange roof and yellow body switch tower is rare. From the author's collection. (Photo by Peter Tilp)

This rare Ives transition No. 230 station is found in unusual colors.

*A few switches from the control
panel of Steve Papa's layout*

*More of Steve Papa's layout, showing his near-
mint power station in the foreground
and a picture of Raquel Welch in the background.*

*Various lamp posts from the Ed Prendeville
collection with the early and late colors of
the 155 freight shed shown in the background.*

Situated in an attic is Tom Sefton's train layout. He literally has trains in the rafters, an interesting and unusual way of displaying a fine Lionel Standard gauge collection.

*On the left we see the large Lionel 840 power station and in the background
four of the Lionel 444 roundhouse sections. You never thought
Standard gauge could look this realistic, did you?*

The double-motored 402 speeds past the small 380 at the crossroads. In the background is the large 920 scenic park. To fully appreciate and enjoy your trains you should set them up and run them, for layouts such as this are a pleasure to behold.

More of Tom Sefton's layout is seen here.
Painted backgrounds add a most realistic effect.

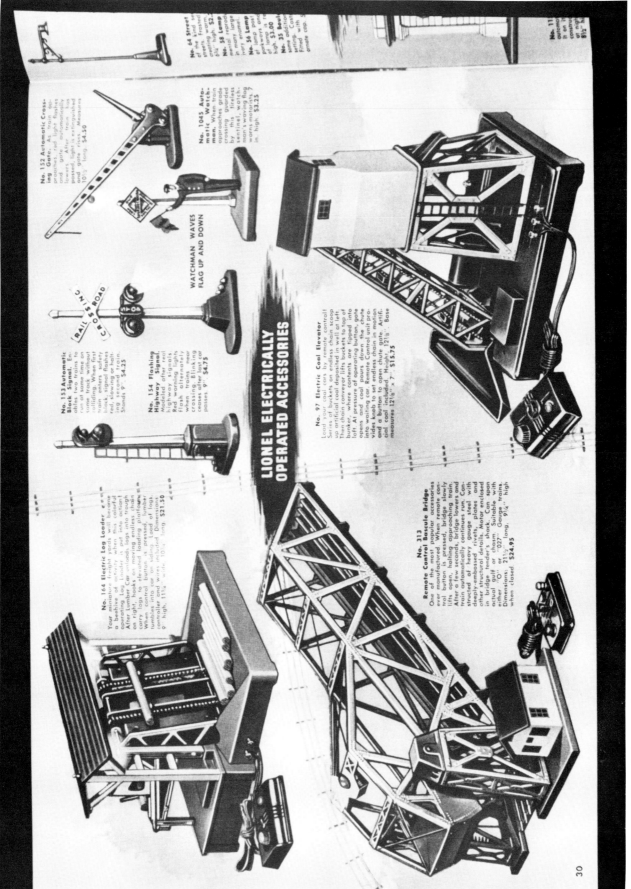

LIONEL ELECTRICALLY OPERATED ACCESSORIES

No. 152 Automatic Crossing Gate. As train approaches and light flashes and gate automatically lowers. After train has passed, light is extinguished and gate rises. Measures 10½" long. $4.50

No. 1045 Automatic Watchman. When train approaches grade crossing guarded by this tireless sentinel, watchman's own working flag warns motorists 7 in. high $3.25

WATCHMAN WAVES FLAG UP AND DOWN

No. 153 Automatic Block Signal. Enables two trains to run at same time on same track without colliding. When first train enters safety block, signal flashes red, slowing and halting second train. Stands 9". $4.25

No. 154 Flashing Highway Signal. Modeled after real highway signals. Red warning lights flash alternately when trains near crossing. Blinking ceases after last car passes 9". $4.75

No. 97 Electric Coal Elevator. Load your coal cars by remote control! Series of buckets on endless chain scoop up artificial coal deposited in well at left. Then chain-conveyor lifts buckets to top of bunker, where contents are tipped into loft. At pressure of operating button, gate opens and coal pours down the chute into waiting car. Remote Control unit provides button to set endless chain in motion and a button to open chute gate. Artificial coal included. Height, 12⅛". Base measures 12⅛" x 7". $15.75

No. 164 Electric Log Loader. Your miniature freight yards will become a beehive of activity when this colorful operating Log Loader is put into action! After Lumber Car unloads logs into trough on right, hooks on moving endless chain carry logs to elevated loading platform. When control button is pressed, lumber tumbles into car on siding. Load of logs, controller and wires included. Dimensions 9" high, 11½" wide, 10½" long $21.50

No. 313 Remote Control Bascule Bridge. One of the most popular accessories ever manufactured. When remote control button is pressed, bridge slowly lifts open, halting approaching train. After a few seconds, bridge lowers and train automatically continues run. Constructed of heavy gauge steel with deeply-embossed rivets, plates and other structural details. Motor enclosed in bridge tender's shack. Can span either "O" or "027" Gauge trains. Suitable with actual gulf or chasm. Dimensions: 21½" long, 9¼" high when closed. $24.95

Three of Lionel's best made and most desirable postwar accessories are pictured here: the 164 chain-driven log loader, the huge 313 bascule bridge, and the 97 coal loader.

as well as the simple 157 station platform, are attractive, even though all-plastic in construction, and are close to scale proportionately.

In 1953 there was the new, large 497 coaling station, a fabulous item that sits over the tracks and has a bin that is raised and lowered by remote control. Also new that year was the 193 blinking water tower, which was basically made as a decorative item for train layouts. By 1954 Lionel came out with a new electric crane, this time a different type, one that could sit over the tracks. The gantry portal crane was numbered 282 and performed the same functions as the 182 magnetic crane made a few years earlier.

In 1955 came the new 415 diesel fueling station. One of the most desirable items was also made that year—the 352 ice depot set. This set, which comes with the 6352 P.F.E. reefer, is known in two variations. Some ice stations have a brown base, considered rarer than the usually seen red base ice depots. Lionel also made the extremely common 110 trestle set that year. These sets were both very good and very bad at the same time. If they were not set up properly, Lionel steamers with their low cowcatchers would short-out at the start of the grade, because the pilots would rub across the middle and outside rails. Basically these trestle sets were good when used with Lionel Magne-Traction diesels; otherwise they tended to give you a pain in a certain part of your body.

Another popular accessory, first made in 1956, was the 342 culvert loader, which loaded metal pipe sections into a red 6342 gondola especially made with a metal ramp and included in the set. The next year, 1957, they made the culvert pipe unloader, which was made to use with the culvert loader. The unloader is somewhat harder to find than the loader. The 464 lumber mill was also made in 1956 and was an interesting item that had the logs go into the mill and appear to come out as finished lumber in a very realistic manner. Lionel also made the 465 sound dispatching station, which came with its own small microphone that year too.

In 1957 we saw the addition of a few new items to the line. One was the 334 dispatching board which had a little man who would run up and post arrivals and departures on a board. The 264 operating forklift platform also was made then; it came with its own special 6264 timber flatcar, which was made to accommodate the square timbers that would be loaded off the forklift. There was the popular 128 animated newsstand, which had the dog running around the fire hydrant. Or the 114 newsstand with built-in horn, or the 118 newsstand with built-in whistle, perfect for sound effects on any train layout. Perhaps most fabulous of all was the 350 engine transfer table and the transfer table extension, also first made that year.

With the added extension, you could transfer engines across four different tracks, just as in real engine yards.

By 1958, with the addition of the 175 rocket launcher, we see Lionel enter the era of Space Age faddism as they began to produce all-plastic junk, such as the 443 and 448 missile-firing sets and the 419 heliport and the 943 exploding ammo dump. The era of quality-made accessories had all but ended.

The most common accessory of all might be a tossup between the 145 automatic gateman made for almost twenty years and the 394 and 494 rotary beacons, seen everywhere and made in almost infinite quantities. The basic signals, such as the 153 block signal, 154 highway flasher, 151 semaphore, and 152 crossing gate, were also made in tremendous quantities. While mentioning signals, I think it's important not to forget the well-made and modeled 450 signal bridge, which is not hard to find, but the 452 gantry signal, which is half of the full signal bridge, is a well-known rare item and brings more than the larger 450 signal. Always a sought-after rarity is the 148 dwarf signal, probably one of the rarest of any postwar accessory items. The green and yellow 192 railroad control tower has been lately recognized for what it is, and that is one of the hardest-to-find accessories of them all.

Other accessories were made that I have failed to mention, not because they are not collected or are insignificant, but simply because describing them would have taken too much space and most collectors don't think the world of floodlight towers and girder bridges. Actually, the best reference sources on Lionel postwar accessories are the catalogs themselves. They are readily available in excellent and even new condition.

There are all sorts of minor variations among the accessories that I didn't mention, such as some 455 oil derricks that have the top part of the derrick painted red, while most come painted all green with just the base painted red. Since very, very, very few collectors bother to collect these types of variations and since most collectors haven't taken any notice of these variations, I felt them to be of too little interest to be mentioned here. A good example of a fertile collecting category going relatively unnoticed can be found in the many different and interesting billboards made by Lionel in cardboard for their 310 billboard sets. In future years they're likely to be recognized as being truly collectible, with a subsequent inevitable price rise, which will cause them to go from junk to desirable items overnight.

Displaying Accessories

When talking about accessories we must also consider displaying them properly and how this should

*Ward Kimball's European train room. Almost makes you want to quit
collecting Lionel and start in on Marklin and Bing. The only problem
is that most of this equipment is just not available at any price.*

Ives 1 gauge, Ives 0 gauge, and a Hubley elevated railway make up just a part of this unique train layout in the Ward Kimball collection.

be done. Most collectors will agree that the best way to display accessories is on a layout, a fully wired-up and working layout, possibly a complete miniature railroad. Too few collectors actually get that far, myself included, and our large and bulky accessories lie scattered on the floor, on shelves, in cases, in closets, under the table, and anyplace else where it becomes difficult to enjoy them.

First, let's talk about prewar accessories and Standard trains. If you line up stations and tunnels and bridges neatly in a row on a shelf, you lose the proportions, the detail, and the character that is so quickly brought out when these items are placed on a well-organized train layout. Standard gauge and prewar O layouts are fabulous, and, since most of these prewar models were well made, the quality of your trackwork really determines how well the trains are going to run. Many collectors try to use the actual prewar tracks when building a "period" layout, but it must be remembered that many of these tracks are slightly warped. When these are used with old wheels, which tend to dish out slightly even when they look fine, you can have quite a few problems. Just think how nice the finished product will look when you're done, with all your elaborate accessories out on display!

When working in O gauge with Lionel track there is the option of working with 072 track (72-inch radius curves) or solid T-rail track, either of which can be costly in terms of what you'll have to pay for switch tracks. In the end it's probably worth it, and you have no choice if you decide to run some large 072 or scale engines on your layout.

Postwar accessories are almost never shelved by most collectors today who choose to collect them. Most of their beauty lies in using them; they are fun and even fascinating to watch. Many people have told me that if it were not for Lionel's operating accessories they would probably be running HO trains today instead of O gauge. Certainly Lionel operating cars and accessories played a big part in making sales years ago, and they have a lot to do with the popularity of postwar trains today. I know that adults enjoy watching many of the accessories operate as much as children. I know I do.

To summarize, let me say that what kind of track you use is really not that important, whether it's O gauge, Super O, 072, Standard, or even No. 1 or 2 gauges. What is most important is that, if you decide you like and want to collect accessories, you should try to display them, if you have the room, on a layout in use with the trains. Then and only then can you begin to appreciate them fully. Set up a period layout with the era or eras you like best, and I'm sure you'll get much greater satisfaction and enjoyment out of the trains and accessories you own. Excuse me, I have to go now; I have to go down to the lumber yard to pick up some 4×8 boards I ordered yesterday. Take care.

10

CATALOG COLLECTING

The vast majority of train collectors also collect catalogs. The reasons for collecting catalogs go beyond the obvious reason, which is their primary use as a reference source. Train catalogs were always a very special and important thing in the toy train industry, and their advertising and public relations value were never underestimated. In years past, many boys and hobbyists each year eagerly awaited the arrival in the mail of their new train catalog. On receiving it they would rush to their rooms to pore over it page by page, noting anything new they soon hoped to get. You can begin to comprehend this legion of devoted train fans and their desire to "get the new catalog" only when you realize that the printings of some catalogs actually ran into the hundreds of thousands and even millions of a single issue!

Toy train catalogs were liked and loved as greatly as the trains themselves, and most young fans would immediately salt them away after reading them so that they could be looked at again and again, sometimes even years later. Train catalogs may represent one of the most important types of childhood literature, because these were magazines that no one forced youngsters to read. Children eagerly sought them so that they could tell "Santa" just what they were hoping to get. The catalogs began to represent the trains themselves, and people, young and old alike, appreciated them greatly. Where in any other hobby or field of the toy industry can you think of a place where catalogs played such an important role?

Catalogs being as popular as they were, most young boys and hobbyists tended to store and file away their train catalogs, often in a place other than where they kept their trains. Later, when these kids became older and the trains no longer interested them, they simply threw the catalogs away. Perhaps they were cleaning their rooms or the attic and on finding the old pile of catalogs they discarded them in the trash, considering them worthless paper. Whatever reasons caused them to be thrown away, it is sad, for, even though most catalogs were issued in enormous quantities, they are sometimes difficult to find today, especially the older issues.

Most collectors can tell you that rarely do they find any catalogs at all when they go to buy old toy trains from their original owners. In the few instances when you do find catalogs with the trains you'll often find more than one issue. Most people tended to save at least one issue from each year, and many times you may find a group covering a ten-year span, with a catalog from each and every year. Since most of the public to this day regards paper items as having little or no value (other than a rare first edition book), you'll probably find it difficult to obtain a large catalog collection on your own. Eventually you'll have to buy or swap among collectors to fill in the holes in your collection.

Types of Catalogs

In the years before 1900 when most toy trains were trackless tin and iron models, regular consumer catalogs were virtually unknown. Catalogs at that time were produced for the wholesale trade only and were rather large and extensive books made up for manufacturers and jobbers. By the 1900s, when track trains were fast becoming the rage, the need for consumer catalogs became immediately apparent, because these new trains on tracks offered untold opportunities to the manufacturers who could supply the track, signals, and stations needed to build a miniature railroad.

Many early train manufacturers issued catalogs, but few of these were exclusive to trains. They usually contained all sorts of electrical novelties, ranging from dynamos, motors, and fans to telegraph sets, experimental apparatus, and gas engines. Carlisle and Finch was the first to issue such catalogs, but other companies, such as Knapp and Voltamp, soon followed. Ives issued the first exclusive train catalog in 1901, and Lionel issued theirs by 1903. While these first catalogs were small black and white affairs, it was not long before the size was enlarged and color was added. Eventually catalog production was developed into an art, with their covers painted by famous artists and each and every set vividly described, some even showing the construction of the locomotives.

There is a general rule among catalogs, which is that the older the catalog the rarer it is. This rule holds true most of the time, for a catalog from the fifties is more easily found than one from the forties,

and one from the thirties is harder to find than either, and so forth. Exceptions might be the Ives 1928 catalog (the year of the bankruptcy), the Ives 1931 catalog (the Ives line was then part of Lionel), the Lionel 1942, 1946, and 1949, all hard to find, and of course any of the special-issue catalogs, such as the advance or export issues. In general, most catalogs of the postwar era are not too hard to find, because many collectors were by then safely hoarding and preserving each year and the paper drives of World War II had long since past. The 1930s are much more difficult, especially those from the beginning of the decade, and the 1930 catalog itself is one of the most sought-after and valuable of all the Lionel issues. The catalogs of the twenties are even harder than those of the thirties and are often found in poor condition. The catalogs of the teens are all extremely rare, and the first catalogs made by Lionel before 1910 are

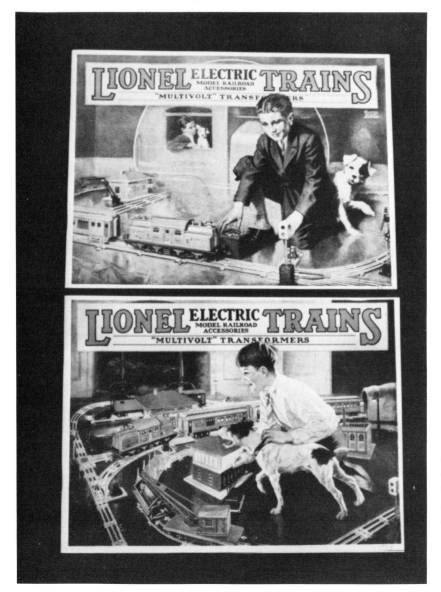

Many of the early Lionel catalogs had interesting and nostalgic painted covers. At top is a 1925 and bottom a 1926 showing the then new 402 set.

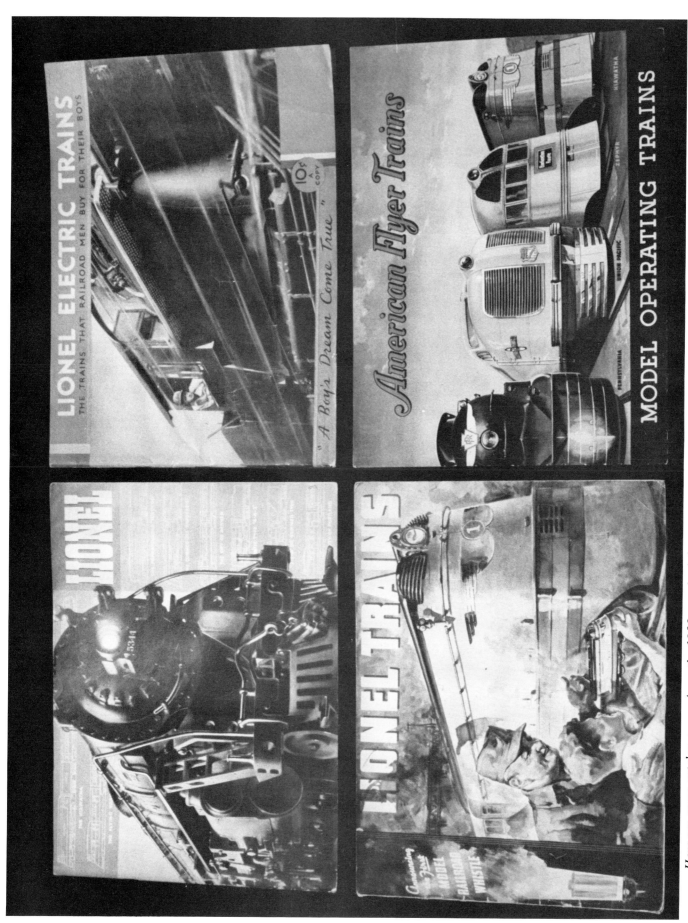

Here are some catalog covers from the 1930s; each of them is spectacular and shows famous locomotives of the period.

*The rare Lionel cardboard train set of 1943 made during the war,
when Lionel production was geared to the war effort
and regular model trains were not being made.*

so rare as to be considered legitimate museum pieces.

Ives catalogs are all hard to find, as the last one was made in 1930. Lionel made a 1931 and 1932 Ives catalog and, although they are small and skimpy, they are also scarce, as are the Lionel-made Ives trains of this period. Ives kept up a practice of including a catalog with every set, even their cheapest sets, and so Ives catalogs are not impossible to find, and some collectors have amassed complete collections of Ives catalogs. Because of the great Ives fire in 1900 and the burning of the company files and catalogs, any Ives catalogs found prior to 1900 could also be considered museum pieces.

Outside of regular-issue consumer catalogs, there are other types of special catalogs. The advance catalogs are of a special order usually made for the trade and issued to dealers and wholesalers. While the earliest types of advance catalogs were very different from the regular consumer catalogs, those made later,

in the postwar years especially, were very similar to the regular issues. These advance catalogs were usually made to coincide with the Toy Fair in New York, where the toy industry would meet with buyers and salesmen and would show a preview of the line far in advance of the fall Christmas season. Advance catalogs are naturally rarer than regular consumer issues and are desirable to collectors, because they sometimes show prototypes and handmade samples, some of which were never actually made. Advance catalogs have features different from those of regular catalogs and are sometimes even more attractive, such as the gold cover of the 1950 advance made in Lionel's golden anniversary year.

Then there are the export catalogs, which were either regular catalogs with the prices changed or entirely omitted or a special catalog written in a foreign language. Lionel made special export catalogs for Great Britain, which included the rare 1694 set,

Interesting Lionel promotional material is a fertile field for collectors. Shown above is a Lionel sound effects record and in front is a card that kids were supposed to stick on dad's breakfast plate, reminding "pop" what the little "devil" wanted for Christmas.

*The cover to a Lionel dealer
promotional booklet that shows many of Lionel's
ingenious marketing techniques.*

*Lionel promotional brochure outlining their
super advertising campaign for 1957. Many
promotional booklets and brochures such
as this have become hard to find.*

and they also made foreign language editions in
Spanish, French, and German, some of which included
both the 1694 and 1764 train sets. The perfect idea
of a vacation for a train collector would be for him
to find one of these sets unexpectedly in a foreign
country. American Flyer also had export catalogs in
Spanish, and even Dorfan made catalogs in Spanish
and Portugese. Marklin made catalogs for many
countries, including Sweden, Austria, Hungary, Switz-
erland, France, and of course the United States and
Great Britain.

There are also various pocket-edition catalogs issued, as well as different-size folders issued at different times by many companies. There are also rare
executives' catalogs issued on extra-heavy paper, as
well as master catalogs especially bound in hard
covers. There also have been catalogs of specials not
listed in the regular catalogs. Still other important
items are the price lists and special inserts made in

some years to go with certain catalogs and very often found missing, as they became lost or discarded over the years.

I guess it can be said that any type of paper or literature made by and for the various train manufacturers is collectible. Certainly letters written by the company, whether form letters or of a personal nature, would be of historical importance and might be extremely significant if they were to tell us some important facts about the company. Collectors undoubtedly might decide to collect instruction sheets as well as instruction booklets, and in times of repair they would of course be a valuable reference. Certainly any envelopes and folders with the company name would be of interest. Anything is likely to be collected and should be collected, for who knows what kind of valuable information might be unearthed just from the catalogs we now own?

Because practically every collector of trains collects catalogs and because many issues are in short supply, catalogs have begun to take on sometimes great value. Many new collectors shudder in disbelief when they hear the prices being asked for many prewar catalogs. Many people cannot comprehend how anyone could pay so much for a catalog when they could buy a fine train for the same price. When you think about it it's not actually that ridiculous, for the catalogs have assumed an importance in collecting as great as the trains. Also they are the primary reference sources on the trains themselves, and our general knowledge of trains is greatly enhanced when we study the catalogs.

Errors and Variations

Many collectors know the catalogs to the last detail, but while they do provide us with the knowledge of what was made, what it cost, etc., they can also at times be incorrect and misleading. Because artists were used to paint and draw the catalogs they sometimes drew what we refer to as an "artist's conception," which could be miles removed from the actual item. In prewar catalogs especially, colors are often completely off, and many colors are rendered either darker or lighter than the actual paint colors used.

Lionel stated in their early catalogs, between 1906 and 1912, that the gauge of track was 2 inches, when the actual and correct measurement of their Standard gauge track was 2¼ inches wide. Probably Lionel had originally intended to make their track 2 inches wide, but an error must have occurred in the early design or construction. Even then they started to call it 2¼ inches instead of 2 inches, and it wasn't until 1936 that they called it by its actual measurement of 2⅛ inches.

The reason for this could have been their method of measuring, which should have been between the insides of the outermost rails instead of from the middle of the two outside rails.

Many mistakes have occurred in train catalogs, some large and some small. In the Lionel 1930 catalog a red 381 locomotive is pictured on the cover, but none is known to exist. In the 1931 catalog the Stephen Girard cars are pictured in the back with the nameplates "Hillside" and "Irvington," which they never came with, although it is well known that these names were used on some of the postwar 027 passenger cars made many years later. Some of the models shown in the 1930 catalog, for instance, are obviously copied from handmade samples, such as the 258 O gauge engine and the unusual-looking 384 Standard gauge loco.

Sometimes mention of an item in the catalogs has created a continual search for the mythical item that was never made. A good example would be the 2624 Madison-type passenger car mentioned in the 1941 and 1942 catalog as being the companion observation car for the series. Well, no factory-authentic Madison-type observation cars have ever been found, although many collectors have fashioned their own observation cars from existing Pullmans.

Another big myth, which came from the postwar era, is the green 6464-50 Minn. & St. Louis boxcar pictured in the 1953 catalog. This car is always found in tuscan red, and the closest anyone ever came to finding this car is when Elliot Smith, who specializes in 6464 boxcars, found a blank car that was of a green plastic mold. He took this green car and had it made up with the regular lettering used on the common tuscan car, and it now looks exactly like an original. While other boxcar variations have turned up that are not shown or pictured in the catalogs, there are no actual or real original green Minn. & St. Louis boxcars known.

One postwar catalog that has a number of errors is the 1946 catalog, which was the first Lionel catalog made after the war. As an example, a prewar black 763E locomotive is shown in the catalog bearing the number 703, a model that was never made in postwar years and a number that was used many years earlier on a different engine. We now know that only the 726 was made and that it was the engine that was listed incorrectly as the 703. Also a 403 switcher is listed in the back that year; none was ever made.

There is also an interesting variation among the 1946 catalogs, for there are actually two distinct varieties. Lionel wanted to return quickly to the toy train market at war's end, so they made a deal with the publishers of *Liberty* magazine and purchased 16

The LIONEL CORPORATION

FIFTEEN EAST TWENTY-SIXTH STREET · NEW YORK 10, N. Y.

March 30, 1954

TO OUR TRADE:

Attention: Toy Buyer

Dear Sir:

We are happy to tell you that our new line is ready and since we have received quite a number of inquiries, thought it advisable to write you and give you some idea as to what it is like.

The volume of business we enjoyed in 1953 was the largest in our history, yet inventories are as low as the previous year. However, in checking inventory reports, we decided to again run those sets that are the heaviest in stock. You will find our #1500, #1503WS, and #2201WS, listed again.

Enclosed is a copy of our Advance Catalog which is fully descriptive of our entire line and also, you will find a brochure listing all of the displays that we will have available this year. In this latter folder, you will find a numerical price sheet, as well as some suggested assortments which you can use as a guide in making up your requirements.

The "027" line once again is offered with the first number at **$19.95** and with sets that show better values, including new locomotives which will range upwards in price to $69.50. Included are new steam and Diesel locomotives, new operating and non-operating cars. Set #1503WS is again sold at **the** same net price. The Diesel switcher is in an outfit at $49.95.

"O" Gauge commences again with set #2201WS at $39.95 but from that point on, the line is much improved over last year. Sets contain operating cars, including the new barrel car and the non-operating new, and much <u>longer</u> freight cars, such as stock and refrigerator with entirely new appearances. Here also is the new <u>improved</u> eight wheel drive locomotive, new and colorful Southern Diesel and the sensational new Fairbanks Morse Diesel. Values unquestionably are greater than in 1953.

New in cars, are Astra-dome in "027", baggage in "O" Gauge, much <u>longer</u> refrigerator, stock and cement cars. Also, a new operating car that unloads barrels.

Interesting facts about the inner workings of the Lionel corporation can be seen in this letter from the Lionel sales department to its wholesalers in 1954. Lionel letters and correspondence are not only collectible but historically significant as well for the information that they sometimes reveal.

In operating accessories, there is a new banjo crossing signal at $5.95, and a wonderful operating crane at $15.95.

Last and certainly by no means the least, there is a new and sensational operating "gang" car at $7.95.

With regard to outfits which are not listed in our current line, we will have to ask your cooperation in order to avoid misunderstanding which might lead to widespread price cutting. Will you please be good enough in the event that you run an advertisement, to state that the train sets are 1953 discontinued numbers.

In doing so, it will not give any other retailer the opportunity to cut prices by making the claim that your advertisement has created the impression that you are cutting on current items.

While on this subject, we want you to know that we instituted a great many successful proceedings against price cutters. Many of the larger discount houses in the country were brought into court because of the violation of the Fair Trade laws in their states and were enjoined from cutting prices again.

Unfortunately, price cutting late in the season did hurt some of our legitimate dealers. It is our intention this year to fight this situation vigorously and at an early date. Right now we have a number of cases pending in the courts. We want you to know that we have not closed our eyes to this situation and when our representative calls on you, he will be more than glad to explain to you how much we actually did accomplish.

Please remember that in order to bring action against violators, it is necessary to have good state enforcement laws. Unfortunately, some state laws are so weak that we find it impossible to bring action against some price cutters.

Our thanks to you for the consideration you have given our product in the past and we do want to take this opportunity to wish you a very Successful Lionel Year.

                              Yours most cordially,
                              THE LIONEL CORPORATION

                              Belser
                              Sales Manager

S. Belser/bb

THE LIONEL CORPORATION

While original catalogs still are an important facet to collecting, reproductions are fine for the information they contain, and the price is right. Even Lionel and Flyer "S" repair manuals are being reproduced.

188

pages of advertising. They then printed the 1946 catalog inside of the regular *Liberty* magazine; this could be considered a 1946 catalog, in addition to the regular Lionel catalog.

In the 1947 catalog we see a gray 2856 hopper car pictured; it was never made, although it is known to come in the regular black color as the scale B&O hopper car. In 1948 we see the new 2333 Santa Fe pictured in an unusual black and red, obviously an artist's conception, for all known models are found in the common red and silver colors. In 1949 the 622 switcher is shown with Lionel lettering, although it is always found with the Santa Fe railroad motif. Then in 1950 we again find this same engine, the 622, shown with New York Central lettering. While I do not believe that any models with this lettering were ever made, I will not say definitely one way or the other, for a prototype model or models may exist that I have not yet seen. Inconsistencies between what was actually made and what is shown in the catalogs exist in minor details for many years, but as long as catalogs are not your sole source of information and you do not regard everything seen in them as gospel, then they can and should be valuable guides to your train-collecting pursuits.

There are other variations among the catalogs themselves, such as some catalogs having inserts and some coming without. A good example would be the Lionel 1932 catalog, which sometimes came with an insert for the Lionel Winner Line of trains. There are of course catalogs known with different variations on the covers, catalogs with regular and glossy paper, and some with variations of the type of color used for the printing, whether black, red, or whatever. Of course, while many of these seemingly insignificant variations hold no interest for you, it must be remembered that perhaps someday they will, and you will carefully examine and compare your catalogs every time you find new ones, hoping to discover some new variation for your files.

Storage

Upon starting to put together a fine catalog collection the question of preserving your collection properly may occur. Certainly it goes without saying that they would not be helped by moisture or dampness or extremes of heat. For extra protection you might even consider housing them in individual manila envelopes or folders, preferably the envelope

they originally were mailed in. They could then be filed or stacked as long as they are not bent or crushed in any way. It would be wise to file them in order, for it is strictly taboo ever to write the date on the face of the catalog, as this will of course adversely affect its value. Also never to be considered are stapling, folding, taping or gluing, as well as punching holes in the catalog for insertion in a looseleaf (don't laugh, I've actually seen it done). In order to insure the value of catalogs and to prevent them from further mutilation, it would be in your best interests to leave the catalog alone no matter how bad it seems. Catalogs should be treated with respect and, since most were printed on quality paper, they have every chance in the world of surviving for many, many years to come without fading, yellowing, or crumbling as is the case with regular newsprint.

Reprints

In recent years there has been a rash of new catalog reprints made available many in fine color. While they have in certain instances tended to depress the prices for some originals, they are also a blessing to the collector. Many early original catalogs cannot be found at any price, but with the tremendous variety of reprints now being made you can get a copy of virtually any year of most of the major American companies. The prices for the most part are reasonable, although it must be stated that the quality of many of these printings varies, with some being far superior to others. All in all, I think these catalog reproductions or reprints are good for the hobby as they have put fine catalog collections within the reach of all collectors since most of these reprints sell at reasonable prices. Also, many collectors like reprints because they do not have to damage their originals from heavy use.

Still no matter how fine a reproduction is, there is nothing like an original and many collectors who want the real thing and who see the history in an original will still hunt down the original catalogs. It may surprise you to hear that there are a number of collectors who value their catalog collection above their train collection and would sooner sell off their trains than their catalogs. Every field of collecting has its specialists, and there are many who have chosen catalogs, which have always been and will continue to be a particularly interesting and absorbing area of collecting.

11

FAKES AND REPRODUCTIONS

Certainly there is no other subject in train collecting that evokes such greatly differing opinions as the many and varied arguments surrounding restorations, reproductions, and fakes. Many collectors hold very definite opinions about how the train-collecting organizations or the collecting community as a whole should restrict the making and selling of these items. Some of their arguments, both pro and con, go back to the very beginnings of the hobby, and yet to this day there are no steadfast solutions as to how to control these items.

The most important thing to remember in this and any other hobby is that original items in excellent original condition are always worth more than any repaint, repaired, or reconditioned items. That is not to say that repaints, restorations, or whatever you wish to call them, are worthless but rather that an original item with its original paint and parts is more desirable in almost any condition than an excellently restored train. There are times, though, when an item will be found already repainted from its original owner or when a train is found very badly chipped, scratched, dented, rusted, or flaking terribly. When trains are found in this "basket case" condition and they cannot be cleaned and repaired to a decent and somewhat presentable state, then there are two basic choices to make. Either you choose to scrap the item in question for its salvagable parts or you can have it restored.

Restoring Trains

One important point to ponder is, "Just how bad does an item have to be before you can call it restorable?" Surprisingly, opinions vary widely, from those who say never restore an item to those who like to restore anything that has even a few noticeable scratches on it. Basically it is a matter of personal opinion, but my own feelings in this regard are that an item should be beyond recall and look rather unsightly before it can be labeled a candidate for restoration. I have always felt that you can wait as long as you want, to decide whether you want to restore an item but once you've gone ahead and actually restored it, you can never again take it back to its original condition.

Once you decide to restore your train you can obviously do it yourself if you feel up to it, or you can have another collector do it for you. There happen to be many collectors all over the country with the talent and skills to restore most trains properly, and many of these fellows will do a fine job for a "price." It is important to determine the price beforehand as well as to find out *definitely* how long it will take to have the job completed. One collector who said it would take "only a few months" had my engine for two full years, believe it or not! To find someone in your area who does restoration work all you have to do is ask around and most collectors can direct you to someone reliable in your vicinity.

If you decide to restore the train yourself you'll first want to remove the paint completely. It is suggested that you avoid the use of lye and corrosive paint removers, which can eat into the metal surfaces and can damage castings. Also these removers are hard to wipe off completely and they tend to prevent new paint from adhering properly. One excellent method of removing paint is to immerse the item in a pot of boiling water, in which you dissolve a household detergent such as Tide. Remove any loose paint with a brush and rinse the item in cold water when you are done.

Sometimes original owners paint over their trains in some often ridiculous color, but they rarely remove the original paint underneath. Often when a train is found like this you can remove the top coat with paint thinner or nail polish remover, but this has to be done carefully and takes a long time. I have seen many seemingly ruined items brought back to life, because the paint used over the original coat is usually thick and doesn't always hold that well to the original baked enamel paints used years ago.

Since collectors sell the different colored paints needed and decals are available to replace almost any original rubber-stamped lettering, you can immediately start to restore. Many fellows don't believe in the spray paints and will mix up their own batch of paints to try for a perfect match. It would be advisable to have an original item immediately available to compare it with as you work. Many collectors feel you should repaint the item in a color in which it was never made so as to distinguish it from an original. Most fellows will tell you that whatever you decide you should mark the item as a restoration in some way. You can either scratch the word *repaint* on the inside or paint only the outside and not the inside of the engine or car, thereby making it easy to tell for future owners. Whatever method you decide to mark it with, most collectors will repaint an item in a rare color. An example would be that, even though the 400E locomotive you want to restore was originally black, most fellows will paint it in the Blue Comet colors or the harder-to-find gray rather than its original black.

Once that 400E is completed, let's say in blue, it should command less money than a common black original 400E will bring. No matter what color a repaint is painted in, it is still not original and should always command less than any decent-looking original. Interestingly, while most collectors prefer originals, there are a growing group of collectors who prefer repaints and find them as appealing as any original. Years ago repaints were lucky to bring half the price of originals, but today they will often command prices of 75 to 85 percent of an excellent original, and I have heard of unusual instances where a collector paid the full price for a repaint simply because he admired the high quality of workmanship on the particular item. Today there is greater acceptability of repaints, and in many quarters they are considered as good as originals. Still, most collectors prefer to collect only items in original condition, and they will happily pay a premium to get items in excellent or like-new condition.

Just as repaints are worth less, so are items that are retouched or touched up in any way. Many times trains will be found that have scratches filled or touched in. This adversely affects their value, unless it is done professionally and the paint matches and blends in perfectly. No matter how ugly the scratches may look, it is always best simply to leave them alone rather than yield to an itchy desire to use a paint-brush.

Is It an Original?

Since restorations have become more and more common and increasingly acceptable, many collectors have begun to do restoration work for others in order to earn extra money and to pay for their hobby. Many of these fellows have become so proficient at restoring that it is very often hard to tell their repainted trains from originals. Many train clubs have a policy of requiring members selling trains to state before the sale whether or not the item is original or restored. Nevertheless, in changing hands and with the sale of many large collections, you will have to find out whether or not the items are original. Because items restored years ago will often be purchased years later by another collector, he often has to find out whether or not he is buying an original item. The problem is that too few collectors actually mark the items they restore and, unless you have been collecting trains for a long time and are familiar with the exact paint colors and various other details of manufacture, you may one day find yourself trying to figure out the great dilemma: Is it or is it not an original?

I have found most collectors generally to be honest and if asked they will usually tell you what they know about an item's history and whether or not it's original. Since in any hobby there are bound to be an unscrupulous few who will attempt to get away with deceit, there will undoubtedly be some who will get burned. Many items are restored and not marked as such in any way, and some of these items are really intended to be nothing less than fakes. With the increasing rapid rise in values and the large sums of money that certain sets have been known to bring, it can be expected that a certain amount of fakery will go on, and it does.

First, let me make clear that I am not talking about reproductions, which are another category altogether. What I am saying is that certain restorations are done so well that they are sold to collectors on the basis that they are exactly like an original. In years to come, when the dust and scratches of time have begun to "age" these items, certain unscrupulous individuals may yield to the temptation to make a lot of money easily. As a result, many "suckers" will be taken to the cleaners. And it's simply because these items are restored so well and look so much like originals that people will be able to get away with it.

You might tend to ask just what items to look out for. Well, let me just say that any and every train of more than a nominal value has been and will be restored, so always know who you buy from. Since many train purchases are made at meets from people who often are total strangers to you, it would be a good policy to get the name and address of the individual you buy from, if you have any doubt at all about the item you're buying. If you have time it is always a good idea to ask the advice of a knowledgeable friend, or even someone you don't know but who looks honest, before you go ahead and make a costly purchase. One of the great problems is that with rare and costly train sets you rarely have the time to think and examine the item before you buy it, because there is often a group of hungry buyers surrounding the table who are hoping you'll pass on the set so that they can have a chance at it. I am sure that many of you fellows know exactly what I am talking about.

Through the years collectors have copper-plated their own Prosperity Special sets, as well as chrome-plating some American Flyer President Specials into Mayflower sets. Since not all originals were brass, the magnet test is not always enough, but original Mayflowers are supposed to have serial numbers inside the cars. (Of course, whether all factory originals have these numbers is another question in itself.) I have not yet seen any replated copper or nickel 1134 Ives steamers that could not be easily spotted as fakes from a block away.

One noted fellow in Connecticut has restored virtually every major Ives set in Standard gauge, and they are often exact, as his work is considered among the best in the country. He has restored many of these sets in quantity, dating back a number of years. Among the items that he has done are white Ives sets, 3245 sets, Black Diamond and Chief sets, 1764 sets, and National Limited sets, among others. One way of telling them from originals if you are not otherwise familiar with them is that original paint on most Ives sets has either chipped or begun to flake in spots such as car ends, roofs, and doors.

Many collectors have specialized in restoring Lionel trains, primarily Standard gauge, and it can often be hard to tell them apart from originals when the work is done properly. The list of items remains endless, but there are simple ways to tell. Even though many overzealous collectors clean and polish their trains, as well as replace every wheel so that they appear shiny as new, most old models usually retain a certain amount of patina or an aged look, which is hard if not impossible to duplicate. Trains in general tend to tarnish and rust. Finishes tend to dull, and

there will usually be telltale signs such as these noticed on original items. Basically, the best method is to try to be familiar with the methods used to paint originals so that you can look for paint runs and spray marks when they should appear. My own personal rule of thumb is that, since most items found in excellent or better condition are usually items that were kept in the original boxes, I try to see if the seller has the correct boxes for the set and if they are in comparable condition. From experience most items in like-new or seemingly mint condition should come with original boxes—if not, look out!

Reproductions

Other train items that we have begun to see more and more of lately are the many different types of reproductions. These fall into two basic categories: those that are not exact copies of original items, although they reproduce the designs of a particular train, and reproductions of old models that are no longer made by the original company. The thing to keep in mind with all reproductions is that they are not collector's items, because they were made recently and lack the age, history, and quality of old toy trains. While many of these reproductions are supposed to be of limited production (limited by how many they can actually sell), they are not collected for what they are and who they were made by, but rather for what they represent. True tinplate trains are collected by manufacturer (Lionel, Ives, Flyer, etc.), and collectors try to obtain the different models made by one or more different companies. Most fellows aren't interested in who makes a reproduction but whether or not it appeals to them or is a close copy of an original model made years before.

This is not to say that in future years reproductions will not be collected themselves, for undoubtedly they will, and some will probably increase in value sometime in the future. Just which ones will show the greatest rise in demand and value is anybody's guess, but I'm inclined to favor those repros that are not copies of trains made years ago but are of new and original design. Most items falling into this category are Standard gauge and geared toward "operators" or those fellows who like to run their trains.

Among the best known of these reproductions are the wide (Standard) gauge trains made by McCoy Manufacturing Company of Kent, Washington. These are the original McCoys (you might even say the "real McCoys"), who were among the very first to reproduce Standard gauge trains in any quantity. They are still going strong, and many collectors have purchased and run the various engines, freights, and

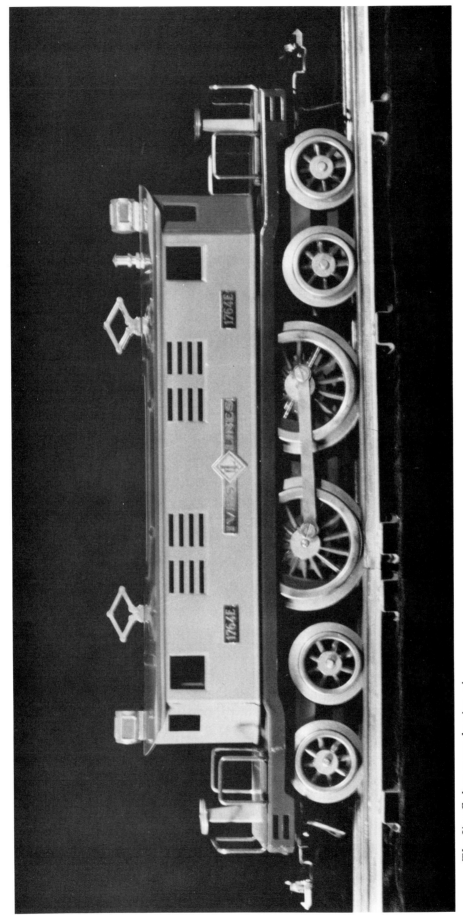

*The Jim Cohen reproduction of
the Lionel-Ives 1764E locomotive
looks amazingly like an original.*

passenger cars made by McCoy. In their early career they made reproductions of the Lionel nickel-plated No. 7 steamer as well as the brass 1912 Special electric loco. They have made many engines and cars of original designs, and they currently make the TCA loco and caboose as well as the Standard gauge convention cars available each year. They have even made a complete circus train with animals in cages and circus flatcars and now make a work train series for the TCA. They also have made a series of TCA Division and Chapter cars especially for Herb Morley.

Other original design equipment items are the ¾-inch scale passenger car kits designed by Tom Randall and currently available from Mike Hill in Illinois. These cars are heavy aluminum models, with the long-size cars a full 28 inches long! There is also a shorter 21-inch series of passenger cars, which are available with closed vestibules or with open ends having the appearance of the old "General" set but this time in Standard gauge. Currently there is no engine made to match the set, although Lionel or others can be used. Another line of this type, although far less elaborate and certainly not made in aluminum, is the Standard Lines Standard gauge models available from Martin Zair in New York. These original design trains are also available in kits or completed ready to run.

One train that never was made before in Standard gauge is the Milwaukee Road Hiawatha passenger set. Well, it is now available, for it is being made by the JAD Railway Lines and can be purchased from John Daniel in South Pasadena, California. It's quite an impressive model and the engine comes complete with its tender ready to run. It makes quite an impressive set when teamed up with the matching articulated passenger cars never before seen in Standard gauge. Other unusual models of this type have been made by others, such as a Standard gauge diesel engine and a Standard gauge GG-1, but these items are usually the result of one individual's handiwork and are all but impossible to obtain. It's new and interesting models such as the Standard gauge Hiawatha that are needed for collectors to operate and even collect, because these types of reproductions are complete original models.

Well known among collectors are the Classic Replica models made by Varney and Sirus in California. These trains are reproductions of models made originally by American Flyer and also some Ives. Overall they are well done and excellently reproduced, no matter how you feel about them. They made reproductions of the Mayflower set, two-tone blue President's Special, and the Flying Colonel set with the Ace plate. These are complete sets with the fully detailed passenger cars correctly painted or

plated, whatever the case may be. The engines come with dummy motors, although real motors can easily be added. Although I would like to tell you that they can be easily told apart from an original, I cannot, for these engines and cars are structurally the same as the originals. They even made some of their first Mayflower sets with brass cars!

They have also made 3245 reproductions in both short- and long-cab versions, and they have correctly painted their Flyer passenger cars to match. They have sold everything from Prosperity Special copper-plated cars to Black Diamond and Interstate light green passenger cars. These are just like the originals, right down to their Ives trucks and couplers, and the paint matches closely. I hoped to find differences, major differences that would easily set these cars apart from the originals, but I found very few. While all the Varney and Sirus observation cars have a cut-out on the rear platform for the light socket that came on American Flyer cars, I have seen some original Ives cars that had this same feature. One difference is that most, but not all, Ives observation cars using the Flyer bodies are found with a brass nameplate on the rear deck, which is usually at least somewhat worn, while the reproductions always come with a lucite insert with the Ives name. There are minor differences between these reproduction cars and the originals, such as different rivets used and the brass window inserts not as rigidly shaped as those on the original cars, but these differences are not that great. While reproductions such as these have enabled many fellows to be able to afford these sets when they couldn't normally afford originals, reproductions such as these may eventually be passed off as originals to new and unwary collectors. When that happens we can no longer call these sets reproductions but only fakes, something which they were never intended to be.

Also other individuals have made copies of former Lionel models, such as Ted Geng's reproduction brass 1912 Special and models of the early 5 and 6 steam-type locomotives. Jim Cohen made an exact model of the Lionel nickel and brass No. 7 locomotive. He also made an exact copy of the Lionel-Ives 1764 twelve-wheel electric locomotive, which is a virtual carbon copy of the original, except that it was sold with a dummy motor.

The one man who has become almost synonymous with the word *reproduction* is Jerry Williams of Williams' Reproductions Limited in Maryland. He first reproduced a fairly accurate model of the Lionel-Ives O gauge 1694 locomotive. Since original 1694 engines are close to impossible to obtain, it was the opinion of most collectors that an engine such as this was needed. Most fellows felt that, in general, Lionel

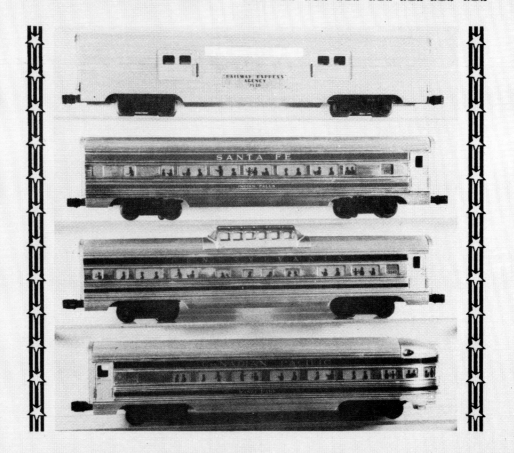

Williams' latest venture is the reproduction of the Lionel striped series O gauge aluminum passenger cars.

GOLDEN MEMORIES
by
Williams' Reproductions Limited

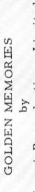

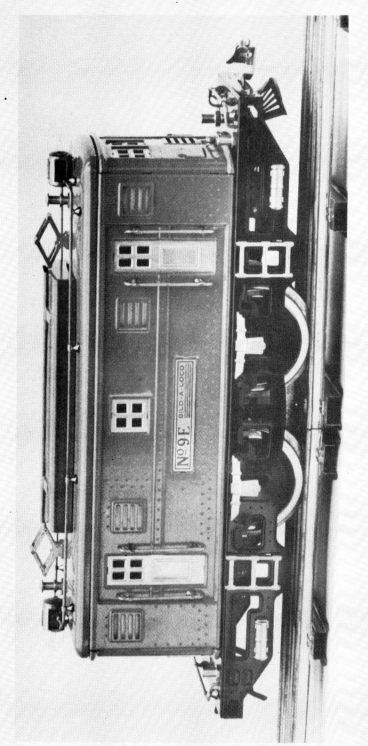

#9E LOCOMOTIVE

These handsome box cab electrics were catalogued from 1928-1936 and are now available in the four original color variations: Orange (illustrated), Two-tone Green, Gunmetal Grey, and the very rare Dark Green. All locos have brass trim except the gunmetal grey which has all nickel trim. The #9E's are the most desirable of all box cab electric engines. These gems will be available at the current price of $160.00 until November 1, 1975 at which time the price will be increased to $175.00. These engines will not be available in the distant future, so procurement at this time is a wise investment. Loco comes complete with all trim and hardware for installing either the BILD-A-LOCO or SUPER motor.

(Include $5.00 shipping)

Williams' Reproductions has turned out many
of the Lionel deluxe Standard gauge electrics,
among them the four color variations of the 9E, the 381E, and the 408E.

STORE: 465 CONGRESS AVE., NEW HAVEN, CONN. (203) 787-2121
AFTER 6:00 P.M.: 684 ELM ST., NEW HAVEN, CONN. (203) 776-7710

LIONEL REPRODUCTION PARTS

Please ORDER BY BIN NO. ONLY in order to speed delivery. List adequate substitutes, when stock is depleted there isn't any more. All items are EXACT SIZE. Destroy my OLD PARTS LIST as NUMBERS have been changed to correspond with PICTURES. No order shipped less than $5.00. Include $1.50 for Postage and Handling Charges, regardless size of order. We also MANUFACTURE some REPLACEMENT PARTS.

No.	Part	Description	Price	No.	Part	Description	Price
1	263	Tender End	3.00	27A	700E-5	Trailer Trk. Frame	3.00
1A	260	Tender End	3.00	27B	773	Trailer Trk. Frame	4.00
2	700E	Outer Ring	3.50	28	700T-4	Bearing Caps	.25
3	700K-16	Boiler Front Comp.	6.50	28A	700T-25	Bear. Cap Screws dz	.50
3A	700E	Boiler Front Center	3.50	29	700E-84	Bolster Steam Coupl.	.50
4	701T-5	Tender Coupl. Mount	1.00	30	700E-16	Ladders	.50
5	773-75	Pilot	2.00	31	700E-3A	6 Wheel Tender Trk. Frame	
5A	700E-11	Open Pilot	2.00			w/bear. Caps & Screw	4.00
6	400	"O" Latch	1.00	31A	700E-3A	6 Wheel Ten. Trk. Fr.	3.00
7	385,392	St. Gauge Latch	1.00	32	400	Boiler Front	4.00
8	700E-239	Crosshead	.50	33	390	Boiler Front	4.00
9	700E-66	Valve Stem Crosshead	.50	33A	384	Boiler Front	4.00
10	700T-24	Straight Coupler	2.50	34	392	Boiler Front	4.00
10A	700T-24	Offset Coupler	2.50	35	700E-125	Drawbar with Chain	1.25
10B	700T-24	Bent Coupler	2.50	36	700T-23	Brake Cylinder	1.00
10C	700T-34	Front Coupler	2.50	37		Strap on Headlight	1.50
11	700E-82	Power Reverse Cyl.	.50	38	700E	6 Wheel Ten. Trk. Axle	.50
12	714T-3	Bolster & Coupler	3.00	39	700E	Trailer Truck Axle	.50
13	700E-46	Eccentric Crank	.50	40	622-5	Black Smokestack	.50
13A	226E-19	Eccentric Crank	.50	41	2460-16	Round Hole Handwheel	.50
14	700T-14	Front Step	.50	41A	2660	Square Hole Handwheel	.50
14A	700E-6	Rear Step	.50	42	752	Vestibule Whl. w/axle	1.00
15	700E-83	Turbo Generator	.50	43	2332-10	GG1 Ladder (R)	.75
16		Scale Hopper Door	.50	44	520-30	Driving Coupler	1.00
17	700E-25	R.H. Crosshead Guide	.75	45	2243-90	Dummy Coupler	.75
17A	700E-62	L.H. Crosshead Guide	.75	46	773-57	Collector Assembly	3.00
18		"O" Headlight	1.25	47	3650-22	Crank	.50
19		St. Gauge Headlight	1.25	48	1661-7	Wheel	.50
20	700E-43	L.H. Drive Rod	1.00	49	636	Plain Wheel	1.00
20A	700E-42	R.H. Drive Rod	1.00	50		Lionel Wheel	.50
21	700E-40	L.H. Side Rod	1.00	51		Scale Wheel	.50
21A	700E-41	R.H. Side Rod	1.00	52	8040-11	Rear Truck Wheel	.50
22	700E-10	Trailer Front Wheel	.75	53	700E-8	Drive Wheel	2.00
23	700E-11	Trailer Spoke Wheel	1.25	54	700E-8	Drive Wheel (R)	1.50
24	700E-249	Pilot Truck Frame	2.00	55	700E-8	Blind Wheel	1.50
25	636	Gear Wheel	1.00	56	2671W-13	Water Scoop	1.00
26		Hiawatha Frt. Wheel	1.00	57	716-13	Truck Bolster	3.00
26A	250	Hiawatha Trailer Truck Wheels	1.00	58		Scale Truck Side	.50
26B	250	Hiawatha Axles	.25	59	2023-110	Truck Side	1.50
26C		Hiawatha Trailer Trk.		60	622-41	Truck Side	1.50
27	700E-5	Trailer Trk. Frame w/ Bear. Caps & Screws	4.00	61	2333-68	Truck Side	1.50
				62	385	Steamchest	10.00
				63	2046-13	Boiler Front	3.50

Almost every kind of part imaginable today is being reproduced by someone, somewhere. Here on one page of Harry Gordon's list we find everything from scale Hudson parts to Standard gauge.

Standard gauge is far too common and no one would dare to reproduce it. Well, Williams did just that. Since most collectors do not own any reproductions and since the large accumulations of many of the older collectors represent quite an investment to them, many fellows got very upset when these items were first announced. Their natural fear, whether they admitted it or not, was that these items might ruin the value of their original trains. Actually, these reproductions, like any other, have very little effect on the train market in general, since most collectors buy only original trains anyway. What they did is offer some copies of some expensive Lionel Standard gauge trains at reasonable prices, and for those who wanted to run their trains but were afraid of damaging their originals they also had a need fulfilled. The simple fact is that in this, as in any other hobby, as prices continue to increase and rise to a certain level it becomes profitable for someone to reproduce copies of the originals. It was going to happen anyway, so why blame Jerry Williams? If you don't like his reproductions then don't buy them; it's as simple as that.

He made the four different color variations of the Lionel 9E electric locomotives. These are fairly accurate reproductions, but one easy way to tell them from the original is that they have a separate roof section, which is tabbed to the sides of the engine, unlike the originals. Probably his most popular model is that of the Lionel 381 twelve-wheel electric engine. This is another nice copy of the original model, but inside, where the originals have a large brass band running from the headlights to the Bild-A-Loco motor, the reproduction is without it. Certainly one could be easily fashioned but there are other little differences between these engines and originals. Since these reproductions are not made from the same types of high pressure tools and dies used on the original Standard gauge models, they tend to have light and uneven rivet details on the engines as well as the frames. Also brass parts, such as the window inserts on the No. 9 locos, tend to fit unevenly and not as snugly as those seen on original engines.

At the writing of this chapter Williams is also threatening to make models of the Lionel 408 electric engine and a number of the Lionel trolley cars, with the large No. 8 "Pay As You Enter" trolley. These reproductions, no matter how well they are made, will have little if no effect on prices in general, and I know that a number of my friends as well as myself have just purchased original number 8 trolleys and paid a top dollar price to get them, even though we knew that reproductions were soon about to be made.

At this writing Williams also intends to make a series of O gauge aluminum passenger cars, copied after Lionel's striped road-name series. There will be no Lionel Lines aluminum cars reproduced, for he has been forbidden from using the Lionel name, which is currently being leased by MPC (Model Products Corp.) from the actual Lionel Corp. As time goes on, more and more new reproductions, copied from originals, will be made, because as long as there are people willing to buy them there will be people willing to make them. Reproductions, copies, fakes or whatever you wish to call them are common to many different hobbies, and whether you like them or not more and more will appear in the future, for the once innocent hobby of train collecting has unknowingly started to grow up.

Fakes and reproductions are not limited to Standard gauge, as many Lionel O gauge collectors can tell you. Many of the Lionel diesel engines have been reproduced, their cabs that is, and many new collectors have unwarily been "taken" with these professionally painted cabs, especially through mail order sales. These reproduction cabs were originally made so that collectors could run these models and not have to risk wear or damage to their expensive originals. The only problem is that these cabs are too well made and look exactly like the originals. What's more, since reproduction number boards are available of the type found on the nose of F-3 diesels, many collectors have added these to their repro cabs, with the correct numbers making it even harder to tell them from originals.

One of the first men to reproduce these cabs and one who has probably made more than anyone else is Ed Kraemer. Since he knows all too well how easy it would be to pass these off to unsuspecting and unknowing individuals, he once wrote and printed an article at his own expense that details the differences between the repros and the original diesel shells. Ed went out of his way to write this article, which is excellent and complete. Since there is little that I could add let me quote from his writings:

Lionel used two types of lettering and line process. First is heat stamping, which is done by applying heat to line and word area through a heat ribbon. The heat causes the plastic, or paint, to soften and rise around the *indented* lines or words. This can be felt by running your fingernail across the lines or words, feeling the indentation. Then there is the rubber-stamp process, which is self-explanatory; *line and word paint density in this process is thin,* and sometimes it has a blurred or smeared outline around the letters. This process is mostly used around rounded cabs or on the nose lines and cannot be felt by running your fingernail across the lines or words.

Postwar Silk-screen Reproductions

No.	Description	Original	Reproduction
0000	Alaska GP-9	About four prototype models made, were hand-painted with water decals	Silk-screened and sprayed
746	N&W Tender	Short or long stripe rubber-stamped	Silk-screened, rivets sanded off
2028	Pennsy GP-7	Brown plastic cab	Brown paint
2240	Wabash AB	Blue plastic cab, words heat-stamped	Painted blue cab, silk-screened words
2242	New Haven AB	Heat-stamped nose and sides	Decal nose, silk-screened sides
2321	Lackawanna FM	Lines and words rubber-stamped	Silk-screened
2328	Burlington GP-7	Lettering and herald rubber-stamped	Silk-screened
2331	Black and yellow Virginian FM	Rubber-stamped, paint is light and clear	Rubber-stamped, heavy and blurred
2332	Pennsy GG-1	Heat-stamped, often tends to fade	Silk-screened, often appears too bright
2341	Jersey Central FM	Heat-stamped, also one side wording has larger spacing than other side	Silk-screened, same spacing on both sides
2345	Western Pacific AA	Heat-stamped	Silk-screened
2348	Minn. & St. Louis GP-9	Heat-stamped	Silk-screened
2349	Northern Pacific GP-9	Heat-stamped in gold leaf	Silk-screened in dull gold
2356	Southern ABA	Rubber-stamped	Silk-screened
2358	Great Northern electric	Lines rubber-stamped, words heat-stamped	Silk-screened
2360	(also 2340, 2330) Pennsy GG-1	Heat-stamped, often tends to fade	Silk-screened, striping may appear too bright
2363	Illinois Central AB	Rubber-stamped	Silk-screened
2368	Baltimore & Ohio AB	Blue plastic cab, heat-stamped words	Painted blue cab, silk-screened words
2373	Canadian Pacific AA	Heat-stamped on top and sides	Silk-screened
2378	Milwaukee Road AB	Gray plastic cab, heat-stamped	Painted gray cab, silk-screened
2379	Rio Grande AB	Heat-stamped	Silk-screened
2625 (2627, 2628)	Madison-type passenger cars	Heat-stamped	Rivets removed around the words for silk-screening; lettering is a very bright white
6467-50	Virginian caboose	Heat-stamped	Silk-screened, Lionel Lines lettering often slightly visible underneath

This list is not 100% complete, since almost anything made in the postwar period can and will be reproduced. Also Lionel MPC made many copies of the original Lionel designs in the 70's which have major and minor differences but might still further confuse the novice collector. The rule still applies when buying excellent to like-new or mint equipment; always ask for the original boxes, which generally confirm if the item is authentic or not.

Silk-Screening

Silk-screening is the method used on the reproductions. This is done by forcing paint through a silk screen, depositing the paint, which is the lines or words, on the surface of the cab. Hardly any height can be felt. Screening is a very clear printing process. There is a very distinct difference between silk-screening and rubber-stamping. There is *definitely no indentation* on the word and line areas as in heat stamping.

Another way to determine the screened process is that for any lines or words printed over detail, such as rivets or detail molded in the cab, the paint has a tendency to smear or blob up. In order to screen clear on this surface, the area to be screened must have the rivets sanded down or removed. In the heat-stamping or rubber-stamping processes, the lines are applied right over the rivets; no need to remove rivets or sand down the area.

There are a number of models that are reproduced such as the Alaska GP-9 prototype, which is sprayed and silk-screened, while the originals are hand-painted and decaled. Many of the 746 Norfolk and Western tenders, which were originally rubber-stamped, are reproduced with the rivets sanded off. The 2028 Pennsylvania GP-7, which came with a brown plastic cab, is reproduced with the cab painted brown. The scarce 2242 New Haven had a heat-stamped nose while repros had a decal nose. The Jersey Central 2341 had the lettering "Built By Lionel" heat-stamped while repros were silk-screened. Also many 2627 series Madison passenger cars were restored with the silk-screen process and can be easily detected because of the rivet details removed around the numbers and words, as well as the bright white lettering usually more dulled on the originals. This is a sampling of what was reproduced, and many more engines and even some freight cars were also silk-screened. The important thing to remember is that you cannot tell these differences at a glance, so if you are about to purchase any diesel at all it is always wise to examine the item closely before you buy it.

Reproduction Parts

One other important type of reproduction consists of train parts. In recent years more and more kinds of reproduction parts have become available, because the supply of original parts started to dry up years ago. These parts range from Standard gauge to 027, from couplers to wheels, plastic, metal—you name it. Reproduction parts are well liked and widely accepted and available within the hobby. Many individual collectors and companies produce these parts in all parts of the country. Wherever the demand exists, eventually a reproduction is made to fill the need. Many reproduction parts represent the only kind available, as original supplies have long since been exhausted. Currently Lionel (MPC) is making many of the sorely needed postwar O gauge parts. Standard gauge and prewar parts have been available for a long time, and everything and anything is made, ranging from wheels and axles, gears, die-cast frames and steam chests, to complete Standard gauge motors.

While it is definitely true that having a part is a lot better than having no part at all, the fact is that reproduction parts affect the value of the trains when they are used. That is to say that a 400E or a 260E with a replacement (reproduction) frame is worth less than the same engine with an original frame. While this doesn't hold true on everything, such as replaced handrails or wheels, most collectors if they have a choice prefer an item that is wholly original. Just as you would be expected to tell someone that part of the train you are selling has been repainted, you likewise should mention if you've replaced the tender top to an 1835 coal tender, for instance, or replaced the marker light to a 2056 postwar locomotive, because these replacement parts may add to the value of these engines, but they are still worth less than if the item is completely original. How much reproduction parts can influence the value of a model varies greatly. Most collectors would not mind if a 400E loco, for example, had a replaced boiler front, for it is common to those engines, as many original boiler fronts have cracked and broken with age. Basically it depends on whether the reproduction part is easily noticeable or not; if it is a close copy of the original then it will probably withstand the scrutiny of most collectors.

Reproductions, restorations, and fakes, whether you like them or not, are here to stay. They are an inevitable part of any hobby that has a substantial following. As prices continue to rise on many train sets, the sets will eventually be reproduced. To paraphrase the words of one noted individual, "As for me, give me an original or give me death." On second thought I'm not that serious a collector!

12

THE FUTURE
OF TRAIN COLLECTING

Before we can talk safely about the future of the hobby and where it's headed, let me mention some things about the present. What is train collecting today, what does it consist of? Well, it's basically a middle-class collecting hobby similar to collecting coins and stamps, guns, old tin and iron toys, even antique cars. Many of these collectibles have attracted people from all walks of life—from the poor to the superrich, all nationalities and ethnic groups, from the very young to the very old and of course both men and women. The same thing has happened with train collecting. One possible difference might be that train collecting has not become dominated by the rich. In fact, most of the largest and finest train collections in the country reside in middle-class homes, and very often the total value of the train collection far exceeds the current market price for the collector's house. Is this unusual? I don't think so. Most collectors are in the hobby because they enjoy collecting the trains themselves, regardless of the prices quoted. They have gotten around the high prices by buying and selling trains at some stage in their career, simply to "support the hobby," as is often heard.

Every train collection is somewhat different, and so are the many reasons why people choose to collect trains. For many people the trains bring back the joy and memories of years past, while others love real trains and have found solace in collecting and displaying these miniature models. Still others, like myself, are compulsive collectors—"born collectors"— who collect anything that appeals to them. Some have found that, as they have grown older, they can afford to buy these trains they longed for so greatly as children. They have great pleasure in being able to fulfill their early desires at last. Of course, others collect simply to "hide" their cash and conceal the many untold dollars on which they never paid taxes.

Many find that the rising prices of the trains in general have given them a very healthy return on their "investment."

Numerous collectors have discovered their own little niche in the hobby and have developed a certain specialty for themselves. And why not? After all, there are so many different facets to train collecting. Some like to repair; some enjoy restoring; many love to build layouts and operate the trains; still others like to research and study the trains through catalogs and any available research material; and many like to become specialists and devote their time and effort to collecting and studying a particular period or make and type of train. Clearly this hobby has much to offer, as shown by the increasing number of new collectors always joining our ever-expanding ranks.

Obtaining Trains

Outside of higher prices very little has changed in train collecting for quite a long time. While the public has in general become increasingly aware and knowledgeable about anything deemed "old" ("old" can often mean a mere twenty-year span), and many of the once common bargains and fabulous deals have thus fallen by the wayside, there are still a surprising number of "finds" for those with the time and persistence to chase after the trains, and there are countless ways of doing this. Whether you decide to put a sign up on your car window that you are looking for old trains or put the sign in a local store window or supermarket, or go to all the local and not-so-local garage sales, or attend the antique flea markets, or hound relatives, friends, and neighbors till you get laryngitis, or check out every possible antique shop in your area, or run a classified ad in your local

A familiar sight in practically every newspaper in America is the familiar ad—Lionel Trains Wanted. Just check the classified section of any major daily paper and there is usually one, two, three, even four or five competing collectors continually outbidding each other. The question is: Has the public become aware of train prices?

paper, you have to find something eventually. With luck, when you do finally come across a load of trains you will be able to buy them at a reasonable price; if not, you can always give up and go see a dealer, either a hobby shop owner who handles collectible trains or one of the many mail order dealers listed in the back of most of the hobby magazines.

Most fellows develop some sort of technique for picking up trains, but, whatever you try, be forewarned that it can be very time-consuming and sometimes quite disheartening. Of course if you don't have the time a lot of money would help, but many fellows enjoy the thrill of buying the trains directly from their original owners. There is also the disappointment when you lose the deal to another collector who got the set for ten dollars more than you offered. That is why you should always try your hardest to get a price from the people before you go over, something which is not an easy thing to do.

Most people start off with "What are they worth? I have no idea." To which you answer, "They're your trains, what do you want for them?" They then say, "You're the expert, you know what they're worth." To which you finally reply, "I'll give you a hundred bucks for them," and they immediately answer, "We'll call you and let you know, because Mister So-and-So is coming tomorrow." On and on goes the old story till the trains get bid up and up, and till they're completely out of sight and you walk away a dejected soul, losing the deal completely and returning home to take it out on your wife. Oh, the terrible taste of defeat known to almost every collector sooner or later when you miss that important deal! It's just part of the initiation process in collecting old toy trains.

Most collectors will very willingly travel for hours to buy a set of trains or attend a train meet that may or may not have an item they're looking for; yet very few will go out of their way to visit another collector unless he has some trains for sale. This is a serious mistake that many collectors make, for, no matter how big or small a collection, there is always something there you have never seen before and always something new to learn. You should try to visit collectors in your area and whenever you travel, and—who knows?—you might even find them willing to sell you something you need. Especially try to visit fellows who collect the same type of trains as yourself; they may add a lot to your knowledge of what is rare, unusual, or common within your field.

Lionel and Others

Most fellows make the mistake of thinking that Lionel is the beginning and end to train collecting.

They might do themselves a lot of good by seeing a collection of American Flyer, Ives, Marklin, Bing, or Dorfan and start to realize what they are missing. You may find yourself thinking that you don't really care at all about these different makes, only to have your tastes change a year or two later when you are out searching for these other makes which you once referred to as oddballs and junk. The majority of collectors today collect Lionel, but it must be kept in mind that Lionel is the most common make, and it presents little or no challenge to assemble a large Lionel collection, while other makes are far more elusive.

Other than specializing in a particular company, gauge, or period, many have directed their collecting pursuits toward getting locomotives rather than sets or individual cars. Engines have always been and will continue to be the center of the hobby as well as the most expensive individual items. This is not to say that some freight as well as passenger cars cannot command the same price as an engine, but rather that, in general, many collectors are basically locomotive collectors, with freight cars and passenger equipment of secondary importance. Still others collect by condition, many of them without ever realizing it. Many will not accept a train into their collection unless it meets their own particular standards. Unlike coin collectors, many do not want a "filler" to fill in a gap unless it is in presentable shape. Condition is very important to many collectors, and only a very rare item will be accepted in lesser condition. Condition is an important factor in determining an item's price, for it is obvious that many will want an item that is in excellent shape, while few will want it if it is in poor condition. Trains in mint (new) or shiny like-new condition can sometimes command twice as much as the same item in very good or excellent shape.

Today the vast majority of collectors are interested in Lionel trains, both prewar and postwar models. Perhaps this is because most hobbyists originally owned a Lionel train set as boys and many naturally tend to feel sentimental about the Lionel company. This sentimentality has caused many collectors to believe that Lionel trains are superior in terms of construction and design to other makes. While it is true that Lionel often did make a better product, many of these strictly Lionel collectors have become blinded to the beauty of Flyer, Ives, Marklin, and, yes, even Marx! When collectors' tastes and esthetic appreciation progress to a point at which they begin to notice the many fine models made by Lionel's competitors, they also begin to realize how much harder they are to find. While some collectors will always look down on certain makes and snobbishly write them off

Still a bargain at today's prices are many odd and interesting variations of 100 series freights. The four 112 gondolas pictured come in different colors in addition to the different styles of lettering shown.

because they do not command the higher prices brought by Lionel items, some have been attracted to other makes just because they are often far less expensive to collect.

"Sleepers"

In any hobby we tend to have "sleepers," which are items that have not become popular and tend to bring a low price, lower than you might normally expect. While all trains in general rise in price, it might be expected that some would rise in value faster than others. This happens all the time, because any hobby is subject to fads, and collectors, in an effort to keep up with any changes in the hobby, tend to watch the other fellow to see what he is doing. If so and so wants a Hell Gate bridge, a Lionel trolley, or a Flyer President Special, you try to beat him to the punch and get it first. As soon as you start to ask around, others get the same idea. Before you know it, everyone is out after the same things and the price starts to go up, for if ten collectors want the same item one of them is going to be willing to pay more than the others. Once the new record price is met the word will spread fast, for the train-collecting community is very close knit and everyone will know to ask even more next time, driving the price up still further to even greater levels of insanity.

As a good example, I can remember once there was a time when five different collectors came up to me and asked if I knew of any brown 408E State sets for sale, and of course I knew of none. At the time I wasn't particularly looking for one, but after the fifth person had asked me for one, I decided to look for a set for myself. I knew that if I didn't find one soon the price would be sure to rise. Of course, when I approached people I knew who owned brown State sets they naturally didn't want to sell.

Since collecting, especially of rare and expensive items, is by its very nature highly competitive, many who cannot afford the astronomical prices or who do not wish to play the game start to look for other things to collect. That is why sleepers remain good buys for only so long. Eventually others pick up on the same idea and the whole price spiral begins again, with the direction always upward.

What are today's sleepers? I wish I knew for sure, but I have a number of guesses that may or may not be correct. Among the sleepers Marx has got to be the king, for since many Louis Marx train sets were sold at next-to-nothing prices, the vast majority have long since been broken and thrown away. Also, Marx trains come in a wide assortment of variations, which

all command often insignificant prices. Another series that is just beginning to be appreciated consists of the small HO trains made by Lionel and American Flyer in comparatively small quantities compared to O and S gauge production. In postwar Lionel the 027 and O gauge black die-cast steam engines are sure to rise in price in future years, probably a great number of years, when collectors have started to grow tired of diesels. In prewar trains we find many O gauge models already rapidly rising and at times approaching the prices fetched for many expensive Standard gauge trains. Of the Standard gauge trains themselves I find many of the American Flyer sets to be good buys at current prices and many of Lionel's earlier Standard gauge items go relatively unnoticed, such as the 18, 19, 190 passenger cars and the 100 and 10 series freights, which often go begging at reasonable prices.

Popular Trains

Enough of the sleepers. What of the popular trains? There are many too numerous to mention, but as always you can bet that Lionel leads the pack. In postwar other than Flyer S gauge there is little else to collect besides Lionel. The most popular Lionel items are the O gauge diesels and electric engines, in addition to the 6464 series boxcars, various road-name cabooses, and large quad hoppers. In Lionel Standard the popularity centers on items made in the Classic period, with the large passenger sets such as the State set and Blue Comet being held in awe by many. Actually, much of the large Lionel Standard gauge sets have become train collecting "status symbols" to many, although I know of many collectors, myself included, who laugh at the thought, for only rare trains deserve that sort of recognition, and hardly anything in Lionel Classic period Standard could be called rare. Always popular are Lionel trolley cars, which generally are quite hard to find, as well as any of the hard-to-find early period train sets, such as 1910, 1911, and 1912 square-cab electrics. Ives's top train sets in Standard gauge, such as the 3245 Olympian and the 3243 white Ives set, always command attention. Actually, any of the transition period sets, such as the National Limited, the circus train, the Black Diamond set, and others, are all very popular and are virtually impossible to buy in original condition. The Flyer Standard gauge President Special sets, as well as the Flying Colonel and chrome-plated Mayflower trains, are popular and also expensive. In prewar, Lionel 072 as a category has always been popular with a large following, and so have the early Ives

*For many the future of train collecting lies in HO trains. These models
from the Joel Cane collection are part of the more than three hundred HO
engines that he is able to confine in only half of one room of his apartment.
Joel also notes that in addition to taking up less space they also "cost
one hell of a lot less" than comparable O gauge or Standard models.*

O gauge models with the many attractive and beautifully lithographed freight and passenger cars that were made.

Rarities

So many trains are popular and the most popular ones command the highest prices. As long as certain items remain popular they are also likely to rise in price, no matter how high the price might seem today. Prices vary, but some items are so rare that they do not even have a set price. There are many rare individual trains, but since it would take too long to mention each one, I will mention the rare categories of trains, some of which were just mentioned before when I tried to elaborate some of today's more popular sets. Lionel 2⅞ gauge equipment certainly is a major contender in this category. Then there are Lionel trolley cars, as well as any of the very earliest Lionel Standard gauge items characterized by thin-rim drive wheels, three-rivet trucks, and knobby roof passenger cars. Of course, any of the early tin, iron, and wooden trains made before the turn of the century would qualify as very rare, so rare in fact that they have not been dealt with in this book, as they are beyond the scope of most present-day collectors. Alcohol burners should also be mentioned here and, in addition to the many models made abroad by Marklin, Bing, Bassett-Lowke, and Carette, there were a number of American manufacturers. These live-steam models were made by Beggs as early as the 1870s, to be followed by Garlick, who was a former Beggs employee. The best known was Weeden, which sold large quantities of their famous Weeden Dart locomotive.

All of the fine Marklin and Bing 1 and 2 gauge models are in general scarce, as is the equipment that went with it, namely, the fine and elaborate accessories made for many years. Ives 1 gauge is also difficult if not very rare, although one or two models turn up more often, such as the 3239 or the 1129. Any of the early and now defunct train manufacturers are all scarce, such as Carlisle and Finch, Voltamp, Howard, and Elektoy, and most collectors wouldn't even know what they were looking at anyway, let alone even try to begin to collect those makes. Ives transition sets in both O and Standard gauges are rare, as well as the Lionel-Ives trains of the 1931-32 period. It is also fairly well known that any of the department store specials made by any company tend to be rare as well as desirable. Also, all of the Lionel 700 series early O gauge engines are rarely seen. Most collectors would rate any Dorfan locomotive found in

excellent condition scarce too, since many of their die-cast engines have long since crumbled.

Another generally rare category would be any errors or mistakes that were unknowingly made in manufacture. Mistakes in coin collecting, such as the 1955 double-die cent, command fantastic prices, and stamp collecting too has its high-priced errors, such as the upside-down airplane on the U.S. airmail stamp, which commands many thousands of dollars. How about train collecting? For the time being, errors have gone relatively unnoticed in the mainstream of collecting. Only items painted in an unusual color, a color in which items are normally not found, tend to .generate any interest. Of course, there are all sorts of errors if you look hard enough, such as a number or lettering stamped twice on a car or engine, or an engine that slipped through without being properly stamped and lettered. In the future any unusual error might become a highly sought-after and desirable variation, as some of them are in the other collecting hobbies, but until then most collectors want the item in nice condition without any oddities. Most errors are looked upon as items that have problems rather than odd and interesting variations, a situation that is likely to change in the future.

Prices

If something you read in this book hasn't already upset you, the next subject certainly will. That is the subject of prices and values, always controversial in any hobby. Every collector has a definite opinion regarding train prices, and quite frankly, no matter what I say about the subject and how I handle it, I am likely to be bombarded with criticism from all ends of the earth. There are a number of collectors, mostly older collectors, who feel that train prices today are absurd and ridiculous and far greater than the trains are really "worth." Then there are others who feel that prices are high in general, with certain items just too high and "overpriced." Then there are some collectors, mostly new ones, who seem to think that prices are not that bad, since people seem to be paying them and, feeling that the trains are a good investment, they buy up sets like water.

Whatever your belief is regarding current prices for trains, most collectors still want to obtain items at a bargain price, but they like to sell their items at the top dollar value. Since I have obviously tried carefully to avoid mentioning prices, you may ask why. First, it's because values change so rapidly that, upon publication of this book, they would be immediately incorrect and therefore prove useless and misleading to you. Second, this book was not written as a price guide but rather as a generalized overview of train collecting today. Third, if you want to know prices I'm not going to tell them to you unless you decide to write me a letter describing something you have for sale.

Prices in general vary, with Standard and other large gauge models commanding the highest prices. Many O gauge engines even today sell for less than $25, with most of the better models bringing between $100 and $300. Some O gauge sets have already surpassed the thousand-dollar mark and I know of one particular Ives 1694 set in the original box that brought $3,000 at auction. A number of Standard gauge engines and sets still sell for less than a hundred dollars, and many sets bring only about $200 to $500. While these prices may seem high to you today, these sets were expensive when they were new, especially if you try to realize just how much money twenty or thirty dollars was in the 1920s and 1930s. During the Great Depression years of the 1930s many men were happily supporting their families comfortably on twenty-five dollars a week! It's no wonder, then, that train sets that sold for sixty and seventy dollars in the Depression will bring a few thousand dollars from collectors today.

Since some of the rarest and finest Standard gauge train sets have already brought prices over five thousand dollars for one set, a number of predictions have been made. There are those that think that prices are already so high that they can go no farther and are even likely to come down. For the most part, many seem to think that they will go even higher.

My own feeling is that prices in general will continue to rise and that eventually prices of ten thousand dollars and better will be paid for some of the rarest Standard gauge sets. I also feel that some of the rarer O gauge sets will one day bring prices of more than five thousand dollars for one set. I believe that prices in general will always rise, but I also think that there will come a time when prices on certain items will fall and others will reach their (temporary) peak, for in anything there has got to be a limit. Some fellows seem to think the "sky's the limit" with today's prices, but they are wrong, for I have seen some collectors go into orbit with their prices while others were definitely circling the moon!

Many collectors are quick to comment when someone asks a high price, saying, "That guy is crazy, his prices are right through the roof," only to have the same item on their own table a few months later and this time not talking too loud as they are asking the same high price, or even higher. I have known many perpetual complainers, and each of them talked about

high prices, but when they had items to sell they were whistling a whole new tune and you'd think they were trying to establish new world's records. Older collectors frequently complain about today's high prices, but when it comes time to sell they inevitably ask and get the top dollar for their trains.

Interestingly, the highest prices for many of the rarest sets have not been paid by wealthy collectors but more often by a middle-class collector who has been in the hobby for a while and feels the item to be worth its expensive price. Perhaps the collector sold many smaller and less expensive sets to pay for the purchase or had saved for a period of time prior to buying it. Since most of the highest-priced trains are not necessarily purchased by the rich, much can be said in regard to this fact, for this has had a very direct effect on the general stability of train prices.

Curiously, as prices have continued to increase in the hobby more and more have become attracted to it. There are a number of reasons for this, one of which would be that old toy trains have started to become well-known collector's items and are no longer laughed at. Having a train collection used to bring comments such as "He's just like a baby playing with those toys," or "What are you doing with that junk?" Now you are likely to hear, "I hear old trains are worth a lot of money, you must have quite a fortune here," or "Wow, these trains are really beautiful," as the collector beams a proud smile and looks over his new "status symbols." Some of course entered the hobby as soon as they found out how rapidly prices were rising, so they could make a good "investment," and of course they heard so much about the trains being worth money that they felt a safe assurance that they would not be throwing their money away or risking it foolishly.

It is a situation common to many hobbies where people become collectors, simply because the hobby has gained stature and they feel they are likely to get a greater appreciation of their money than they could normally receive in a bank. While it is true that many collectors frown on this, it is also true that everyone, whether he is willing to admit it or not, is not averse to making money, and therefore practically all collectors will buy items for resale when they get the chance.

Of course then there are the usual gripes about so-and-so who is strictly a dealer and only in it for the money. While most collectors are in effect dealers, for practically everyone in the hobby buys and sells to some extent, there continues to be a growing number of collectors who enjoy the hobby so much that they have decided to make it their full- or part-time avocation and so have opened up a hobby shop.

Many hobby shop owners did not start with the idea that they were going to make a quick killing, but rather felt they would enjoy having their own business involved in something they enjoy, namely, model trains.

There are still many collectors who hate and despise dealers and use them as scapegoats by continually blaming them for rising prices and anything wrong they see in the hobby. This is simply not true, and in fact there is much to be said for the dealer, for he sells trains and is often the only available source of supply for many who would just as soon buy from a collector if they knew of one who was willing to sell them something. Dealers are much like any other group of people; there are all kinds, from the very friendly to the cunning and the cutthroat. The answer is very simple: if you don't like dealers, then don't buy from them and don't sell to them, but keep in mind that "one bad apple doesn't spoil the whole bunch."

The facts are simply this: Train collecting has become a well-known and established hobby and as such is continually growing, with the net result being that train prices will inevitably continue to rise, for better or for worse. It often seems that today's high prices are tomorrow's bargains and rightly so, for I know of many who overpaid when they bought certain sets, only to be offered a substantial profit a short while later; such is the nature of collectors and the often unpredictable and fickle nature of prices. That is why there are no price guides on toy trains that are worth the paper they are printed on, for by the time they are printed and distributed they are immediately inaccurate, rendering them virtually useless.

How are prices determined? In order to know that you must understand the closeness of the hobby and the fact that most train collectors tend to socialize with other collectors. Most serious and active hobbyists make at least one or two calls a day to other fellow collectors and dealers and you can bet the subject is trains. They don't want to know about your wife, your kids, your job, or your family, just what's new and who is buying and who is selling. I venture to say that if a fellow picks up a train collection of any significant size, it would take no longer than a day or two for every detail to sift from the East Coast to the West Coast, and by a week later every major collector in the country would know the news.

It's because of the relative closeness of the train-collecting community and the fact that most active members attend train meets regularly that train prices become firmly established. Prices are not made

by the random whim of one collector asking an exorbitant price but are established by supply and demand and popularity, all of which combine to give us a price. Each item, with its asking price and what it actually sold for (taking price) and to whom (either a sucker or a knowledgeable collector), is carefully analyzed and discussed by collectors with all the seriousness of a Wall Street stockbroker.

Buying and Selling

Collectors keep on top of today's prices, for they need to know what to pay when buying and what to ask when selling. Many also like to know just how much their collection is worth (whether they admit it or not), just in case they decide to sell it or not. Every hobby has its lifelong collectors; I like to think of them as "true" collectors, and of course there are those who leave the hobby as quickly as they came. They immediately sell off their collection, although, surprisingly, very few know how to go about doing this.

Basically unless a collection is small and you know every individual price you should try to avoid breaking it up and selling it piecemeal. When a collection is broken up in this manner, you tend to sell all the good pieces first and end up getting stuck with all the junk. You should never sell your best pieces first, because they tend to "carry" the collection as a whole and make it possible for you to sell the collection as a lot.

Much can be said on behalf of having your collection appraised first before you decide to sell, something that very few collectors have the sense to do. Naturally, consult someone you trust and arrange a set fee in advance, but the cost of the appraisal should be more than offset by what you stand to gain.

You should avoid another big mistake made by all too many in a big rush to sell their collections: Never sell your collection to the first man there. I know from experience, for I have had many collectors quickly write me off when I tried to buy from them, only to see them get less from somebody else. Often collectors conclude too quickly that "he would never pay my price," or "he doesn't have the money," and their assumptions are often wrong and sometimes very costly.

Since most major train collections do not come up for sale too often and collectors tend to keep the better items for last and sell their junk first, there is generally a lack of fine items for sale at most times. This is a continual thing, for most fellows, when they get something good that they want to sell, just make one or two phone calls and the item is immediately sold. Because of this most of the train sets that are rare or in spectacular condition are sold too quickly, and unless they are priced extremely high they usually never make it to the train meets or on sales lists. This has tended to discourage many collectors who have many common sets but are in need of some of the rarer items to fill in their collection. The one conclusion that many of these collectors come to is to trade for what they need.

Trades

There are all types of trades and all kinds of horse traders in the hobby for sure, but what are the hazards of trading? First, there comes a time when a fellow wants what you have but doesn't own the particular item or items needed to complete the trade. Second, you must be realistic and not expect to come up on the trade but offer items in an equal class, both in terms of rarity and equivalent value. Third, since many trades are made over the phone or by mail, once a deal is agreed upon you must be sure to pack and ship your merchandise properly. Many collectors will only trade and refuse to sell anything, which is both foolish and ridiculous. The majority of trains are obtained by buying them for cash, and money happens to be the common denominator in civilized nations all over the world, so it can be rightly argued that you should sell anything. The only problem is that since fewer and fewer fine trains are available, many feel that if they sell for cash the money is useless to them, because they cannot buy what they want. My philosophy is to wait for what I want and to buy the item as soon as I find one for sale. I then proceed to sell off something else in my collection, and the end result is equivalent to a trade. Whatever you decide, trading has been and will continue to be an important facet of the hobby and, with luck, a pleasant one.

Many new collectors continue to get taken on trades, because they are not fully aware, for example, that one diesel painted one way is worth more than another or that a black GG-1 is worth at least double the price of a similar condition green model. Many friendships have been made and broken as the result of trades; it therefore becomes imperative to check the advice of a few collectors before treading on unsteady ground.

Always keep in mind when shipping trains to insure them for their full value, and make sure you use a heavy carton packed within a carton and filled tightly with crushed newspapers or other packing materials. Items that jut out, such as couplers and side rods, should be individually wrapped before packing. Remember that shippers tend to throw cartons around, in addition to stacking boxes on top of boxes, and your trains might just be on the bottom.

The Future

How about the hobby itself, where does train collecting stand today? Collecting old trains as well as all types of old toys is fast gaining a lot of public recognition, for it is no longer confined to just a few railroad hobbyists, but collectors of trains are everywhere, in all parts of the United States, Canada, and, yes, all over Europe, where many of the finest collections lie. Many people know that trains are worth money. Of course, they don't know exactly how much but they certainly have a rough idea. This is in one way good, for at least from here on fewer and fewer train sets will be thrown away by the public. In fact, higher prices have even caused train collectors themselves to treat their models with more respect, and, where many hobbyists formerly would cut up engines or cars to make larger models for their layouts or where they might add on details and deform an otherwise fine original item, you can be sure this is happening less today.

As train prices go higher and higher the news media, from television to newspapers and major magazines, will print stories and prices in their articles, but as train collecting is one of the largest collecting hobbies today we cannot expect to prevent the hobby from growing up, and that means higher prices, commercialism, and unfriendly and impersonal attitudes. Every hobby that becomes large eventually grows up, and with it comes many changes and, whether we like them or not, if we want to collect we must learn to live with them.

Not all train collectors are railroad buffs as you might imagine. Scratch the surface of almost any collector and you'll find him interested in many other fields of antiques and Americana. Old toy trains are by their very nature an important kind of Americana, for the railroads played a strategic role in helping to build our nation. They also are the toys synonymous with Christmas, and almost every boy owned a train set at one time. You would naturally expect any hobby that concerns itself with the collecting and preserving of old toy trains to be a popular one, and you'd be right.

What does the future hold for train collecting? Continued growth and popularity and an increasing acceptance by the public that there is more to collecting trains than simply running them around an

Additional models of HO trains from the Joel Cane collection.

oval at Christmas time. Possibly the collecting emphasis will shift from postwar to Classic to· early periods, but inevitably as more and more people enter the hobby there will be fewer scarce models around and prices will continue to go up. Some, of course, will resist the increased prices and the "new collectors," as others have in the past, but others will work even more feverishly to build up a bigger and better collection. To pay or not to pay—each collector must make the decision for himself. If you want bargains, fine, we all do, but keep in mind the words of Herb Morley, who once said, "A great collection isn't built on bargains." No truer words were ever spoken.

BIBLIOGRAPHY

I used a number of sources for reference, all of which I would recommend to any interested hobbyists. The most obvious sources are naturally the toy train catalogs of various manufacturers, going back as far as I could find them. I also found some pertinent information in some older and out-of-print hobby magazines. The Train Collectors Association also produced a Lionel numbers list of enormous value, as well as the informative articles found in their publication, the TCA Quarterlies. The Toy Train Operating Society also has an informative magazine issued monthly known as the *TTOS Bulletin*. Any and all of these sources are of great help to old and new collectors alike, for it is often heard in the hobby that there are too few reference books devoted to the serious study of toy train collecting. The following publications and books were used in my research and comprise most of what exists on the hobby. Be advised that the best books of all were written by Louis Hertz and have long been out of print.

1. Carstens, Harold H. *The Trains of Lionel's Standard Gauge Era*. Ramsey, N.J.: Model Craftsman Publishing Corporation, 1968.

2. Hare, Frank C.; Burke, James; Wolken, I. Stephen. *Toy Train Treasury*, Vol. 1. Pittsburgh, Pa.: Iron Horse Productions, 1974.

3. Hertz, Louis H. *Riding the Tinplate Rails*. Ramsey, N.J.: Model Craftsman Publishing Corporation, 1944.

4. Hertz, Louis H. *Messrs. Ives of Bridgeport*. Wethersfield, Conn.: Mark Haber & Co., 1950.

5. Hertz, Louis H. *Collecting Model Trains*. New York: Simmons-Boardman Publishing Corporation, 1956.

6. Kowal, Case. *Toy Trains of Yesteryear*. Ramsey, N.J.: Model Craftsman Publishing Corp., 1972.

7. McComas, Tom; Tuohy, James. *A Collector's Guide to Postwar Lionel Trains*. Wilmette, Ill.: TM Productions, 1974.

8. Morley, Herb G. *TCA Catalog Series 1-E (Lionel Standard Gauge Trolley Cars)*. Pittsburgh, Pa.: Train Collectors Association, 1961.

9. Park, Russell C. *American Flyer Wide Gauge*. Princeton, Ill. Tribune Printing Co., 1971.

10. TCA Ives List Committee. *TCA Catalog Series 2 (Ives Trains List)*. Pittsburgh, Pa.: Train Collectors Association, 1967.